THE THEATRE OF TRUTH

Psychodrama, Spontaneity and Improvisation:

The Theatrical Theories and Influences of Jacob Levy Moreno

by

Eberhard Scheiffele

Doctor of Philosophy in Logic and the Methodology of Science

University of California, Berkeley

Professor Hans Sluga, Chair

Jacob Levy Moreno, M.D. (1889-1974) is known today as the founder of psychodrama, which he defined as "the science which explores the 'truth' by dramatic methods." He has been mostly studied by psychologists, who generally emphasize his important contribution to psychology, in particular to group therapy and action methods. This dissertation investigates Moreno primarily as a theatre artist.

It starts with a philosophical analysis of the concepts of acting, improvisation and spontaneity and then consolidates the elements of Moreno's theory of the nature and function of theatre, which are dispersed throughout his writings and have never been thoroughly collected in one place. This approach allows a critical comparison with two dramatic theorists who anticipated some of Moreno's ideas: Aristotle from whom he adapted the concept of catharsis and Goethe whom he saw as a forerunner of both therapy through drama and spontaneous production.

The dissertation also examines how Moreno discovered the healing power of drama while he directed his *Theatre of Spontaneity* in Vienna in the early twenties, a project which he revived in New York in the early thirties. Next, it traces Moreno's influence on American theatre, observing especially the spread of his two main ideas: the therapeutic use of dramatic enactment and his call for spontaneity in theatre, therapy and education.

Analyzing the dramatic and artistic way Moreno wrote and acted, I conclude that he was at heart a theatre person. Despite his pervasive influence, he failed however in his larger and perhaps overly idealistic vision of creating a global therapeutic community.

The appendix contains Moreno's earliest theatrical text, *The Godhead as Comedian*, translated for the first time in its entirety from the 1919 German edition. Also included is a look at Moreno through his appearance in the *New York Times*.

THE THEATRE OF TRUTH

Psychodrama, Spontaneity and Improvisation:
The Theatrical Theories and Influences of Jacob Levy Moreno

by

Eberhard Scheiffele

A dissertation submitted in partial satisfaction of the

requirements for the degree of

Doctor of Philosophy

in

Logic and the Methodology of Science

in the

GRADUATE DIVISION

of the

UNIVERSITY of CALIFORNIA, BERKELEY

Committee in charge:

Professor Hans Sluga, Chair
Professor Mel Gordon
Professor James Bierman

1995

The dissertation of Eberhard Scheiffele is approved:

_____ 11/7/95
Chair   Date

_____ 11/9/95
                                                                      Date

_____ 27 Nov. 1995
James Burnian   Date

University of California, Berkeley

1995

THE THEATRE OF TRUTH

Psychodrama, Spontaneity and Improvisation:
The Theatrical Theories and Influences of Jacob Levy Moreno

by

Eberhard Scheiffele

To Heinz-Dieter Ebbinghaus,

Aaron Osborne,

Gregg Fritsch,

Mel Gordon,

Hans Sluga,

Kara Randall,

for showing me the beauty of

Mathematics,

Modern Dance,

Acting,

Theatre,

Philosophy,

and Love,

respectively.

CONTENTS

v

ACKNOWLEDGEMENTS

My thanks are foremost due to the members of my dissertation committee. Specifically Mel Gordon for his often weekly dose of inspiration, support and wisdom. Somehow he always found the best balance of challenge and encouragement. Hans Sluga for numerous insightful philosophical discussions, for his thorough reading of the manuscript, and for his astute feedback. Jim Bierman for first bringing my attention to Moreno's work, and for his subsequent support. In fact, it seems that after quite some time of searching, I was fortunate enough to find the ideal dissertation committee. The three members are not only exceptional each in their own right, but they also complement each other in a way that proved most fruitful to my work.

I want to thank the following practitioners of theatre and psychodrama for discussing their work and related topics with me: Judith Malina from the Living Theatre, Moreno's wife Zerka, and also Hyia Bolsta, Philip Coleman, Jonathan Fox, Gregg Fritsch, Herb Propper, Wolfgang Scheiffele, Jonathan Siders, Lewis Yablonsky, and Ruth Zaporah. Of course I am indebted to Jacob Levy Moreno for having started it all.

Special thanks go to my partner Kara Randall for honoring my needs for both love and space during the work on this project.

Last but not least, I like to thank my parents for their tremendous support and especially my mother, Susanne Scheiffele. for taking such an active interest in my research and for providing me with instant access to German and Austrian bookstores, libraries, and other resources.

PREFACE

Jacob Levy Moreno, M.D. (1889-1974), a psychiatrist, an existentialist and a theatre director, is mostly known today as the founder of group psychotherapy, psychodrama and sociometry. His philosophy centers on the validity of immediate experience and the importance of living one's convictions in action. He displayed complete confidence in human potential and proclaimed "God is spontaneity" [Moreno, 1946 frontispiece] - the source of creativity, catharsis and human progress.

Psychodrama, which Moreno defined as "the science which explores the 'truth' by dramatic methods" [Moreno, 1946 p. a] is a form of group psychotherapy, that utilizes guided dramatic action to examine problems or issues and seeks to facilitate personal growth and healing of mental illness through heightened spontaneity and catharsis. It is now used throughout the world in a broad range of settings, from schools and mental health clinics to business management and the military.

Moreno and many of his followers claim that his ideas have influenced most systems of experiential psychotherapy, such as gestalt therapy, encounter groups, transactional analysis and reality therapy [Moreno & Moreno, 1970 p. 7ff; Yablonsky, 1981 p. 136ff]. Most writings on Moreno have been produced by psychologists who generally emphasize his important contribution to their field, in particular to group therapy and action methods. Many of these writings point out that Moreno's contributions to psychology have not been given the recognition they deserve. His contribution to theatre however is even less understood. It is hardly mentioned at all, except by Moreno himself.

This dissertation investigates Moreno primarily as a theatre practitioner and theorist. It, first of all, consolidates the elements of Moreno's theory of the theatre which are dispersed throughout his writings and have never been thoroughly collected in one place. Then it traces Moreno's influence, especially on American theatre, beginning in the thirties.

The introduction shows how Moreno was perceived by the public at different times through his appearance in popular newspapers and books. While he became initially recognized as a theatre person in Vienna in the early twenties , he is now mostly known in the field of psychology.

The first chapter contains a philosophical discussion of the main concepts and provides a framework for later chapters. It defines acting and improvisation and introduces a scale indicating the amount or degree of acting/improvisation involved.

Spontaneity is the most important concept in Moreno's entire philosophy - his proposed cure for the problems of modern society. It is a state of consciousness that manifests itself in behavior which is immediate, adequate and novel. Moreno suggested ways in which it can be tested and trained.

The second chapter presents Moreno's critique of traditional theatre. For this he created the term *cultural conserve* to emphasize the repetitive, mechanical, uncreative performance of past, dead events. The actor is not expressing himself in the here and now, rather he is engaged in recreating a past expression of some playwright's creativity. The audience is even further removed as a mere spectator of actors portraying the sufferings of scripted characters.

The best known case of improvisation before Moreno is the *Commedia dell'arte*, popular in Italy in the seventeenth century. After Moreno's comments on this form of theatre are presented, the amount of improvisation and spontaneity involved is examined.

Among the theorists that came before him, Moreno mentions mainly Aristotle and Goethe. From Aristotle he adapted the concept of catharsis, but gave it a new interpretation focusing more on the actor than the spectator. Moreno's account is compared with other writers, such as Gerald Else, Samuel Butcher, Leon Goldon and Augusto Boal.

Goethe wrote *Lila*, a play about curing the madness of the heroine through a dramatic enactment that anticipated many elements of the treatment of psychosis in psychodrama. While Moreno was correct that Goethe knew about improvisation, in fact Goethe's directorial view of acting was mostly the opposite of Moreno's. Improvisation played only a minor part in it.

The third chapter presents the main components of Moreno's theory on the nature and function of theatre. It distinguishes 14 categories, falling into two groups according to the two main notions that Moreno advocated: healing through dramatic enactment and spontaneity.

The initial section explains that for Moreno the goal of therapy is not only the cure of specific mental illness, but a transformation or liberation of the whole being towards a higher level of vitality, authenticity, expressiveness, spontaneity and creativity. This effect is facilitated through catharsis in both actor and spectator, analysis plays a comparably minor role. The theatre has to touch the participants on a personal level and build a sense of community, smashing the barrier between audience and actors. To this end, Moreno designed the open stage, first exhibited at the *Internationale Ausstellung Neuer Theatertechnik* in Vienna, 1924. The stage is placed in the center, accessible from all sides; there is no backstage to hide. The physical architecture supports the metaphysical, psychological function of the stage as a place where the actor is encouraged not only to be personal and truthful, but to be who he is, more deeply and explicitly than in real life. He enters what Moreno coined Surplus Reality where acts are richer in inspiration than in life itself and where everything is possible, a safe place to be dangerous. This includes the realm of fantasy, dreams, hopes, fears, etc., and thus Moreno emphasized the validity of subjective experience, carrying the actor/patient's autonomy to a maximum.

The next seven elements all support spontaneity. First, the spontaneously creative state of consciousness is the prerequisite as well as the result of good theatre. It is a state of heightened spontaneity in which the actor is able to embody his own inspirations immediately and to react to those of others. To reach this spontaneity, Moreno developed techniques for warm-up that are part of every enactment and increase the level of spontaneity in everyone involved. He also proposed the use of spontaneity training to enhance the actor's spontaneity permanently, beyond the scope of a particular production. For Moreno, spontaneity and memorized lines are incompatible, hence his demand for the elimination of the playwright. His theatre is instead guided by the new dramatist who spontaneously facilitates the production as it unfolds in front of the audience. He guides actors and audience through a warm-up, assigns roles to the actors and gives cues for beginning, end and major shifts. Like the actors he has to be spontaneous to react to new developments or audience reactions.

Moreno introduced the concept of encounter for the coming together of two (or more) actors to experience one another openly and immediately. It is intense, unrehearsed, personal communication in the here and now, an intuitive reversal of roles, a realization of the self through the other, an experience of total reciprocity. He first used the concept of *encounter* (Begegnung) in 1914 and claims to have influenced Martin Buber, whom he met as part of the intellectual circle in the cafés of Vienna. Buber went on to write his well-known *I and Thou* in 1923 and is commonly seen as the originator of the idea of encounter.

The fourth chapter focuses on Moreno's influence on some important American theatre companies. It traces historically the people he met, as well as the related ideas. After revealing Moreno's connection with the Group Theatre (New York, 1931-1941) which is known for introducing Stanislavsky's system to America, and Viola Spolin (Chicago, New York and Los Angeles, 1906-1994) who is known for promoting improvisation in theatre and education, most of the chapter is devoted to the *Living Theatre* (New York, 1948-   ), including an interview with Judith Malina, the co-founder and leading director. This avant-garde company incorporated many of Moreno's ideas, such as audience participation, truthfulness and therapeutic goals, but also went further in its call for a non-violent anarchist and sexual revolution. In addition they were indirectly influenced by Moreno's effect on gestalt therapy.

The fifth chapter evaluates the implications of the research and appraises Moreno's impact on theatre today. Analyzing the dramatic and artistic way Moreno wrote and acted, I conclude that he was at heart a theatre person. His two main ideas, the therapeutic use of dramatic enactment and his call for spontaneity in theatre, therapy and education, are now more prevalent in America than ever, as exhibited by the spread of improvisation in education, training and performance and by Drama Therapy becoming a recognized field of study and practice. Despite his pervasive influence, Moreno failed however in his larger and perhaps overly idealistic vision of creating a global therapeutic community.

The a p p e n d i x contains Moreno's earliest theatrical text, *The Godhead as Comedian*, translated for the first time in its entirety from the 1919 German edition. While written in an esoteric, poetic language, it already contained many of the ideas which he later fully developed. Also included is a look at Moreno through his appearance in the *New York Times*.

We end with a c h r o n o l o g y , highlighting the events in Moreno's life which are relevant to his work in theatre.

Unless otherwise mentioned, translations from German are mine.

INTRODUCTION: MORENO KNOWN AS A PSYCHIATRIST

Moreno's books and monographs are almost exclusively published by his own publishing house, Beacon House, Inc. that he started in 1941 and which is now in the process of dissolution. These writings are extensive and often repetitive. They are available only in major university libraries and rarely in bookstores. For these reasons Jonathan Fox [1987] edited a collection of some of Moreno's major writings under the title *The Essential Moreno*. The volume focuses on the foundations and applications of psychodrama and sociometry. Moreno's work in theatre is mentioned only in passing:

> Despite the publication of a book on the subject as early as 1923, however, his writing on theatre is not as cogent as his other work. Thus his contribution to theatre consisted of personal influence upon a like-minded few who were not interested in artistically produced plays but in native inventiveness and spontaneous dramas "as they spring up in everyday life, in the minds of simple people." [Fox, 1987 p. xvii]

1. Psychology Books

There are a number of readily available books on psychodrama, many written by Moreno's students, e.g. [Blatner, 1988a; Blatner, 1988b; Leutz, 1974; Yablonsky, 1981], all working in psychology or sociology and honoring Moreno's contribution to these fields.

Lewis Yablonsky, a professor of sociology and a long-time student of Moreno, devotes a chapter in his book *Psychodrama* to Moreno's influence on other therapies and writes:

> The introduction and usage of psychodrama in other therapeutic approaches has already occurred in a spontaneous fashion. Several specific cases make this point: Fritz Perls acknowledged that Gestalt therapy was in large measure derived from psychodrama; in Transactional Analysis, ego states of parent, adult, and child are often enacted in a psychodramatic fashion; a number of neo-Freudian psychoanalysts have patients act in psychodrama and then interpret the action in classical psychoanalytic terms; many of the principles and techniques of Dr. William Glasser's Reality Therapy overlap with psychodrama; psychodrama has been fundamental to the encounter approach since its inception and has been widely utilized in various sensitivity and encounter groups. [Yablonsky, 1981 p. 137]

Yablonsky briefly mentions Moreno's theatrical experiments with the Living Newspaper and the Impromptu Theatre [ibid. p. 200, 279]. He does not acknowledge any influence of Moreno on the field of theatre, although he includes a chapter entitled *Psychodrama: Theatre and Life* [ibid. p. 213-238]. In it he emphasizes the differences between psychodrama and theatre and displays a negative view of theatre, reiterating some of Moreno's criticisms of traditional theatre (cf. chapter II). "Although live appears to be spontaneous, many robotlike people are as role-bound to their lives as are actors in the theatre" [Yablonsky, 1981 p. 218].

Almost every dictionary of psychology mentions Moreno, if not under his name then under psychodrama. He is listed as a psychiatrist, the father of psychodrama and sometimes of group therapy in general. In the monumental classic *The Discovery of the Unconscious : The History and Evolution of Dynamic Psychiatry* we read: "The year 1932 has remained famous in the annals of psychiatry as the year in which the term 'group psychotherapy' was introduced by J. L. Moreno" [Ellenberger, 1970 p. 854].

Most comprehensive books on group therapy contain a section on Moreno. Mark Ettin in *Foundations and Applications of Group Psychotherapy* mentions Moreno throughout and devotes a section to him [Ettin, 1992 p. 93ff].

In 1976 an entire volume of *Group Therapy* was dedicated to Moreno [Wolberg, Aronson, & Wolberg, 1976]. The publication is part of "an annual series of invited original articles by prominent theoreticians and practitioners of group and family therapy. Each volume is dedicated to a distinguished person who has made seminal contributions to the field" [ibid. p. ix]. The volume on

Moreno, a collection of twenty-four articles, is classified into four categories. It contains sections on Action Techniques, Systems Theory and Psychoanalytic Group Therapy, but opens with an account of the *Contributions of J.L. Moreno*. This part of the volume is made up by articles from Moreno's wife Zerka, his son Jonathan, Arlene Wolberg and Neville Murray.

In the preface we learn not only of the importance of Moreno's contributions, but also that they have not been fully appreciated.

> The present volume honors Jacob L. Moreno, who died in 1974 at the age of 85 after a long and exceptionally productive career. Although Moreno succeeded in reaching a wide audience during his lifetime via his prolific writing of books and articles, his editing of professional journals, and the memorable demonstrations he conducted throughout the United States and many parts of the world, it is only recently that group therapists have begun to appreciate and to comprehend the profound impact of his contributions. [Wolberg, et al., 1976 p. ix]

Zerka Moreno agrees in her article *My Dedication: J. L. Moreno*: "I am convinced that his genuine contribution will not be fully realized, recognized or appreciated for a long time to come, possibly not for another half a century" [Wolberg, et al., 1976 p. xv].

Arlene Wolberg divides her article *The Contributions of Jacob Moreno* into sections on Sociometry, Role and Action, Psychodrama and Group Therapy and then concludes:

> In summary, we may say that Moreno's work has given us many of the technical and theoretical foundations of teaching

and learning: psychotherapy and experimentation in the field of social science. He has devised testing measures which clarify man's relations with man, or the dynamics of groups. His contributions have been monumental and lasting and have given us propositions that provide possibilities for research for years to come. [Wolberg, et al., 1976 p. 12]

2. Theatre Books

While Moreno claims to have influenced some major American theatre companies[1], few theatre historians have written about him. Theatre dictionaries or textbooks generally omit Moreno and his theatre companies. Among the dozen or so authors in the field of theatre history, theory and criticism who comment on Moreno, Eric Bentley's and Robert Sarlós' writings are the most significant and substantial.[2]

Eric Bentley is an American drama critic, translator, editor, playwright, and director and most recognized for his translations and commentaries on Brecht's plays. In his book *The Life of the Drama* he joins the commentators from the field of psychology in describing Moreno, not as a theatre person, but as the founder of psychodrama [Bentley, 1964 p. 64] and in the chapter on enactment he gives a description of psychodrama "because it offers the most vivid evidence imaginable of the intimate link between theatre and life" [ibid. p. 187].

Then in 1969 Bentley wrote his essay *Theatre and Therapy* which he composed after visiting Moreno's psychodrama sessions in New York. "My piece on therapy represents exclusively what I

[1]"Slowly my ideas began to influence the Group Theatre and the [American] followers of Stanislavski" [Moreno, 1983 p. c].
"Think of Moreno's influence upon the so-called Living Theater and Open Theater" [Moreno & Moreno, 1970 p. 4].
[2]Others are [Boal, 1995; Courtney, 1974; Courtney, 1990; Innes, 1993; Ogden, 1987; Schutzman & Cohen-Cruz, 1994]; there are also some in German, e.g. [Brauneck, 1982; Buer, 1991; Burkart, 1972; Dietrich, 1974; Feldhendler, 1992; Lazarowicz & Balme, 1991; Lesák, 1988; Marschall, 1988; Pörtner, 1967].

learned from Moreno's psychodrama" [Bentley, 1969 p. 321]. He seemed very impressed by what he saw: "At the Moreno Institute, therapy was the acknowledged and sole aim in view, yet the sessions there were emotionally affecting and intellectually interesting to a much greater degree than the New York theatres" [ibid. p. 322].

His essay begins by pointing out how the Living Theatre's audience involvement and therapeutic goals remind him of Moreno[3], and then he analyzes Moreno's ideas using the "I and Thou" terminology, usually associated with Martin Buber.

He refers to many of Moreno's ideas that I discuss in chapter III and goes to great lengths contemplating the difference between drama and psychodrama (and life). He concludes "...that one of the chief differences between drama and psychodrama is this: while drama is judged, fairly enough, by the effect the actor has on the audience, in psychodrama the highest priority goes to the effect the audience has on the actor" [Bentley, 1969 p. 329]. As we will see later, Moreno's goal is a therapeutic effect on both actor/protagonist and audience.

The last section of Bentley's essay examines Moreno's critique of scripted theatre (cf. chapter II).

> The psychodramatist inevitably looks with horror upon the written text. Dr. Moreno contemptuously terms it a "cultural conserve," and sees it exclusively as a hindrance to spontaneity, the highest value in his philosophy. From the

---

[3]More on the relation between the Living Theatre and Moreno in chapter IV.3.

viewpoint of therapy, I believe his point is well taken.
[Bentley, 1969 p. 332]

Moreno's demand for the elimination of the playwright (cf. chapter III.2.5) is one of the most controversial elements of his theory and is debatable even from a therapeutic viewpoint. While Bentley might be correct in saying that in most cases, "If one had a serious mental illness, no amount of theatregoing in even the greatest of theatres could be expected to help very much" [Bentley, 1969 p. 334], it is documented that written plays have been put on in mental institutions with great therapeutic effect, especially when the patients were involved as actors [Schattner & Courtney, 1981].

In fact, it is one of the discoveries of Drama Therapy (cf. chapter V.2) that therapeutic change can be achieved without ever directly addressing the patient's issues. Some patients are indeed more open to this approach than to regular psychodrama or other modalities.[4]

Bentley then discusses catharsis and the function of art and concludes with an attempt at describing the spontaneity of an actor in a play:

> On the face of it he has surrendered it to the playwright....But the actor still meets the eye of another actor, not of a character, which is to say that both actors are still present: their own bodies and all that two human beings have that is not body. And they continue to use all of this, in live contact,

---

[4]For example prison inmates as reported in *Humanizing Offenders through Acting Therapy* by Ramon Gordon in [Schattner & Courtney, 1981 p. 312].

as "I" and "Thou."... That the character may *seem* to have a spontaneous existence, the actor must *actually* have a spontaneous existence. [Bentley, 1969 p. 338]

While Bentley's essay is an insightful comparison of psychodrama and theatre, it says very little about Moreno's influence on theatre as a field.

In contrast, Robert Sarlós in his *Jig Cook and the Provincetown Players* fully acknowledges Moreno's contribution to the field of theatre. When he first mentions him he writes:

> Jacob Levy Moreno and Martin Buber recognized the need for personal "encounter" in religion. Almost simultaneously, Moreno applied this concept to theatre and to psychotherapy, sensing that all three fields relate to the human need for psychic catharsis that depends on some sort of coming together, and finding apparent corroboration of his perception in Aristotle's *Poetics*. [Sarlós, 1982 p. 39]

He goes on to explain some of Moreno's "gospel" [ibid. p. 56], especially on spontaneity, creativity and encounter. In passing he suggests Moreno's influence on American theatre. "Moreno revived his *Stegreiftheater* (Wien, 1921) as Impromptu Theatre (New York, 1931), with a probable impact on founders of the Group Theatre whose theatre he shared" [ibid. p. 40][5].

He discusses Moreno mainly because of the many similarities he finds with Jig Cook, the leader of the Provincetown Players.

---

[5]Sarlós is probably referring to the Guild Theatre, where Moreno officially opened his Impromptu Theatre in 1931 [Marineau, 1989 p. 123].

...and the revolution of encounterculture was joined. Jig Cook and J.L. Moreno were among the precursors of this revolution. They recognized how crucial trust and interdependence, spontaneity and release were in an increasingly mechanized and impersonal world; correctly identified those elements as building blocks of the theatrical creative process, and therefore focused on theatre as a uniquely suited laboratory of human emotions within the intimate group, and eventually beyond its boundaries. [Sarlós, 1982 p. 40]

Moreno's gospel - for he considered it nothing less- rested on three assumptions: first, that spontaneity/creativity is "a propelling force of human progress," second, that "faith in our fellowmen's intentions" is necessary, and third, that on these two axioms "a superdynamic community" can be based. These convictions were developed in what Moreno calls his "axionormative period" - 1911 to 1923 - and they appear to be articulated equivalents of Jig Cook's passionate requirements of the beloved community of life givers. [ibid. p. 56]

Yet another ideological kinship between Cook and Moreno is manifest in their common belief in the necessity of bridging the Dionysian and the Apollinian. Unlike Cook, however, Moreno seldom touched alcohol and was firmly opposed to the use of drugs to enhance creativity. ... Parallels between Cook's fragmentary statements and Moreno's quasi-scientific writing are probably no more than coincidences in the development of human understanding of relations between society and creativity. But if the creative process is best understood in its own peculiar atmosphere, then the intimation must be allowed that the minds of these two men shared a source of inspiration. Cook sailed for Greece and Moreno for America, but their spirit commingled in their followers: it can be detected in ideals of several groups of artists, from the Group Theatre to the Living Theatre. [ibid. p. 57]

Sarlós' book is probably the most extensive publication commenting on Moreno as a theatre person. While he touches on many aspects of Moreno's work in theatre, he clearly leaves many questions open - some of which will be explored in this dissertation.

3. Vienna Period

The first time Moreno became known to a larger audience was in 1918 in Vienna when he started publishing a monthly expressionist, existentialist, literary journal called *Daimon*. It became *Der Neue Daimon* in 1919 and *Die Gefährten* in 1920. The list of contributors is impressive and contains many famous writers of the period, some of them influential in theatre. Besides Moreno's own contributions, it contained articles by the Czech writer Max Brod, the playwright and novelist Franz Werfel, the writer Paul Kornfeld who later worked as dramaturg for Max Reinhardt in Berlin, the philosopher and theologian Martin Buber, the expressionist dramatist Georg Kaiser, the playwright, painter and scenic designer Oskar Kokoschka, the French playwright Paul Claudel, the poet and pioneer of absurd drama Iwan Goll and many others.[6]

Like most of his early writings, Moreno's own numerous contributions were written in a poetic, sometimes mystical language; they nevertheless exhibited many of his later ideas. *Der Neue Daimon* [1919] also contained Moreno's first exposition on

---

[6]The complete list from 1918-19 also includes E. A. Rheinhardt, Jakob Wassermann, Francis Jammes, Gütersloh, Friedrich Schnack, Otokar Brezina, Ernst Weiss, Alfred Wolfenstein, Franz Blei, Giovanni Pascoli, Dr. Alexander Schmid, Bela Balazs, Rudolf Fuchs, Egon Wellesz, André Suares, Nicolaus Cusanus, Lorenz Grabner, Eugen Hoeflich, Karel Hlavacek, Leopold Reissinger, Hermes Trismegistos, Hetta Mayr, Petr Bezruc, Georg Kulka, Robert Müller, Chajan Kellmer, Ernst Bloch, Mynona (pseudonym for Salomo Friedlaenders), Blaise Pascal, Hugo Sonnenschein, Albert Ehrenstein, Julius Slowacki, Fritz Lampl, Ernst Weiss, Otto Stoessl, Carl Ehrenstein and Hermann Kesser.

the nature of theatre which has never been translated in its entirety. Since it clearly establishes Moreno as a theatre person early on in his career, a complete translation is included in the appendix.

Possibly Moreno's first public theatrical performance took place in Vienna on April Fool's Day, 1921, and was reviewed the next day (without mentioning his name) in the *Wiener Mittags-Zeitung*. The event was ridiculed by audience and critics alike.

Dadaism in the House of Comedies.

A late night performance on April 1 in the *House of Comedies*. This means: The management of the House of Comedies took no responsibility. They had rented the auditorium to a physician who lives in a famous spa-resort on the south railroad line[7], where he might also practice, but who primarily sees himself as poet-philosopher and who chose specifically the first of April to bombard a lenient and easygoing audience with his rather obscure way of thinking. The author introduced himself as a king's jester who is searching for the king of the world, that king who must not be elected but recognized, because he exists as an idea and truly lives in the heart of humanity. The form chosen for this, with three long,

---

[7]From 1919 to 1924 Moreno was appointed as health officer in Bad Vöslau, about forty kilometers south of Vienna, where he soon became famous as a *Wunderdoktor* [Marineau, 1989 p. 58], see also [Moreno, 1995 p. 90ff]. My mother recently had an opportunity to visit Bad Vöslau and met some people who still remembered Moreno. At the house in Maithalstrasse 4 where he lived, she found a commemorative plaque with the following inscription:

"DR. JACOB L. MORENO
GEMEINDEARZT VON VÖSLAU
1918-1925
ENTWICKELTE HIER
SOZIOMETRIE
GRUPPEN-PSYCHOTHERAPIE
PSYCHODRAMA"

bombastic speeches, forced, naturalistic, crude explicitness and an almost pathological imagination, was equally uninteresting as the style of presentation, which was an inadvertent but clearly recognizable caricature of the dramatic accent of Novelli[8], Kainz[9], Lewinsky[10] and Schildkraut[11]. At first, the presentation was received with quiet delight, later there were strong gestures of displeasure. Next to loud whistling one could hear rather crude heckling. This was followed by ironic applause which kept the speaker from continuing his speech. But there were also friends, who were supposedly followers of *Werfel*[12] and defended the poet. Many left the auditorium loudly, up in arms over the wasted evening. But enough people remained who enjoyed the humor of the event and anticipated the small possibility that the story might have a punch line after all. They became equally disappointed as those who believed that the speech by the poet was only a prologue to a dance performance, and only the fall of the iron curtain made the audience aware that they were fools, just as much as they looked at the speaker as a fool.

[*Wiener Mittags-Zeitung*, Saturday, April 2, 1921]

---

[8]The name probably refers to Ermete Novelli (1851-1919), Italian actor and company manager [Banham, 1992 p. 720].

[9]Josef Kainz (1858-1910) was an Austrian actor who joined the Vienna Burgtheater in 1899 and "was undoubtedly the most popular actor of his day due to his aristocratic appearance, his phenomenally flexible and accurate voice, and his unusual physical dexterity" [Banham, 1992 p. 535]; see also [Sucher, 1995 p. 352].

[10]Josef Lewinsky (1835-1907), a masterly player of villains, was among the greatest actors at the Viennese Burgtheater [Banham, 1992 p. 133f].

[11]Rudolf Schildkraut (1862-1930) acted in Vienna at the Raimund Theater and the Carl Theater before joining Max Reinhardt's Deutsche Theater Berlin in 1905, where he became known for his explosive portrayal of Shylock [Sucher, 1995 p. 620]. None of these names are mentioned elsewhere in Moreno's writings.

[12]The famous novelist and dramatist Franz Werfel (1890-1945) was according to Moreno's autobiography one of his closest friends. They met in the Viennese coffee houses and then worked together in the Stegreiftheater. Years later they renewed their friendship when Werfel came to Hollywood to work on the screenplay for *Song of Bernadette* [Moreno, 1989 p. 71].

Moreno opened his *Stegreiftheater* (Theatre of Spontaneity) in Vienna, Maysedergasse 2 in 1922 [Burkart, 1972 p. 19; Marineau, 1989 p. 72]. Its popularity grew and in 1924 much was written about it in the newspapers. On April 26, 1924 the following announcement appeared in the newspaper *Der Tag* in Vienna:

A Stegreif-Theater in Vienna.
The Viennese experimental stage is preparing for the opening of the Stegreif-Theater in the fall. This afternoon a meeting will take place in the small concert-hall, where the Misters A. B. *Blum, Rodenberg* and Peter *Lorre*[13] will speak about the diverse disciplines of acting spontaneously.[14]
[*Der Tag*, Wien, April 26, 1924, p. 6]

Paul Stefan wrote on May 18, 1924 in *Die Stunde*:

Young actors under the direction of the "father" (as Dr. Jakob Moreno *Levy* calls himself in his writings) perform two or three times a week in a hall, Meysedergasse 2. The throng is

[13]Peter Lorre (1904-1964) is possibly the most famous actor associated with Moreno - they met through his brother William Moreno. The episode is mentioned in Lorre's biography: "William brought Peter to Jacob, and introduced the young man. Peter needed a job; perhaps he had talent. A maverick himself, Moreno took to the independent youngster and agreed to test his ability.
Placed in an improvisational situation, the aspiring actor showed promise. Moreno asked Lorre to become a regular member of his acting troupe. In the workshop, he created his own stories, roles, and dialogue. He lived out his problems and his fantasies. ...
Moreno had given Peter a chance to develop and hone his talent, and provided the setting for the actor to find himself. However, by 1924, Peter was ready to move on. Before he went, he needed a stagename; Ladislav Loewenstein would not do. Moreno gave him the name Peter Lorre" [Youngkin, Bigwood, & Cabana, 1982 p. 24].
[14]"Ein Stegreif-Theater in Wien.
Die Wiener Versuchsbühne bereitet für den Herbst die Eröffnung des Stegreif-Theaters vor. In einer heute nachmittags im Kleinen Konzerthaussaal stattfindenden Zusammenkunft werden die Herren A. B. *Blum, Rodenberg* und Peter *Lorre* über die diversen Disziplinen des Stegreifspiels sprechen."

large, the themes are brought along or suggested by the
audience. ...
There is a "truth-chair": whoever sits on this furniture must
show himself the way he really is. ...
I assure you that this can be more amusing and engaging
than the well-respected classics, including Strindberg.
[*Die Stunde*, Wien, May 18, 1924, p. 6]

Moreno quotes from similar articles in *Neues Wiener Journal,
Welt Blatt, Prager Presse, Berliner Börsen Zeitung, Leipziger
Neueste Nachrichten, Rheinische Musik und Theater Zeitung,
Ariadne, Il Sereno,* and *Haagsche Courant* [Moreno, 1983 p. 103f].

During his time in Vienna, Moreno became most famous for his
controversy with the architect and stage designer Friedrich Kiesler
(1890-1965). Both presented their ideas for stage design at the
Internationale Ausstellung neuer Theatertechnik (international
exhibition of new theatre techniques) in Vienna in 1924. The
illustration of Moreno's *Theater ohne Zuschauer* (theatre without
an audience) below was drawn by the architect Rudolf Hönigsfeld
and is taken from the exhibition catalogue [Kiesler, 1924 p. 67].[15]
(For a further discussion of Moreno's stage design see chapter
III.1.5).

---

[15]The drawing only has Hönigsfeld's name on it, not Moreno's. The
catalogue also contains the following letter, apparently written by Moreno:
"'Die Analyse des Komödianten mußte die Rahmen, In welche sein Spiel
gepreßt ist, fragwürdig machen: die gegebene Dichtung - die Regie und
Kulisse - die wiederholte Aufführung. Es erwies sich: die Technik macht das
Leben mächtiger , aber nicht produktiv. Sie, geeignet Im Bunde mit
Analyse und Bewußtsein das Unbewußte aufzubrauchen, aufzulösen, kann
es nicht mehren; denn nur durch unbekümmertes Tun wird fort und fort
Unbewußtes erzeugt. Daher muß das Korrektiv einer Theaterform, dessen
Vorbild die Maschinenarbeit ist, einseitig In Ihr Gegenteil umschlagen: das
Stegreiftheater.' (Einsendung des 'Vaters' [Dr. M. Levy] vom 5. September
1924 an den Herausgeber.)" [Kiesler, 1924 p. 1]

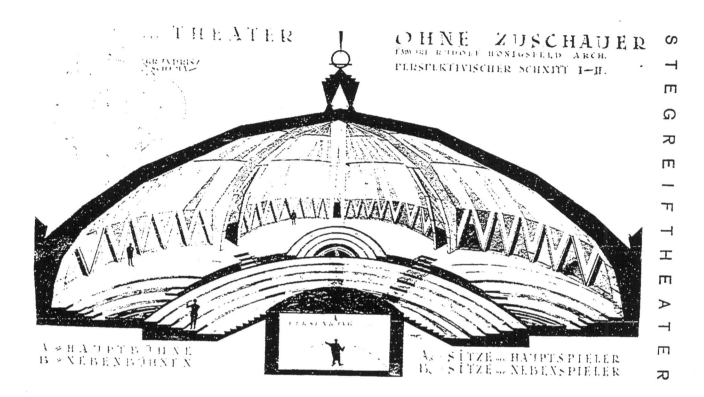

The controversy ("Plagiatstreit") between Moreno and Kiesler started after the first presentation of Kiesler's *Raumbühne* (space stage) on September 5, 1924. A few days later Moreno sent a declaration to the press "in which he claims authorship of the idea for the Raumbühne and accuses Kiesler of plagiarism" [Lesák, 1988 p. 113]. This was followed by a series of open letters between Kiesler and Hönigsfeld published in *Der Tag* [ibid]. The dispute culminated on the day of the opening of the exhibition on September 24, 1924. Moreno interrupted the ceremony and shouted: "I declare hereby publicly that Mr. Kiesler is a plagiarist and a scoundrel."[16] Soon other artists announced their solidarity with Kiesler or Moreno. Even caricatures depicting the two antagonists could be found in the local press; the following is taken from [Lesák, 1988 p. 155]. On the top of a model of Kiesler's Raumbühne we see Moreno and Kiesler fighting:

Die Raumbühne, Karikatur von Ladislaus Tuszynsky, aus: Der Götz von Berlichingen, 3. Oktober 1924

[16]"Ich erkläre hiermit vor aller Öffentlichkeit Herrn Kiesler für einen Plagiator und Lumpen" (Sensationeller Zwischenfall bei der Eröffnung der Ausstellung neuer Theatertechnik, *Illustrierte Kronen-Zeitung*, Wien, September 25, 1924, p. 2, quoted from [Lesák, 1988 p. 114]).

Kiesler finally sued Moreno and the trial brought the incident back into the newspapers. On January 20, 1925 we read about the trial and its prehistory in *Der Tag*, Vienna, p. 8:

Before the judge

Who had it first?

> Strafbezirksgericht 1.
> OLGR. Dr. Weiß.
> Klagevertreter: Dr. Preßburger.
> Geklagtenvertreter: Dr. Schnepp.

The idea of the *Raumbühne*. The academic painter Friedrich *Kiesler* and the physician and writer Dr. Jakob *Moreno-Lewy* fight over priority. When on September 24 at the opening ceremony of the exhibition "New Theatre Technique" president Vetter welcomed mayor Seitz and introduced to him Kiesler as the creator of the model of the Raumbühne, Dr. Moreno shouted loudly into the auditorium:
"I declare hereby publicly that Mr. Friedrich Kiesler is a plagiarist and a scoundrel!"
Kiesler sued for *slander* and denied that his *Raumbühne* had anything in common with Dr. Moreno's *Stegreifbühne*.
The accused admitted making the remark and offered to deliver a proof in several ways.

Radio and crocodile.

Dr. Moreno explained now that he worked out the basic idea for a Raumbühne in 1923 together with the architect *Hönigsfeld* and that the model Kiesler exhibited was nothing but a copy of that idea. Kiesler had attended his lectures on the topic and had also known his theatrebook.
The defense presented letters from experts who agreed that it was indeed plagiarism. Supposedly Kiesler had also copied a

poster by the painter Klinger. To support the point he made about Kiesler being a "scoundrel" he brought up Kiesler's behavior towards the puppet theatre *Der Gong* and also his behavior towards the writer Ludwig *Kascha*. The plaintiff pointed out statements by important people who say that the accusation of plagiarism is completely unfounded. Besides, he has had the idea for the Raumbühne much earlier than the accused and, long before the publication of the theatrebook, he wrote about it in the "Berliner Tageblatt". A well-known critic from Vienna had also declared that the two projects are related to each other as much as *a radio and a crocodile*. All the other statements made by the accused were equally absurd.

In order to complete the long proofs presented by both parties, the judge had to adjourn the trial.

(Quoted from [Lesák, 1988 p. 159])

The radio and the crocodile could also be found in a caricature of the trial, which appeared in *Die Stunde* on January 1925. The following reprint is from [Lesák, 1988 p. 159]:

Der Prozeß um die gestohlene Idee. Karikatur von Peter Eng. aus: *Die Stunde,* 25. Januar 1925

Moreno never retreated from his original position and in his autobiography he calls Kiesler "one of my students" and writes: "Unknown to us, Kiesler built a model which was almost identical to ours and then took credit for the creation of a revolutionary new style of theatrical architecture" [Moreno, 1989 p. 77].

None of the sources consulted stated the final outcome of the trial. Held [1982] in his study of Kiesler's theory and scenic design writes: "Unfortunately, trial records in Austria are destroyed after 30 years. Kiesler claimed that decision was in his favor. The 1947 revision of Moreno's book makes no claim to primacy" [Held, 1982 p. 35]. However, in his autobiography Moreno describes his argument before the court and ends with the sentence: "I was vindicated" [Moreno, 1989 p. 79]. So the controversy continues - it now also includes the outcome of the trial, which both claim ended in their favor.

The episode certainly helped Moreno's name to become widely recognized, though not necessarily in the best light. Through the exhibition he became known to many theatre people, for example all the important Bauhaus[17] artists were invited to Vienna [Lesák, 1988 p. 166]. Incidentally, both Moreno and Kiesler emigrated to New York within a year [Lesák, 1988 p. 7]. For a more complete report of the controversy, including a list of relevant newspaper articles, see [Lesák, 1988 p. 112-120, 209, 212][18] and also [Held, 1982 p. 31-37].

[17]Xanti Schawinski claimed that Moreno's Theatre of Spontaneity had influenced the Bauhaus theatrical experiments [Moreno, 1995 p. 84; Pörtner, 1967 p. 11].
[18]The accounts in [Marineau, 1989 p. 82ff] and [Marschall, 1988 p. 14f] seem to be mostly based on Lesák.

4. New York Period

In 1931 Moreno briefly published a little-known journal titled *Impromptu*. Only two issues appeared, no. 1 in January and no. 2 in April. The preamble states:

> This magazine is pledged to three principles of publication:
> FIRST: to interpret and elaborate a philosophy of the creator as an anti-mechanical corrective to our age.
> SECOND: to state the already known Impromptu techniques, and to enlarge the knowledge about them through collaboration with many experimental groups.
> THIRD: to be the recording organ for creations accomplished with the aid of various Impromptu techniques on the spur of the moment. [Moreno, 1931 p. 3]

Most of the articles were devoted to the use of improvisation in theatre and education and were written by Moreno (some translated from earlier publications). It also included texts by drama critic A. B. W. Smith, Viennese authors Hans Kafka and Robert Müller, writer J. J. Robbins (mostly known as translator of Stanislavsky), psychologist Helen C. Jennings, magazine writer Robert Mitchell and composer and music teacher Theodore Appia.

Moreno's attempts to explore and spread his ideas through the medium of theatre were ultimately not successful enough for him. for soon after this period he became more and more focused on his work in psychology, becoming the founder of many more journals, associations and institutes.

For a look at newspaper articles on Moreno during his New York period (from his immigration to the United States in 1926 to his death in 1974), the *New York Times* is clearly the most important and widespread - articles in other papers were usually similar.

In the *New York Times* Moreno appeared only in the years 1929, 1931, 1933, 1935, 1936, 1938, 1941, 1947 and then not again until his obituary in 1974. This reflects the fact that by the end of the thirties he had already introduced most of his innovative techniques and subsequently concentrated on disseminating his ideas.

For a detailed look at the *New York Times* articles consult the appendix. Only the first two refer to Moreno as a theatre person. From June 1931 onwards he is usually called a psychiatrist.

In summary we find that very little has been written about Moreno as a theatre person. While his theatrical work made some headlines in the early twenties in Vienna, the public, especially in America, now knows him primarily as a psychiatrist and the founder of psychodrama.

I. DISCUSSION OF MAIN CONCEPTS

To give the following discussion as much exactness as possible, we first need to clarify some of the main concepts used in later chapters.

1. Acting

The question about what it means to be acting and how one can best accomplish this elusive task has puzzled most practitioners and theorists of the theatre at one time or another. Among the many attempts to answer this question, Sanford Meisner's definition stands out in my mind, both for the theoretical clarity it allows and for its usefulness in actor's training. It is particularly pertinent to our discussion of Moreno, since both emphasize truthfulness and spontaneity.

Sanford Meisner was a member of the Group Theatre (cf. chapter IV.1) in the thirties in New York. For the last fifty years he has directed the Neighborhood Playhouse School of the Theatre and his teaching has influenced a few generations of actors.

It was not until 1987 that a book was published documenting his method of teaching. There we can read Meisner's now widely known definition of good acting as "living truthfully under imaginary circumstances" [Meisner & Longwell, 1987 p. 15]. This seems paradoxical at first - how can we be truthful while imagining we are someone or somewhere else?

If we take this process apart for the moment in order to explain it, we see that the actor's first task is to imagine the given circumstances, such as his character (including previous events and relations with other characters), time and place of the action (including sensorial experiences such as smell or temperature), sometimes a fourth wall and sometimes the audience will be part of the imaginary world, etc.

The actor's next task is to then allow himself to react to these circumstances. One of Meisner's basic principles is: "Don't do anything unless something happens to make you do it." So if the actor cries, it shouldn't be because it is written in the script or because the director told him to, it can only be because of what actually happened on stage (that is to say in the actor's imaginary world - a combination of what he imagines the other *characters* and himself to be and what the other *actors* actually did, themselves living as characters in an imaginary world).

The character rarely *tries* to cry (unless he is in a scene in which he wants to manipulate someone by crying), usually he tries *not* to cry, but is driven to it by circumstances. Similarly the actor shouldn't make it his objective to cry, but rather allow himself to cry only if the emotion comes out of the circumstances.

At times he might have to hold back, but this is only effective if he first allows himself to feel the emotion. While it is moving to watch someone hold back emotions, it usually isn't as interesting to watch someone who simply doesn't feel any emotions, who isn't affected by what happens around him. "But in order to hold back, you have to have something to *hold*." [Meisner & Longwell, 1987 p. 176].

The actor can only play circumstances, not emotions. "You must have a reason why you want to do it, because that's the source of your concentration and eventually of your emotion, which comes by itself" [Meisner & Longwell, 1987 p. 39]. If the director wants the actor to be more angry, she doesn't simply tell him to be more angry, but rather to concentrate on the circumstances, e.g. something the other character did to him or what he wants of the other character. There is a certain language that should be used when talking to an actor that encourages truthfulness, creativity and aliveness. Of course not all directors speak this language and a good actor should be able to translate directions into his own language.

For example, if the director tells the actor: "When the waitress comes in you stand up and look at her angry," the actor has to be careful not to just stand up like someone who has been told to stand up (which would presumably make the actor unbelievable to the audience); rather he has to translate the director's request into a statement about circumstances and motivations, something like: "When you see the waitress, she reminds you of your girlfriend who betrayed you and you want to make her afraid of you."

Initially the actor uses concentration and control to put himself in the imaginary circumstances. Then he is to simply follow his impulses, to allow himself to *be affected* by what happens in front of him, to loose control. All this to an even greater degree than in real life. "You're allowed to do things onstage that you don't do in life. You're permitted to express yourself on stage and don't need to hold yourself back as you must in life" [Meisner & Longwell, 1987 p. 162]. Moreno called this *Surplus Reality* (cf. chapter III.1.6); it is an environment in which the actor can be more free, expressive and truthful than in life.

In Meisner's system the actor doesn't suddenly become someone else when he starts to act. Contrary to some popular notion, acting is not about hiding yourself, deceiving or feigning. On the contrary, "Acting is the art of self-revelation" [Meisner & Longwell, 1987 p. 145]. On the stage you can be yourself even more fully than in life. "Be yourself! Accept whatever comes out spontaneously!" [Meisner & Longwell, 1987 p. 173].

The tendency of acting students to pretend to be somebody else and to act from their intellectual ideas of what the character should do or feel, rather than to follow their impulses, is a problem which Meisner frequently encounters in his classes. His response: "I had to give him an inoculation. What was the inoculation? *No acting, please.*" [Meisner & Longwell, 1987 p. 128]. This somewhat paradoxical phrase is frequently heard in acting classes and is of course meant to point out bad acting.

"Don't be an actor," Meisner says. "Be a human being who works off what exists under imaginary circumstances. Don't give a performance. Let the performance give you." [Meisner & Longwell, 1987 p. 128]

Moreno sometimes uses the word *actor* in a similar negative way, as in the following passage, which refers to his psychodrama techniques, but also echoes Meisner's statement:

The aim of these sundry techniques is not to turn the patients into actors, but rather to stir them up to be on the stage what they are, more deeply and explicitly than they appear to be in life reality. [Moreno, 1946 p. c]

Of course this is exactly what good acting is all about.

After having investigated Meisner's definition of good acting, it is only natural to ask: what is the definition of acting as such, without any value judgments? What is the essence of acting, whether good or bad and also independent of acting style?

First of all we note that it is impossible to decide if someone is acting by observation alone; for example we might watch a play and someone falls down, screaming apparently over a broken leg. Now it is possible that the actor actually slipped and broke his leg by accident and screamed because of the pain. Then we wouldn't say that he was acting (even if his fall was written in the play). On the other hand, if the actor fell and screamed because it was written in the play or because of what he imagined, we would say that he was acting. But especially with a good actor we might not be able to see the difference.

Similarly if during a play we see someone walking on stage, picking up a broken glass and walking off, we might not be able to tell, if it was an actor who is part of the play, or a stage-hand doing his job of preventing injuries. If we know the play we might have more of a clue, but it could be an original or even improvised performance.

So how do we decide if the person is acting? We could ask him what he was doing and presumably he would be able to tell us whether he actually broke his leg. Or we could look at his X-Rays. But even if his X-rays show that he actually broke his leg, we wouldn't necessarily conclude that he wasn't acting. Maybe he was acting just like the night before, but for some reason he actually broke his leg this time.

If we ask the actor whether he was acting and assuming he answers honestly, we could hardly argue with his answer. In other words if the actor *thinks* he is acting, it usually implies that he *is* in fact acting. Acting is something the actor does consciously.

So the main criterion for acting is what was going on in the actor's mind. This leads us back to Meisner's definition of good acting. If we take the judgment out, we are left with: <u>Acting is living under imaginary circumstances.</u>

One might suggest to replace living with performing, however while there is no theatre without an audience, it is certainly possible to act without performing, e.g. if I practice a monologue in my living room. Even more obvious is that we can perform without acting, e.g. when we play piano or give a lecture.

To see if our definition captures the notion of acting, we must ask: Is it possible to live under imaginary circumstances without acting? The only cases that come to mind are psychotics or someone who has taken drugs like LSD. Such a person might be considered to be living under imaginary circumstances, e.g. thinking he can fly, but not to be acting. Why not? Because acting is something the actor does *intentionally*, something he can choose not to do. And a psychotic doesn't have that choice. (If he did we would indeed say that he is acting, that he is faking his mental illness.)

So to exclude these cases we can modify our definition as follows: <u>Acting is intentionally living under imaginary circumstances.</u>

To this one might object: What if someone is taking LSD with the intention to live under imaginary circumstances? Should he be considered acting? Certainly not, the point is that when under the influence of the drug he is no longer doing anything to act. And as anybody who ever had such an experience can tell you, he can not just stop either. To be acting one has to be able to stop if one chooses to.[19]

The next question we have to ask is: Is it possible to be acting while not living intentionally under imaginary circumstances? We often hear that teaching is like acting. So is a professor giving a

---

[19]A possible exception might be an actor who suffers from a *histrionic neurosis*: he can no longer distinguish between his own self and the role he plays. We might meet such an actor on the street and he starts (unintentionally) acting like Hamlet. Would we then say he is acting?

lecture acting? I would argue that this depends precisely on whether imaginary circumstances are involved. Teaching is certainly like acting in many respects, e.g. it involves projection, communication, etc. But if a professor is lecturing to her students, sharing her knowledge and enthusiasm for the subject with the people who are actually in front of her, we wouldn't usually say that she is acting - she is just being herself in the actual time and place of the lecture. She might of course be considered to be performing.

But if somehow we knew that she really hates the subject or her students, while in the lecture she acts *as if* she likes the subject, we would consider her to be acting. But then she is also intentionally focusing on the imaginary circumstance that she is someone who likes her subject.

Another case we might be asked to consider is an actor using "tricks", such as in the following example from Vakhtangov's system:

> A performer who is directed to pace the stage and think of avenging his father's death, for example, may not be stimulated by the director's suggestion and find no inner reality in the action. But he could pretend to himself that the purpose of his pacing is to find a weak floorboard in order to fall through the stage and sue the theatre's management! [Gordon, 1987 p. 83]

Clearly the actor is still living intentionally under imaginary circumstances - the point is that the circumstances that he imagines are different from the circumstances that he appears to be living in. One could of course question whether he is living truthfully and therefore whether this is good acting.

While for many the criterion for good acting is how it looks to the audience, independently of how this look was achieved, for Meisner it is part of good acting to be truthful and to focus on the imaginary circumstances. So the actor portraying Hamlet in the above example wouldn't be considered a good actor in this view. Of course Meisner is also very concerned with the perception of the audience, but he thinks the best way to *look* believable is to *actually* be truthful.

Michael Kirby in his essay *On Acting and Not-Acting* defines acting as follows: "Acting means to feign, to simulate, to represent, to impersonate. ... represent, or pretend to be in, a time or place different than that of the spectator" [Kirby, 1972 p. 3].

This definition raises some difficulties: Feigning and pretending are often used to denote bad acting and while we want to include bad acting in our definition of acting, we do not want to emphasize it. According to Meisner "you can't fake emotion" [Meisner & Longwell, 1987 p. 87]. Meisner and other teachers often ask their students not to pretend. "The foundation of acting is the reality of doing" [Meisner & Longwell, 1987 p. 16]. For example, if you are supposed to listen to the other character it is important that you *really* listen, instead of pretending to listen. Then you allow yourself to react to what you *actually* hear.

Dance performances may or may not contain elements of acting. Words like simulate or represent could be applied to dancers or mime even when they are not acting. For example dancers might have been given movements that simulate or represent a struggle that the choreographer had with his brother (or more abstractly with his inner child). The dancers however might not even know that and simply perform what they consider to be abstract movement. We would not consider them actors. It seems impossible to imagine a case where an actor is acting (as opposed to representing) a character without knowing it.

While for these reasons I prefer the definition we arrived at above, most of Kirby's analysis can be transferred to our definition. Kirby's main point in his essay is that there is a whole continuum between acting and not-acting. He suggests "a scale that measures the amount or degree of representation, simulation, impersonation and so forth in performance behavior" [Kirby, 1972 p. 9] and gives examples of performances with different amounts of acting. His complete scale looks as follows [Kirby, 1972 p. 8]:

NOT_ACTING				ACTING
Non-Matrixed Performing	Non-Matrixed Representation	"Received" Acting	Simple Acting	Complex Acting

Using our definition the amount of acting can be seen as the amount of imaginary circumstances involved. The imaginary circumstances can be divided into time, place, situation and character. Or where, when and who am I. Situation may include who the other characters are and what the objectives are. Character can be further divided and includes such elements as age, profession, habits, sexual preferences, personal tastes and opinions, ailments, etc. and also upbringing up to what happened before the scene, relations to other characters, etc.

To illustrate the different degrees or amounts of acting, let us look at a hypothetical but typical psychodrama session and observe how the protagonist moves from no acting at all to complex acting.

As the group session starts, the participants move into the room and either sit in a circle (in which case the center functions as a stage) or sit in front of a stage of some sort. As they gather they might be introducing each other and socialize - clearly there is no acting at that stage.

After a warm-up a protagonist might be asked to come onto the stage to work on his issues. The director might first ask him to say if he is aware of any sensations or feelings he is having right now. The protagonist might answer that he feels some tension in his neck and that he is nervous since he is on the spot. There are no imaginary circumstances involved and hence the protagonist is not acting. However, he has moved a step closer on the scale to acting, since he is now performing in front of an audience. Kirby calls this *Non-Matrixed Performing*. "When the performer ... is merely himself and is not imbedded, as it were, in matrices of pretended or represented character, situation, place and time, I refer to him as being 'non-matrixed'" [Kirby, 1972 p. 4].

Next the protagonist might report that he feels hostile to his parents. The director then may ask him to choose two people (*auxiliary egos* in Moreno's terminology) to represent his father and mother and to start telling them how he feels about them. The people representing the father and mother at first just stand there without any instructions. They are merely being themselves and don't *do* anything to act nor do they imagine any circumstances, other than the actual ones, like that they have been asked to stand on the stage. Nevertheless, they are one step closer to acting, since they represent father and mother. This is what Kirby calls *non-matrixed representation*. "In 'non-matrixed representation' the referential elements are applied *to* the performer and are not acted *by* him" [Kirby, 1972 p. 5].

The protagonist in the above scenario has to focus on at least one imaginary circumstance, namely that he is talking to his parents. So he is acting, but his acting is very simple; since he is playing himself, he doesn't have to act any other elements of character. He might also not act any other place and time if he imagines his parents are with him on the stage at this time. So this is the very first step towards simple acting.

Now suppose the director asks the protagonist if he remembers a typical scene with his parents. The protagonist might remember that his parents used to play cards while he had to play by himself. The director now sets up a scene asking the protagonist how he remembers his living room and using props to indicate furniture, etc. Then he tells the people representing the parents simply to sit on a table and play any card game they know (lets assume someone has actually brought real cards that are being used). Meanwhile the protagonist plays by himself next to the table, possibly giving a soliloquy about his feelings of isolation.

The players representing the parents are still not acting. They are being themselves playing with actual cards in the here and now and are not *doing* anything to appear to be someone, somewhere or someplace else. For them there are no imaginary circumstances involved. However, they have moved another step closer to acting, since now they clearly *appear* to be someone else in another place and time. Kirby calls this *received acting*.

> As "received" references increase, however, it is difficult to say that the performer is not acting even though he is *doing* nothing that we could define as acting. ... When the matrices are strong, persistent and reinforce each other, we see an actor, no matter how ordinary the behavior. This condition, the next step closer to true acting on our continuum, we may refer to as "received acting." [Kirby, 1972 p. 5]

The protagonist has also moved further on the scale towards acting. His acting is more complex - he is imagining to be in a different time and place, that the people playing cards are his parents, that the props are furniture, etc. He is still playing himself, though probably younger, and he doesn't have to act many elements of character. He also has the advantage that he can rely on his memory, instead of imagining the details of his character.

To go another step further we can suppose that the director asks the protagonist what he would have liked to have done when his parents were playing cards and how he thinks his parents would have reacted. He might respond that he felt like taking the cards away from them and telling them to stop playing. He thought his parents would get furious if he did that and would yell at him or even hit him. The director would then set up the scene and instruct the protagonist to demonstrate to the other actors exactly what they should do to portray his parents. Then the scene would be enacted, hopefully giving the protagonist some relief.

For the protagonist this would only be a small step further on the acting scale, the main difference being that he entered what Moreno calls *Surplus Reality*, where it is possible to enact not only what has happened, but also what one wishes or fears might have or will happen. This requires a higher degree of imagination, but the protagonist can still work from what he remembers.

The auxiliary egos have now entered complex acting, so to speak surpassing the protagonist on the acting scale. They now have to imagine place, time, situation and character. How much character they act will depend on how much information they are given and how skilled and experienced they are.

We have thus seen that all the different degrees of acting can occur even within one psychodrama session.

As quoted above, Kirby states that he has found "a scale that measures the amount or degree of representation, simulation, impersonation and so forth in performance behavior." Measurement involving a scale is usually defined as "the assignment of numerals to objects or events according to rules" [Stevens, 1946]. But is this really possible here or is the use of the term measurement too optimistic? Kirby certainly doesn't give any such rules.

What kind of scale do we have here? Clearly we do not have an *interval or ratio scale* (for definitions see e.g. [Stevens, 1946]), since it wouldn't make sense to talk of one person (or event) acting twice as much as another person or of the difference between performance A and B being twice as much as the difference between performance C and D.

This suggests that we might be looking at an *ordinal scale*, which is simply a ranking of observations along some dimension. The only statements we can meaningfully make are about *more* and *less*, not about *how much* more. Many of the scales psychologists use are of this sort, e.g. preference or intelligence.

However, even such a scale requires that we have a *total* order, i.e. that any two events are comparable. If we have two instances of performance behavior, can we always say which one has a higher degree of acting? It seems quite impossible to compare any totally different performances. But even with related performances difficulties arise: Let A be a psychodrama scene as above in which the protagonist talks to his parents in the actual time and place. Now there are different ways in which the amount of acting can be increased. Let B be the same session with his brother and sister added. Let C be the scene where the parents are acting elements of character. Let D be the scene where we are taken into the past and a living room, etc. Now B, C, D are all comparable to A. But how could we possibly decide which of B, C, D contains the most acting?

Two performances X and Y are only comparable when the corresponding sets of imaginary circumstances I(X) and I(Y) are comparable. For I(X) and I(Y) to be comparable we have to be able to decide which one contains a larger amount of imaginary circumstances. This is clear only if one is a subset of the other, as in the above example where we have $I(A) \subset I(B)$, or in cases where one only contains a few elements and the other a large number. In general however, our notions are not precise enough to actually count the number of circumstances. So we only have a *partial* order. Transitivity holds since if I(X) contains a higher amount of circumstances than I(Y) and I(Y) contains a higher amount than I(Z), clearly I(X) contains a higher amount than I(Z).

But if we only have a partial order it is not possible to assign numbers to all events in a consistent manner - if it were we could use the numbers to compare *any* two events and we would have a total order. Of course the simple set of the five categories that are listed on Kirby's scale is totally ordered and the order is evident from the diagram.

2. Improvisation

Next we will try to find a definition of improvisation. While in daily life it can also mean something like "do a job without appropriate tools," in a performance context it usually refers to a performance or elements of a performance that are not rehearsed and not planned in advance. So a first attempt at defining improvisation could be "performed without planning".

Clearly it is possible to improvise without acting, e.g. in a dance or music improvisation. It is also possible to act without improvising, e.g. when performing a scene in exact the same way night after night.

How do we decide if something is improvised? As with acting we can not always decide through observation whether someone is improvising. If we see a scene between actors that we don't recognize, we have no way of telling if they have rehearsed it. For this reason some improvisational performance groups decided to find a way of proving to the audience that they improvise. In Theatre Sports for example, the actors might ask the audience where they would like the next scene to take place, thus making it obvious that there is no way they could have rehearsed it.

For the same reason Moreno in his Living Newspaper (cf. Chapter III.2.2) enacted scenes from the daily paper as it appeared.

> The dramatized newspaper has another asset from the point of view of an art of the moment: the absolute evidence of true

spontaneity it has for the onlookers - and not simply for the actors, as in some form of the spontaneity theatre - because of the daily news character of the material projected. A good dramatized newspaper tries to produce the news as quickly as it can be gathered by the reporters; thus the production may change in content from hour to hour. [Moreno, 1983 p. 38]

Improvising is something the performer *does* and so he could usually tell us, if asked, whether he was improvising. The opposite of improvised is planned or rehearsed ahead of time. So is every element of a performance either planned or improvised? Suppose at a certain point in a performance the actor has to get up and cross the stage. Sometimes he starts with his left foot and sometimes with his right foot. While he doesn't plan this we also wouldn't say that he is improvising. It is merely *arbitrary* and neither he nor the audience is likely to pay any attention to it.

How do we distinguish arbitrary behavior from improvisation? We feel that improvisation is something that the actor does intentionally. It involves certain choices. The actor *chooses* to do something on the spur of the moment. When he merely starts walking with his right foot, we do not feel that he made a choice, that he had a reason (not even an unconscious one) or that he reacted to something. Nor do we see any creativity involved.

So the (element of the) performance has to be made up, created or composed as it is performed and neither composed in advance nor not composed at all, as in arbitrary movements. In improvisation there is no or hardly any time between composition and performance. This leads us to define improvisation as <u>composed and performed on the spot without planning.</u>

While there can be elements of a performance that are not intentional (but rather say habitual, like an actor constantly blinking his eyes), we wouldn't consider such elements part of the composition or creation. Thus the above definition implies, as I think it should, that improvising, like acting, is done *intentionally* by the actor. If the actor does something habitually, we wouldn't call that part improvised, even though at first it might appear to be. Some improvisation teachers put great emphasis on the student getting away from habitual responses and rather exploring new territory (e.g. Ruth Zaporah in her Action Theatre).

As is the case with acting, there is a continuum between improvising and not-improvising, with different degrees or amounts of improvisation. A performance can be placed on the scale according to how many of its elements are improvised.

A good indication is also the amount of variety between two performances of the same piece (if there is only one performance we could consider a hypothetical second performance prepared in the same way as the first). This is not conclusive however, since the variations could be due to arbitrariness rather than improvisation. In this case the variations, even if there are many, would not alter the impression of the piece. Still we might consider this closer to improvisation then if there are no variations.

Instances of the above frequently occur in *happenings*. These are performance installations in which performers are given certain tasks to perform and usually involve no acting, i.e. the performer does not do anything to suggest character or place and time. A performer might for instance be asked to sweep the floor at a certain point in the performance. He might do it differently each time, however, the variations do not affect the quality of the piece and he does not compose or create anything. He reacts to other performers only in so far as he has to get out of their way. He does not engage with them in a creative exchange.

Let us investigate the improvisation scale. It starts on one end with performances that contain no improvisation and no variation at all. Each performance looks exactly the same and the actors have been told exactly what to do up to the smallest detail and everything is rehearsed to perfection. This is of course an ideal that can not be completely obtained. There will always remain small variations, such as when does the actor breathe in and out. We will call these performances <u>completely rehearsed</u>.

The next step would be performances that are completely rehearsed, but improvisation has been used to create the performance in rehearsal. By this I mean that many elements of the performance were first improvised and then whatever worked well was kept. Such a performance would still not contain any variation, but presumably it would look more improvised since the actors would use elements that first happened in improvisation. This category can of course again be divided according to how much improvisation is used in the rehearsal process. A certain amount of this is very common in rehearsal of plays, as when an actor does something that he came up with on the spot and the director tells him to keep it. We call this category <u>rehearsed using improvisation</u>.

Next we consider performances that contain variations, but they are not due to improvisation, but to arbitrariness. As explained above many happenings fall in this category. Again we can subdivide these performances according to how much variation there is. We call this <u>arbitrary variation</u>.

Next we consider performances with variations that alter the piece substantially. There are such performances which nevertheless seem like the responses are automatic. This occurs when there is variation but in fact all the possibilities are well rehearsed and the performer keeps falling back on responses he has used before. For example a question and answer session after a lecture can be very different each night. Nevertheless, the lecturer might be so well prepared that she has considered and rehearsed answers to all questions usually asked. So while there is a lot of variation, the performer mostly relies on what has been rehearsed. We can call this <u>rehearsed variation</u>.

This should not be confused with the fact that performers get more skilled at improvisation as they practice. The first time someone is asked to create on the spot in front of an audience they often freeze. As they get more experience, they become more comfortable and more creative in coming up with original ideas. This is very different from becoming more proficient since all the possibilities have been anticipated and practiced.

Next we consider variation that is due to elements which are composed for the first time as they are performed. This starts with <u>simple improvisation</u> in which only certain elements are improvised, such as movement or timing or the ending. For example, in an otherwise rehearsed performance at a certain point an actor has to ask someone in the audience: "Can I borrow your shoes?" While he always uses the same line, he can completely change the way he asks by using movement, facial expression, intonation, etc. If he creatively makes those choices according to whom he talks to and what kind of shoes they are wearing, we would conclude that this part was improvised.

As more and more elements are improvised, especially when the lines are not memorized, we enter <u>complex improvisation</u>. For example the Santa Cruz performance group *Ummh....Ghee....Ummh* performs scenes based on cues from the audience in which time, place, character, relationships, objectives, beginning, middle and end are all created on the spot. All movement and dialogue are improvised. They also use accompanying musicians and lighting technicians who improvise.

At the end of our scale we have <u>**all improvisation**</u>, where every element of the performance is improvised. This is of course an ideal, since all performances will contain at least some elements that are anticipated (e.g. in what space the performance will take place) or arbitrary (e.g. how many steps a performer takes to cross the stage).

We have arrived at the following scale:

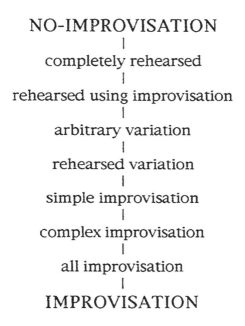

NO-IMPROVISATION
|
completely rehearsed
|
rehearsed using improvisation
|
arbitrary variation
|
rehearsed variation
|
simple improvisation
|
complex improvisation
|
all improvisation
|
IMPROVISATION

Our earlier analysis of the acting scale with respect to measurement easily translates to this improvisation scale and we won't repeat it here (instead of the set of imaginary circumstances consider the set of improvised circumstances).

Improvisation does not only occur in the theatre or on stage. For example, when a professor gives a lecture she could be using any degree of improvisation. If everything is totally planned and she is reading from a script, her speech is *completely rehearsed*. If she started with improvising her speech many times and then kept the elements that worked best, it is *rehearsed using improvisation*. If she walks around during her lecture, but otherwise says everything in the same way as last time, we have *arbitrary variation*. If she answers different questions each time, but has rehearsed all her answers, we have *rehearsed variation*. If she prepares most of her lecture, but uses different examples each time according to how her students respond and makes those examples up on the spot, we are looking at *simple improvisation*. If she prepares hardly anything (other than the fact that she knows a lot), maybe starting by asking the students what topic of the news they would like to discuss, she is engaged in *complex improvisation*, maybe getting close to the ideal of *all improvisation*.

3. Spontaneity

Spontaneity is the most important concept in Moreno's entire philosophy, not only in his dramatic theory. "Spontaneity and creativity are regarded as primary and positive phenomena and not as derivatives of libido or any other animal drive" [Moreno, 1946 p. 49]. He also considers it the prerequisite of good therapy: "Mental healing processes require spontaneity in order to be effective" [Moreno, 1946 p. XII].

His belief in spontaneity as the cure for most of modern man's problems can hardly be overemphasized: "Conscious evolution through training of spontaneity opens a new vista for the development of the human race" [Moreno, 1946 p. 47]; it is almost religious and in fact he proclaimed: "God is spontaneity" [Moreno 1985, frontispiece].

So what exactly is this so important concept? Unlike acting and improvisation it is not something a person *does*. Rather it is an internal *state* of consciousness. Like other abstract ideas such as intelligence or love, we can not expect to define it in a short sentence. It has to be investigated or, better, experienced from different angles to be understood.

First we might ask, how do we recognize spontaneity, how does someone look like who is spontaneous, what are the results of spontaneity? This is also one way in which Moreno attempts to define spontaneity:

> My operational definition of spontaneity is often quoted as
> follows: The protagonist is challenged to respond with some
> degree of adequacy to a new situation or with some degree of
> novelty to an old situation. [Moreno, 1946 p. XII]

The important word in this definition is *new*. Spontaneity is the ability to come up with new responses and to be able to deal with new situations in which we can't rely on previously rehearsed responses. Someone who is spontaneous would be able to surprise us, but they would also be very effective - it is not just newness for its own sake, but paired with adequacy or progress. For Moreno spontaneity, together with creativity, is the primary source of human progress.

Moreno called spontaneity-creativity a twin concept and states: "It was an important advance to link spontaneity to creativity, the highest form of intelligence we know of, and to recognize them as the primary forces in human behavior" [Moreno, 1946 p. XII]. He considers spontaneity to be the source or catalyzer of creativity and thus they are not identical. But is it possible to have one without the other?

> In the case of Man his s may be diametrically opposite to his c;
> an individual may have a high degree of spontaneity but be
> entirely uncreative, a spontaneous idiot. Another individual
> may have a high degree of creativity but be entirely without
> spontaneity, a creator "without arms". [Moreno, 1953 p. 39]

The idea of the "spontaneous idiot" is surprising in light of Moreno's emphasis on adequacy of response, but it is an exception to the rule. Spontaneity and creativity are usually linked, but not in a linear way. Creativity is also linked with productivity and it is possible to be very spontaneous without producing much, especially not much that lasts beyond the moment. "The visible definition of creativity is the 'child.' Spontaneity by itself can never produce a child but it can help enormously in its delivery" [Moreno, 1953 p. 39]. To produce a book or an opera it takes more than just spontaneity, one needs to plan the composition from beginning to end, spend many hours bringing the ideas to the paper, etc.

When someone produces mathematical theorems, she can be considered very creative, but her level of spontaneity might be high or low. Her ideas might take long concentrated thinking, which is not usually considered a sign of spontaneity.

What is the relation between spontaneity and improvisation? In line with the above definition Moreno writes: "The chief sign of talent for spontaneity is the ability of rapid emergence of an idea and the rapid transposition of an idea into action" [Moreno, 1983 p. 74].

"Rapid emergence of an idea and the rapid transposition of an idea into action" - that sounds very much like our definition of improvisation: "composed and performed on the spot without preparation." So we may paraphrase Moreno as follows: "The chief sign of talent for spontaneity is the ability to improvise."

Clearly spontaneity and improvisation are not the same thing - they are not even the same *kind* of thing - one is a state, the other an action. But they are very much linked together. Good improvisation requires a high level of spontaneity in the participants. A high level of spontaneity implies the ability to improvise.

Is it possible to improvise without spontaneity? Moreno seems to think it is:

> An old role player of the legitimate stage can simulate spontaneity in improvisations; but analysis would show that he plays from the residues of a repertory of rehearsed roles, that the creative surplus which he derives from clichés is exhausted after a short period and his inability to produce and compose independently and immediately, is exposed. [Moreno, 1983 p. 74]

The kind of improvisation that Moreno describes here falls in the category which we have called *rehearsed variation* above. When we read Moreno we have to be careful at times. His view of traditional theatre is so disapproving that he often uses the words *acting* or *improvisation* in a negative way (as we have seen for acting above). The way we have defined improvisation, it does indeed seem to require spontaneity - complex improvisation a higher level than simple improvisation.

On the other hand when we see improvisations we often feel that some are more spontaneous than others. These are usually the ones we liked better and which contained a higher level of ingenuity (but not necessarily a higher amount of improvisation).

This suggests that there is a value attached to spontaneity - the more the better! While there is good and bad acting or improvisation (whatever exactly that is), we don't speak of good and bad spontaneity. It is always good and we like to see and experience as much of it as possible.

So spontaneity is tied to good improvisation and this suggests a possible definition of spontaneity: <u>Spontaneity is the ability to improvise (well)</u>. This is at least an important aspect of spontaneity, in the same way as "intelligence is the ability to reason (well)" captures an important aspect of intelligence.

It is possible for there to be complex improvisation without much spontaneity, presumably it would be bad improvisation. Suppose we have a subject with a low level of spontaneity and we ask him to improvise a scene where he lives in the jungle in Africa. We also assume that he has never seen Africa and not even thought of it much. He can't possibly engage in *rehearsed variation*, since he has nothing to draw from. But surely he will come up with *something* and not all his movement and talk will be arbitrary. So he is engaging in improvisation, albeit not a very interesting one.

Next we ask whether it is possible to have spontaneity without improvisation. According to Moreno this is true since it is possible to have spontaneity without doing *anything*. "Spontaneity can be present in a person when he is thinking just as well as when he is feeling, when he is at rest just as well as when he is in action" [Fox, 1987 p. 43]. Moreno doesn't explain this further, what he might mean is that spontaneity is a *potential*. It can be present even at rest as long as *if* something would require the individuals response, he would respond spontaneously.

Moreno at times compares spontaneity and intelligence: "When compared with many other mental functions such as intelligence and memory, the sense for spontaneity is seen to be far less developed" [Moreno, 1946 p. 47]. He is well aware of the over-emphasis on intelligence in modern civilization and the distrust or fear of spontaneity often displayed.

Both intelligence and spontaneity are abstract concepts which are difficult to define. They denote mental functions or abilities for certain actions. They can and should both be trained (for more on Moreno's spontaneity training see Chapter III.2.4). They can also both be tested. In the case of intelligence this is of course well known and intelligence is sometimes ironically defined as that which an intelligence test measures. Moreno often refers to the spontaneity tests that he developed and used. They are supposed to measure the adequacy of response of subjects to novel situations. A detailed description of such a test can be found in [Moreno, 1946 p. 93ff].

"Put a subject into a life situation and see how he acts" [Moreno, 1946 p. 93]. To facilitate his test Moreno built a room on a stage with many details that were explained to the individual, such as doors, furniture, telephone, a baby, etc. The director then gives the subject instructions that are to be taken as facts. At first there is a warm-up period in which the subject performs simple tasks, like being told that the floor needs to be cleaned. Suddenly she is instructed that there is an emergency, such as a fire breaking out. The judges observe whether the individual is able to respond effectively, putting out the fire or calling for help, not forgetting the baby, etc.

If the subject dealt with one emergency with some success, she is exposed to another more difficult situation. At the end the individuals get scores according to how many levels they handled and how effectively they responded. Moreno recommends using these tests alongside intelligence testing in prison, the military and other places. However, he doesn't describe a clear scoring system that would allow the comparison of tests taken at different times and locations. It seems that to design such a test would be even more difficult than in the case of intelligence.

It is also theoretically more problematic to assign a spontaneity score to individuals. An intelligent person can be expected to be always intelligent, and test scores at different times will fluctuate only slightly. But the spontaneity level of a person can vary even throughout one day. He might have no spontaneity in the morning and very much in the evening.

The level of spontaneity is also easily effected by what environment the person is in and by what activities they are involved in. Especially a person who spends a lot of time in an environment which is deadening spontaneity, such as many offices, has to go through a warm-up in order to access his spontaneity. Moreno developed a theory as well as many techniques for warm-ups which will be explained further in Chapter III.2.3.

How can one attempt to measure spontaneity or intelligence? Isn't that even more difficult than to measure acting or improvisation, which, as we have seen above, is strictly speaking impossible? The point is that we were trying to measure the acting level of *any* event or behavior (at least any performance event). Now it is clearly impossible to measure the spontaneity or intelligence level of *any* event. However spontaneity and intelligence scores are to be assigned to *individuals* and are supposed to measure an internal quality that can manifest itself in many ways. To test those it is enough to have a series of *some* events whose levels are on an ordinal scale. The events could be mastering a certain percentage of assigned intelligence or spontaneity exercises. For the test to be practical and reliable, the exercises must be well-defined and repeatable at different times and places. The test would measure the amount of spontaneity or intelligence an individual has by just looking at one possible manifestation. We would then use this to predict how much spontaneity or intelligence the individual has available in any other situation.

It is meaningful to assign intelligence and spontaneity scores to individuals, although especially in the case of spontaneity we expect some intra-individual fluctuation over time. Some individuals clearly are more intelligent or spontaneous than others. But it wouldn't make sense to assign scores according to our acting or improvisation scale to individuals. Almost every individual is capable of engaging in a low as well as in a high amount of acting, though not necessarily good acting. Everyone can act as if they are Napoleon in France, which is complex acting, even if it is done poorly.

Moreno often mentions that many of his ideas go back to his earliest experiences of engaging in play-acting with other children in the houses and gardens of Vienna [Moreno, 1946 p. 2; Moreno, 1983 p. 84]. It was probably also there where he first saw spontaneity at work. He believes that the child is born with natural spontaneity and only later begins to loose it.

> ...Children, said Dr. Moreno in an interview, are endowed with the gift of spontaneous expression up to the age of 5, while they are still in an unconscious creative state, unhampered by the laws and customs laid down by a long succession of preceding generations. After that they fall heir to accepted methods of expression; they become imitative, turn into automatons and in a large measure are deprived of natural outlets of volitional creation. [Moreno, 1983 p. 106]

So the learning of spontaneity is foremost an *unlearning* of conditioning, roles, clichés, customs, in order to gain back what we lost since we were children.

> The actor must therefore learn to unchain himself from old clichés. By means of exercises in spontaneity he must learn how to make himself free gradually from habit formations. He must store in his body as large a number of motions possible to

be called forth easily by means of an emerging idea. [Moreno, 1983 p. 66]

The highest levels of spontaneity and creativity Moreno locates in the "geniuses of the human race" [Moreno, 1946 p. 48]. He sees the potential genius even in the infant and sharply distances himself from Freud, who looked at genius as a pathology, a sublimation of libido.

The purest of all expressions of spontaneity can be found in God. "God is an exceptional case because in God all spontaneity has become creativity. He is one case in which spontaneity and creativity are identical" [Moreno, 1953 p. 39].

To further understand spontaneity we also need to ask ourselves: What is the opposite of spontaneity? The opposite of spontaneous behavior is predictable, rigid, mechanical, habitual, etc. The clearest embodiment of this is the *robot* who can perform many tasks, but totally lacks in spontaneity and creativity.

Lewis Yablonsky, a student of Moreno's and a well-known psychodramatist in his own right, devotes an entire book to this "robopathology" [Yablonsky, 1972]. He has also a section in his *Psychodrama* [Yablonsky, 1981 p. 247ff] in which he writes:

> I coined the word *robopath* to describe people who have suffered the affliction of social death in their lives to the point where they enact robot roles. Although psychodrama is a method for dealing with a variety of human dilemmas and problems, it was conceived by Moreno in its most significant sense as a vehicle for counterattacking the growing problem

of robopathology in individuals and the larger problem of the death of a humanistic society. [Yablonsky, 1981 p. 247]

Robopaths are what we also call zombies - the living dead - people that go through live without any aliveness, they only go through the motions mechanically. They have no spontaneity or creativity left and never do anything new. Like machine robots these human robots might be quite efficient in certain functions. Some professions and work environments in our society almost demand such behavior, they do well especially in a bureaucracy.

The three main components of spontaneous behavior we found can be called: immediacy, adequacy and novelty. These taken together capture most of what we mean by spontaneity, so here is a closer look at each.

IMMEDIACY: Spontaneous behavior has to emerge *in the moment*. It is *automatic* or *reflexive* (but not mechanical). It happens without premeditation - the subject often doesn't know how it happened, he surprises even himself. It happens instantly without thinking. If it is a response, there is no time between action and reaction. If too much time passes, say between a question and an answer, we wouldn't call it spontaneous, even if it is novel and productive.

This state of immediacy is a familiar idea in some eastern religions. It is a primary goal in Zen-Buddhism. The Samurai in Kendo (Japanese form of fencing) empties his mind so that he can respond to an attack instantly - as fast as a mirror reflects its image. There is not one second in which he thinks about the best way to counter the attack. To accomplish this, he often needs years of training. This state is very *elusive* - if one tries too hard to obtain it, one will never reach it [Herrigel, 1951].

A similar idea is *the Way of the Water*, from Taoism. Go with the impulses and allow yourself to be taken by surprise without hesitation. As Alan Watts illustrates so beautifully, when we put a hole in a bucket of water, the water flows out instantly, it does not pause to think about what it should do next [Watts, 1975].

ADEQUACY: Spontaneous behavior also has to be *appropriate* to the situation. A response to an emergency has to be *effective*. A spontaneous contribution to solving a problem needs to be *productive*. Without this quality the behavior becomes arbitrary or random. For example when we suddenly fall on the floor we wouldn't call that spontaneous, even if it is immediate and novel.

NOVELTY: Spontaneous behavior doesn't follow familiar patterns. It should be *original*, either a new response to a familiar situation or a response to an unfamiliar situation. When repeated it looses spontaneity. For example if we see a professor telling a witty joke, we might say she is spontaneous, but if we then find out that she told the same joke yesterday, we would have to reverse our statement.

For another illustration suppose that we punch someone and the person screams and turns away. We wouldn't call this spontaneous, even if the response is immediate and adequate.

We have thus shown that each of these three components of spontaneity is essential. If one of them is lacking, we are also lacking in spontaneity.

II. MORENO'S CRITIQUE OF TRADITIONAL THEATRE

Moreno is a harsh critic of the theatre that came before him (and of most that came later as well) and calls it alternately legitimate theatre, rigid, dogmatic theatre, conventional, traditional theatre.

1. Cultural Conserve

Moreno defines *cultural conserve* as "The finished product of a creative effort (a book, a musical symphony, etc.)" [Moreno, 1983 p. 125] and states that "the pathology of our theatre is part of a larger process of disintegration, the pathology of our culture as a whole of which the most characteristic symptom is the 'cultural conserve' " [Moreno, 1983 p.19].

This concept expresses Moreno's contempt for traditional productions which are mechanical repetitions, removed from the creative act of the playwright.

> The legitimate theatre has its metaphysics in a time already past, outside of the precincts of the stage. The dramatic work, at the moment when it was created during the fleeting moments of the past, was not even then a thing of the present because it was not meant for the present. It was directed towards a future moment - the moment of its performance on the stage - and not towards the moment of its creation. [Moreno, 1983 p. 37]

Moreno's critique can appear devastating, as when he states: "The conventional theatre is, at its best, dedicated to the worship of the dead, of dead events - a sort of resurrection-cult" [Moreno, 1983 p.18].

The influence of cultural conserves is all too pervasive in our culture. "The audiences had been brought up in all departments of living, the sciences and the arts, to use and rely upon cultural conserves and not to trust their own spontaneity. The only spontaneity they had learnt to appreciate is that coming from the 'animated' conserve" [Moreno, 1983 p. 7].

The clearest and most widespread example of the cultural conserve in our present culture is television, which is indeed lacking in spontaneity and renders the audience passive - more so than any theatre.

From his experiments with spontaneity tests in which he observed subjects reacting to unexpected situations, Moreno found that:

> In the civilization of conserves which we have developed, spontaneity is far less used and trained than, for instance, intelligence and memory. ... Conditions of high cultural and technological organization coincide alarmingly with increased immobility of thought and action. [Moreno, 1983 p. 40]

According to Moreno, the theatre has become too predictable: "In the legitimate theatre the development of the drama is pre-established in all its phases" [Moreno, 1983 p. 52]. Theatre loses its aliveness with too much emphasis on slick productions with little room for variety and experimentation (which are considered mistakes).

> For this theatre is concerned with the most faithful rendering of every word. Its value depends upon faithful reproduction. It is the justification of life that is already over; it is a modern example of the cult of death, a cult of resurrection, not of creation. [Moreno, 1983 p. 47]

Today most of his critique also applies to film and other art forms. In fact motion pictures can be seen as being twice removed from spontaneity: The scenes being filmed were already predictable performances of rehearsed lines, but the audience is still further removed by not attending the performance and instead seeing a recording at a later time. The actor doesn't even get a chance to establish a connection with the audience.

For Moreno the performance of traditional theatre has a deadening effect not only on the audience who feels removed, but also on the actor.

> Rehearsing by memory has in many cases overlaid the natural sources of spontaneity by clichés and these blockings tend to become a permanent condition for him. The legitimate role-player has to be untrained and deconserved before he can become a spontaneity player. [Moreno, 1983 p. 74]

The lifeless, mechanical, predictable acting of the conventional actor makes him appear like a *robot*. This kind of behavior is becoming more and more common in our society and is even being demanded as the ideal in many professions.

In this sense Moreno's theatre can also be understood as an antidote to the *robopathic* actor (and audience). When Yablonsky (who coined the term "robopathology", cf. chapter I.3) talks about "the growing dehumanization of people to the point where they have become the walking dead. This dehumanized level of existence places people in roles in which they are actors mouthing irrelevant platitudes, experiencing programmed emotions with little or no compassion or sympathy for other people" [Yablonsky, 1981 p. 250], we are reminded of Moreno's description of the conventional actor.

For Moreno the cultural conserve, the robot, the machine, the bureaucrat are all symptoms of the same fundamental disease, the lack of spontaneity and creativity in our society.

> Following the course of man throughout the various stages of our civilization, we find him using the same methods in the making of cultural products which are used later and with less friction by the products of his mind, his technical devices. These methods have always amounted to this - to neglect and abandon the genuine and outstanding creative process in him, to extinguish all the active, living moments, and to strive towards one unchangeable goal: the illusion of the finished, perfected product whose assumed perfectibility was an excuse par excellance for forsaking its past, for preferring one partial phenomenon to the whole reality. [Moreno, 1953 p. 595]

Today the technical devices, especially film, have perfected what the conventional theatre already had as its goal: performances with no mistakes that could be repeated over and over. Theatre with this goal however can never compete successfully with film, movies will always be more perfect and repeatable; this might indeed be the reason why film and television is threatening to replace theatre in our culture.

Thus we need a theatre with a different orientation. The goals of Moreno's new theatre which are discussed in chapter III can not possibly be reached by film. While many people might nevertheless prefer the more passive experience of film, at least this new theatre still has its unique function.

2. Actor as Playwright's Tool

Moreno's contempt for the playwright is categorical and total. "The root of the theatre disease is expressed in one phrase: rigid given lines" [Moreno, 1983 p. 108].

According to Moreno, "the actors have had to give up their initiative and their spontaneity. They are merely the receptacles of a creation now past its moment of true creativity" [Moreno, 1983 p.18]. In this way they become tools to express the playwright's creativity, although not in the moment of creation.

> The script of the stage play - a product of the mind - is presented to the actor. It consists of words. The actor must not oppose his (secondary) mind to this product: he must sacrifice himself to it. The role stands before him with an individuality of its own. ... The deep stage-fright experienced by many of the greatest mimes is caused by the conflict between the private self and the imposed role, between spontaneous creativity and drama conserve.
>
> Instead of himself, the actor personifies something which has already been personified as a role, by the dramatists. There are three possible relations between an actor and his role. In the first, he works himself into the role, step by step, as if it were a different individuality. The more he extinguishes his private self, the more he becomes able to "live" the role. In this case, the role is like the personality of someone he might wish to be instead of himself. His attitude toward the role is one of identity. In the second, he finds the mean between his conception of the role and that of the author. His attitude, in this case, is one of synthetic integration. In the third, in disgust, he forces the specific role into his own individuality

and distorts the written words of the dramatist into a *personal* style of his own. In this case his attitude is one of disfiguration. [Moreno, 1983 p. 41f]

These are all the possibilities Moreno considers for the relation between the actor and his role. None of these allow for the actor to be true to himself and spontaneous, while doing justice to the play. He doesn't entertain the possibility of "living truthfully under imaginary circumstances" [Meisner & Longwell, 1987 p. 15], which was discussed at length in chapter I.1.

> The professional actor of the legitimate stage is all but spontaneous. He has to sacrifice his own self and the roles he might like to contrive, to the self and the roles which a playwright has elaborated for him and in the process of his adaptation to these roles he may well develop a form of personality disorder which can be called a "histrionic neurosis." His own spontaneity has to recede for the spontaneity of another mind. [Moreno, 1983 p. 83]

Apparently Moreno sees no therapeutic value for the actor playing roles in written plays. This seems surprising if one considers the fact that role-playing is a major component of psychodrama. Moreno is well aware of the therapeutic effect of acting out different roles on the psychodramatic stage. "But the individual craves to embody far more roles than those he is allowed to act out in life, and even within the same role one or more varieties of it" [Moreno, 1946 p. V].

Moreno also acknowledges that there are times when it is indicated to have a protagonist act out roles seemingly unrelated to his personal life.

> A further method of breaking resistance is the "symbolic technique", starting on a symbolic production so that fear of private involvement is eliminated as a cause of resistance. The director addresses the group thus: "There is a conflict between husband and wife because of certain irregularities in the behavior of the husband. He may be a gambler, a drunk, or whatever. They have an only child, a son, who is uncertain on whose side he should be." At this point the director turns towards the group and asks, "Who wants to take the part of the husband, of the wife, or of the son?" These roles being noncommittal for the private lives of the members of the group, the director may more easily provoke some of them to participate. [Moreno, 1946 p. IX]

So the main reason Moreno is critical of acting in plays is not so much because the parts might be unrelated to the actors own life, but because for him memorizing lines and being spontaneous and authentic on stage are incompatible. This also explains why his critique applies to all written plays and not just to plays dealing with issues foreign to the actor.

3. Actor/Spectator Separation

According to Moreno, "The strict separation between the stage and audience is the marked characteristic of the legitimate theatre" [Moreno, 1983 p. 31]. The audience is rendered passive with little influence on what happens on stage. In this setting they experience even less spontaneity and catharsis then the actors. They merely watch the lives and conflicts of characters, which are often foreign to them and far removed from their own life experience.

"In modern times the theatre is seen only from one pole, the stage. The other pole, the audience, is left in the darkness during the performance, not only actually, but also symbolically" [Moreno, 1983 p. 31f]. By now of course there have been many performances with audience involvement, most notably by the Living Theatre (cf. chapter IV.3). Traditional plays however are still often rehearsed and performed without reference to the audience reaction.

On the other hand every actor knows that no matter how hard he tries to fight against it, the audience affects his performance, for better or for worse. Likewise most theorists affirm the importance of the audience. "All types of theatrical performance require an audience" [Brockett, 1992 p. 22].

The separation of the audience obviously reaches its peak in film and television, which leaves absolutely no possibility for the audience to get involved. Despite this (or because of it?), film and television now threaten to replace theatre in our culture.

4. Improvisation before Moreno: Commedia dell'arte

While Moreno devotes a lot of room in his writings to his critique of traditional theatre, we note that he rarely mentions specific productions, companies, directors or playwrights. In fact he hardly mentions going to the theatre himself. We are left to guess that he probably did, since theatre was one of his main interests and for most of his life he lived near Vienna or New York.[20] Surely there must have been some performances that he liked better than others, some that showed at least some level of spontaneity or authenticity. Or did he dislike all of it?

His critique is very general and applies to all theatre using scripts. By implication it applies to most theatre that Moreno was exposed to or knew of. Before he started his own theatre in Vienna in 1921, theatre history contained only a few instances of improvised theatre performances.

The only example Moreno comments on is *Commedia dell'arte.* This form emerged in Italy towards the middle of the sixteenth century. It is not based on written scripts but on scenarios, providing merely given circumstances, lines of actions, motivations and outcome. The basic character-format is well

---

[20]There is a report of Moreno going to the theatre in White's biography of Jean Genet: "*The Balcony* generated plenty of serious discussion in puritanical America. Two psychiatrists (one of them the celebrated J. L. Moreno, the founder of psychodrama, the other the author of 'The Callgirl: A Social and Psychoanalytical Study') discussed the play on-stage after a performance; they were joined by a professor of sociology" [White, 1993 p. 422]. The episode is not mentioned anywhere by Moreno and so we do not know what he had to say about the production.

established and remains mostly the same, containing lovers, masters and servants, including such classics as Arlecchino or Harlequin, Pantalone and Dottore.

Within this framework there was some room for improvisation and especially in its early stages the actors would be able to change dialogue depending on their inspiration and the response of the audience. As the form developed, more and more of the dialogue and *lazzi* (frequently used comic stage business) became standardized.

Oscar Brockett in his widely used textbook *The Essential Theatre* writes about Commedia dell'arte: "Nevertheless, performances undoubtedly created the impression of spontaneity because no actor could be certain what the others would say or do, and each had to concentrate moment by moment on the unfolding action and respond appropriately" [Brockett, 1992 p. 152].

Moreno is more critical and places the Commedia dell'arte somewhere between scripted theatre (no improvisation) and his true spontaneity theatre (all improvisation). He analyzes it as follows:

> The lines themselves were unwritten and it is in this feature that the improvisatory character of the form came to expression, but because the same situations and plots, and the same types of roles were repeated again and again, the improvisatory character of the dialogue which prevailed when a cast was new disappeared little by little, the more often they repeated a given plot. They became slaves of their own recollection of the way they created each role, with the result that, after a given period of time (which, in the

laboratory, can be predicted with accuracy) hardly a sentence or joke in the dialogue was any longer spontaneous. [Moreno, 1983 p. 55]

This again illustrates Moreno's point that memorizing lines automatically leads to a loss of spontaneity. Moreno rejects the idea that psychodrama or his theatre of spontaneity was derived from Commedia dell'arte:

> Psychodrama has apparently no precedent in historic times. On the surface, the nearest approach to it in the history of the drama is the Italian Commedia dell Arte. The plot was written out but the dialogue was improvised by the actors. The characters recurred invariably in these plays, e.g. Arleckhino, The Captain, The Doctor. But the aim of the Commedia dell Arte was entertainment not therapeusis. Even as a theatre for spontaneity it limited spontaneity to improvisation of the dialogue, which, as the situations and conflicts always recurred, was bound to end in clichés of a cultural conserve sooner or later. Working within the framework of the legitimate theatre and without a system of spontaneity training, the Commedia dell Arte died a slow death. [Moreno, 1946 p. 12]

In terms of the improvisation scale introduced in chapter I.2 this view suggests that Commedia dell'arte started as *simple improvisation*, the dialogue being the main improvised element, then developed into *rehearsed variation* as the actors became familiar with all possible responses. Towards the end it more and more lost even these variations, becoming almost *completely rehearsed.*

Moreno's analysis is consistent with most modern theorists' views of the Commedia dell'arte. Kathleen McGill in an analysis from the point of view of rhetoric entitled *Improvisatory Competence and the Cueing of Performance: The Case of the Commedia dell'Arte* concludes:

> Taviani is correct in insisting that the competence of improvisation is *premeditated*. The "learnable skill" of improvisation is to fill the mind with a repertory of possible responses from which to draw. [McGill, 1990, p. 121]

This phrase is very close to our definition of *rehearsed variation* in chapter I.2. After her careful analysis of Commedia dell'arte McGill states without further justification that her findings are "applicable to improvisation in general" [McGill, 1990, p.121]. This is clearly too big of a jump (and would collapse the improvisation scale from chapter I.2). She excludes the possibility of novel responses to novel situations and hence of spontaneity.

Her confusion could be based on the fact that she did not distinguish between two ways in which a performer gets better at improvisation with practice:

a) More and more of what happens becomes familiar and he remembers how to respond.

b) He becomes faster and more comfortable at coming up with new ideas which he immediately embodies.

In 1990 Richards & Richards in their *The Commedia dell'arte* devote a chapter to the problem of "Improvisation and Performance". In it they state: "Although improvisation was early recognized abroad to be a distinctive characteristic of performance all'Italiana, exactly in what it consisted remains elusive" [Richards & Richards, 1990 p. 186]. After stating some of the questions that can not be answered, such as how much was prepared beforehand and how did improvisation function in performance, they continue with the following paragraph which best summarizes what is known about improvisation in Commedia dell'arte:

> Perhaps the one thing we can say with confidence about improvisation is that it was not entirely spontaneous; it was not devised wholly impromptu and off-the-cuff while the players were actually on a stage in performance. Spontaneity was of course a feature of improvised playing, and Perrucci, Riccoboni, Gozzi and others all remark on this as a strength that distinguished it from premeditated acting: but what they seem to suggest is that improvised acting gave the *impression* in performance of being more spontaneous than premeditated acting. The actors did not, then, simply spawn new plot-lines, dialogue and *lazzi* as they went along. Successful improvised performance, when done not as an amateur *jeu d'esprit* like that of Troiano and his colleagues, but as a professional activity for a paying audience, was the outcome of long deliberation by, and close collaboration between, members of a troupe accustomed to playing together, and familiar with each other's stage *personae*. Disciplined performance did not exclude the introduction of unpremeditated verbal arabesques and the elaboration of 'business' on the spur of the moment; it was indeed spontaneous to the extent that it permitted a certain free play in performance for the expression of the performer's character, temperament, particular specialist skills, and personal performance ways with assimilated materials. But it was rooted in careful preparation. [Richards & Richards, 1990 p. 187]

Their analysis of the end of Commedia dell'arte is very much in agreement with Moreno:

> Equally striking is the number of eighteenth-century complaints about the extent to which stage dialogue had become facile, monotonous and repetitious - so much so that many of Carlo Gozzi's contemporaries thought that performances by then were basically premeditated, the same stock sentiments, attitudes and jokes being regurgitated from play to play. [Richards & Richards, 1990 p. 188]

Next they include a section with documents from commentators, mostly dating from the seventeenth century. One such comment is introduced as follows:

> But much of Perrucci's incidental comment is interesting, more particularly the suggestions that improvised playing was widespread, at all cultural and social levels, that vulgarities characterized the performance of street entertainers and mountebanks, and that improvised playing at its best should be considered superior to acting off scripted texts - a view quite widely held by seventeenth- and eighteenth- century commentators. [Richards & Richards, 1990 p. 201]

Indeed, if we look at some of these comments, they argue, like Moreno later, that the improvising actor is more alive and authentic, e.g. Riccoboni in 1728: "The player who acts *all'improvviso* performs in a more vivacious and natural way than the player who has learned a part. Feeling comes more readily, and thus one can better say what one has composed oneself, than what is drawn from others by the help of memory" [Richards & Richards, 1990 p. 204].

Goethe gave an even more enthusiastic account of his visit to the theatre:

> Yesterday I went to the Commedia, Theatre St. Lukas, which was a great joy, I saw an extemporaneous piece with masks, performed with much temperament, energy and brilliance,... With an incredible variety it entertained for more than three hours, the audience participates and the crowd merges with the theatre into a unity. During the day on the square and at the waterfront on the gondolas and in the palace, the seller and buyer, the beggar, the boatman, the neighbor, the advocate and his opponent, everyone lives and bustles about and is concerned, speaks and asserts, screams and insists, sings and plays, swears and blares. And at night they go to the theatre and watch and listen to their daily life, artistically arranged, exaggerated, intertwined with fairy tales, removed from reality through masks, brought back through common behavior. (J. W. Goethe (1786) in [Esrig, 1985 p. 11])[21]

In this wonderful account we see many of the elements of Moreno's new theatre which are discussed in chapter III, such as spontaneity, immediacy, audience involvement, elimination of the

---

[21]"Gestern war ich in der Komödie, Theater St. Lukas, die mir viel Freude gemacht hat, ich sah ein extemporiertes Stück in Masken, mit viel Naturell, Energie und Bravour aufgeführt,... Mit unglaublicher Abwechslung unterhielt es mehr als drei Stunden, die Zuschauer spielen mit, und die Menge verschmilzt mit dem Theater in ein Ganzes. Den Tag über auf dem Platz und am Ufer auf den Gondolen und im Palast, der Käufer und Verkäufer, der Bettler, der Schiffer, die Nachbarin, der Advokat und sein Gegner, alles lebt und treibt und läßt sich es angelegen sein, spricht und beteuert, schreit und bietet aus, singt und spielt, flucht und lärmt. Und abends gehen sie ins Theater und sehen und hören das Leben ihres Tages, künstlich zusammengestellt, artiger aufgestutzt, mit Märchen durchflochten, durch Masken von der Wirklichkeit abgerückt, durch Sitten genähert."

playwright, Surplus Reality, themes reflecting the life of the community. In fact the described replaying of daily lives in a different setting very much reminds one of psychodrama.

The various accounts of Commedia dell'arte show that, while as a whole it is very different from Moreno's ideal of theatre, some performances exhibited many of the elements later developed by Moreno.

5. Theorists before Moreno

From all the theorists that came before Moreno, his writings acknowledge only two as forerunners of his ideas: Aristotle and Johann Wolfgang von Goethe. Moreno's well-known "megalomania" [Marineau, 1989 p. xiii] might explain why he liked to see himself in line with these universal geniuses. Early on he started thinking of himself as a messiah, in line with other geniuses and saints, including Jesus. Ironically some of his followers are of the opinion that his lack of recognition is partly due to his megalomania (e.g. [Blatner, 1988b p. 40]).

Moreno referred to Aristotle for the first time in 1924, but somehow avoided using the term catharsis.[22] In his later works, especially *Psychodrama: First Volume* [1946], he described how he had adapted the concept catharsis from Aristotle and developed it into one of the main tenets of his theory.

The situation with Goethe differs in that Moreno did not add his comments on Goethe to his *The Theatre of Spontaneity* until

---

[22]"Diese vielfache Ortsbestimmung des Theaters gestattet, die gewonnene Auffassung von der Ansicht des Aristoteles (in der Poetik - Die Aufgabe der Tragödie ist, durch Furcht und Mitleid eine Befreiung von derartigen Gemütsbewegungen zu bewirken.) abzugrenzen. Sein Urteilsgrund ist die *fertige* Tragödie. Ob nach seinen Worten die läuternde Wirkung im Leser (Zuhörer) oder in den tragischen Personen der Dichtung eintritt: der Streit darüber währt bis in die Gegenwart; er sucht irrtümlich von der *Wirkung* aus den Sinn des dogmatischen Theaters zu erschließen.
Der Urteilsgrund dieser Schrift ist kein fertiger Prozeß, sondern die gleichzeitige Materialisation einer in Bildung begriffenen Dichtung. Und es tritt eine (unbedingte) heilende Wirkung ein: doch nicht im Zuhörer (erwünschte Wirkung), noch in den dramatis personae eines imaginären Werkes, sondern in den Dichtern, den Stegreifspielern der Tragödie, die sie bilden, indem sie sich zugleich von ihr befreien" [Moreno, 1924 p. 81].

the second, enlarged edition was published in 1973, at a time when his theories had already been fully developed. He felt that Goethe had anticipated some of his ideas for therapeutic theatre and spontaneity, rather than directly influenced him. We will first take a closer look at Aristotle and then return to Goethe.

5.1 Aristotle

Moreno refers to Aristotle in a number of places in his writings, mainly in connection with the idea of catharsis. This concept is used widely today in a number of contexts, but is not easy to define. Nevertheless, if we observe a psychodrama there is usually considerable agreement on whether and when a catharsis occurred. But wherein does the catharsis consist? The patient experiences some kind of emotional breakthrough. Maybe he is able to cry about a loss for the first time. Buried or repressed emotions emerge to a climax of full expression. This can be accompanied by reliving a (possibly until then repressed) memory. But this is not necessary - for example in Rebirthing it is common that the subject goes through an emotional catharsis without knowing "what it is about". The feelings just come up without a conscious content. Still the subject often experiences the characteristic relief and liberation after the climactic experience -

a feeling of having let out something that has been held in for too long. As Moreno used to say: "Every *true* second time is the liberation from the first" [Moreno, 1983 p. 91][23].

When we speak of catharsis, there is usually some form of reference to a past event, something that happened at a time when the subject was not able to fully experience her feelings, as in a childhood with restrictive parents. Without such a reference to the past, for example if I have an emotional outburst simply because of what has just happened, we would rarely talk of catharsis. But again if it is the first time I cried in years it probably would be a catharsis (unless I simply have not had a reason to cry in years).

After these preliminary speculations about the meaning of catharsis it is useful, in order to shed some further light on our topic, to go back to its origin, to Aristotle. Moreno quotes Aristotle as follows:

> It remained for psychodrama to rediscover and treat the idea of catharsis in its relation to psychotherapy. The famous definition of tragedy in the sixth chapter of "De Poetica" ends with the statement "A tragedy is filled with incidents arousing pity and fear wherewith to accomplish its catharsis of such emotions." [Moreno, 1946 p. 13f]

The sentence Moreno cites is commonly known as "*The Poetics* VI, 1449 b 26"[24]. Before I investigate Moreno's comments further,

---

[23]This idea can already be found in [Moreno, 1924 p. 77]: "Jedes wahre zweite Mal ist die Befreiung vom ersten."
[24]"The *Poetics* occupies pages 1447 through 1462 in the second volume of the edition of Aristotle prepared for the Berlin Academy by Immanuel

I will give a brief overview of interpretations of Aristotle's use of catharsis.

5.1.1 Interpretations of Aristotle's catharsis

Some of the better-known translations of 1449 b 26 are:

• "Tragedy, then, is...through pity and fear effecting the proper purgation of these emotions" [Butcher, 1951 p. 23].

• "Tragedy, then, is...through a course of pity and fear completing the purification of tragic acts which have those emotional characteristics" [Else, 1967 p. 25].

• "Thus, Tragedy is...effecting through pity and fear [what we call] the *catharsis* of such emotions" [Hutton, 1982 p. 50].

• "Die Tragödie ist...die Jammer und Schaudern hervorruft und hierdurch eine Reinigung von derartigen Erregungszuständen bewirkt" [Fuhrmann, 1982 p. 19].

While the translations are fairly similar, interpretations differ widely even today. "Judging from the deluge of commentary, Aristotle's statement on the nature and function of catharsis is probably the most controversial sentence ever written" [Scheff, 1979 p. 20].

Indeed Brunius [1966] has written an entire book about this sentence, entitled *Inspiration and Katharsis: The Interpretation of Aristotle's* The Poetics *VI, 1449 b 26*, where he states:

Bekker (1830). Thus the reference 1449 b 26 means: page 1449, right-hand column, line 26 in Bekker." [Else, 1967 p. 14]

It was not my intention to give a complete report of "Stand der Forschung". It cannot possibly be done. Aristotle's *Poetics*, 1449 b 26 inspired about 1425 different interpretations before 1931. Since then the number of new contributions has increased tremendously. [Brunius, 1966 p. 9]

Butcher also agrees:

The other and more fundamental difficulty relates to the meaning of the *katharsis*[25]. Here we seek in vain for any direct aid from the *Poetics*. A great historic discussion has centered round the phrase. No passage, probably, in ancient literature has been so frequently handled by commentators, critics, and poets, by men who knew Greek, and by men who knew no Greek. [Butcher, 1951 p. 243]

Else has a similar view:

The great virtue, but also the great vice, of 'catharsis' in modern interpretation has been its incurable vagueness. Every variety of moral, aesthetic, and therapeutic effect that is or could be experienced from tragedy has been subsumed under the venerable word at one time or another. [Else, 1957 p. 439]

Saint-Evremond even suggested that Aristotle himself did not know what he was driving at [Brunius, 1966 p. 81]. The term "catharsis" appears only once in the extant part of the *Poetics*, and then not in a context that offers a firm handle to interpretation [Else, 1967 p. 6]. There is no evidence that Aristotle himself gave it as much importance as some of his commentators.

---

[25]While I use the now more common Latin spelling "catharsis", some authors adopted the Greek "katharsis".

In trying to sort through the multitude of speculations about catharsis, I will follow Kruse who came up with three basic categories: clarification, purgation, and cleansing [Kruse, 1979 p. 164].

5.1.1.1 Catharsis as Clarification

Under this view catharsis is the enlightenment or intellectual and moral insight we experience from learning something - according to Aristotle associated with pleasure. This view has recently been reiterated by Leon Goldon:

> Aristotle's view of art as *mimesis* demands that *katharsis* represent that moment of insight which arises out of the audience's climactic intellectual, emotional, and spiritual enlightenment, which for Aristotle is both the essential pleasure and essential goal of mimetic art. [Golden, 1992 p. 2]
> Tragic katharsis is, first and foremost, a learning experience about the cause, nature and effect of pity and fear. [ibid. p. 31]
> We have, then, firmly rejected the widely-held view that the final clause of Aristotle's famous definition of tragedy refers to the medical "purgation of pity and fear" or to some hybrid form of purgation and purification of those same emotions. [ibid. p. 32]

Even Goldon does not completely exclude the emotional component, how else could he speak of "emotional enlightenment"?[26]

There are not many critics who interpret Aristotle's catharsis as clarification. It is important to point out that even those who

---

[26]Golden devotes an entire chapter to discussing his interpretation of catharsis and comparing it with others [Golden, 1992 p. 5-39].

have the view that the function of tragedy *should* be insight and learning often express their view in opposition to Aristotle. For example, Bertold Brecht's interpretation of Aristotle falls into the purgation category: "And the catharsis of which Aristotle writes - cleansing by fear and pity, or from fear and pity - is a purification..." [Brecht, 1964 p. 181], even though his own view of the function of theatre stresses insight:

> This dramaturgy does not make use of the 'identification' of the spectator with the play, as does the aristotelian, and has a different point of view also towards other psychological effects a play may have on an audience, as, for example, towards the 'catharsis'. Catharsis is not the main object of this dramaturgy.
> ...In fact, it has as a purpose the 'teaching' of the spectator a certain quite practical attitude; we have to make it possible for him to take a critical attitude while he is in the theatre (as opposed to a subjective attitude of becoming completely 'entangled' in what is going on). [Brecht, 1964 p. 78]

5.1.1.2 Catharsis as Purgation

This is probably the most widespread interpretation and views catharsis as emotional purgation or therapeutic release. One of the most important proponents of this view is Samuel Butcher, who appeals to the metaphor of the medical use of the term, where catharsis denotes the removal of a painful or disturbing element from the organism. He writes:

> Applying this to tragedy we observe that the feelings of pity and fear in real life contain a morbid and disturbing element. In the process of tragic excitation they find relief, and the

morbid element is thrown off. As the tragic action progresses, when the tumult of the mind, first roused, has afterwards subsided, the lower forms of emotion are found to have been transmuted into higher and more refined forms. [Butcher, 1951 p. 254]

Kruse comments: "The second point of view ... assumes that pity and fear are, in many respects, disturbing and uncomfortable emotions. Therefore, they should be eliminated" [Kruse, 1979 p. 164]. While this statement is correct as far as it applies to Butcher's view, it by no means applies to all interpretations in the "emotional purgation" category. Hutton for example writes:

Thus *catharsis* appears to be nothing but the feeling of relief that comes from giving way to the emotions in an intense emotional experience. ... The discharge of the emotions is in any case a temporary psychological effect without moral consequences; one does not become fearless and pitiless from attending the theater, any more than a melancholy man is permanently transformed into a jovial one by drugs or music. [Hutton, 1982 p. 89]

So one certainly does not have to divide emotions into desirable and undesirable ones in order to interpret catharsis as emotional relief. In fact Hutton goes on to say: "The word *catharsis* ... adds to pity and fear the necessary idea that they give pleasure, and pleasure of a harmless, psychological kind, without moral consequences" [Hutton, 1982 p. 89]. This view is also echoed by Jacob Bernays in 1857, who is paraphrased by Butcher as follows: "The stage, in fact, provides a harmless and pleasurable outlet for instincts which demand satisfaction, and which can be indulged here more fearlessly than in real life" [Butcher, 1951 p. 245].

As we will see later, Moreno's interpretation of Aristotle (which has to be distinguished from his own use of the term catharsis) also falls within this category.

5.1.1.3 Catharsis as Cleansing

Under the first two interpretations catharsis is something that is brought about in the audience (or to a lesser extent in a reader) and it is possible that it happens to some spectators but not to others at the same performance of the same tragedy. The third understanding, catharsis as cleansing or purification, locates catharsis within the plot and makes it a property of the text.

Gerald Else is the most prominent and probably the initial proponent of this view. It is hard to believe that as late as 1957 he came up with a totally different interpretation of Aristotle which is now gaining more and more acceptance:

> The "catharsis" is a purification of whatever is "filthy" or "polluted" in the *pathos*, the tragic act. [Else, 1967 p. 98]
> The spectator or reader does not *perform* the purification...
> The purification, that is, the proof of the purity of the hero's motive in performing an otherwise 'unclean' act, is *presented* to him. [Else, 1957 p. 438]

For example in *Oedipus* the tragic act is the killing of a person who is close kin (here the father). This inherently polluted or filthy act is considered unpolluted or pure if it was performed in ignorance (of the kinship). For Else catharsis would then be the process of proving that the act was pure in that sense. To some extent this is achieved by the entire plot, but the innocence of motive is especially guaranteed by the remorse of the doer, which shows that if he had known the facts he would not have done the deed. Oedipus of course convinces us by blinding himself and thus becomes eligible for our pity and horror.

While Else's view in itself is consistent and rather convincing, his lengthy critique of the catharsis-as-purgation view (as represented by Bernays) is rather weak. First he admits that his interpretation is in conflict with Aristotle's explanation in the 8th book of the *Politics* which clearly implies that "catharsis" means some kind of purgation of the subject's emotions. This is where Bernays drew his ideas from, but Else insists that the *Poetics* should be interpreted out of the *Poetics*. He than continues his critique:

> And there is another objection to Bernays' interpretation, which would long since have been recognized as fatal if the authority of the *Politics* passage had not been accepted as beyond dispute. His interpretation, no matter how adapted or refined, is inherently and indefeasibly *therapeutic*. It presupposes that we come to the tragic drama (unconsciously, if you will) as patients to be cured, relieved, restored to psychic health. But there is not a word to support this in the *Poetics*, not a hint that the end of the drama is to cure or alleviate pathological states. On the contrary it is evident in every line of the work that Aristotle is presupposing *normal* auditors, normal states of mind and feeling, normal emotional and aesthetic experience. [Else, 1957 p. 440]

Now clearly Aristotle has not intended drama to be geared towards mental patients. However this is not at all implied in Bernays' view. In our time most "normal" families are considered dysfunctional and therapy is considered to be beneficial to a great number of people. It is not much of a stretch to assume that in Aristotle's time also many "normal" people experienced emotional distress or repression and could benefit from some emotional release. Else confuses different usages of the term "therapeutic". He suggests that "therapeutic" can not be applied to "normal" people, but only to pathological patients. He does not go into what he means by normal, but presumably it should mean something that implies that the majority of people are normal. Bernays interpretation however can be called therapeutic only in a broader sense in which healing, growth, emotional relief, self-expression and insight are beneficial to almost everyone.[27]

Else's next point reads as follows:

> There is still another fatal objection to Bernays' theory, and to any theory which is based like his on the concept of the musical catharsis: that the musical part of tragedy is precisely the one that Aristotle minimizes, not to say ignores, in his theory of tragedy. If the catharsis is in any sense a musical experience, the *Poetics* is the work that least provides a place and mode of operation for it. [Else, 1957 p. 440]

Else fails to explain why it should follow from Bernays' view that catharsis is a musical experience. The apparent reason why

---

[27]This is also how Moreno uses the term *therapy*, as discussed in chapter III.1.1.

he says that Bernays' theory is based on the concept of the musical catharsis is the fact that Bernays' interpretation is largely based on Aristotle's use of the term in the *Politics*. There the term is explained as a form of emotional relief and is applied to a musical experience. Now Bernays is simply saying that besides music there are other things like tragedy that can induce catharsis. By no means does it follow that catharsis has to be a musical experience.

Else's last objection is not very convincing either:

> Connected with this is another deficiency in the reigning explanations of catharsis, not only in that of Bernays but in all the others. They all assume - tacitly, for the most part - that the catharsis is an experience which comes *in the theater*. But Aristotle insists again and again, not merely that tragedies can be read with pleasure or profit, but that "the capacity of tragedy [i.e., its capacity to do its 'work,' produce its effect] exists even without a competition [= actual performance] and actors" (6.50B18); that the plot should be so constructed that one who merely hears it (i.e., not the full play) will feel pity and fear. [Else, 1957 p. 441]

This is again a rather weak point. While it is true that Bernays, Butcher and others usually speak of the theatre, their theory by no means discourages the possibility of a reader (or for that matter a television spectator) experiencing catharsis, perhaps of less intensity.

To summarize my impression of Else's new interpretation of catharsis: While he is convincing in arguing that his interpretation is possible, consistent and maybe useful, he did not succeed in showing that the purgation interpretation has to be rejected.

Looking back at the three different categories we can say the following: The first, clarification, insight or enlightenment, is certainly not the whole story. It doesn't address why the evocation of pity and fear is essential. John Gassner however made a convincing argument that enlightenment, next to pity and fear, is the third component of the process of purgation and is precisely what distinguishes tragedy from mere melodrama [Gassner, 1965 p. 517].

So we are left with two interpretations, both of which are plausible and consistent. Kruse's solution is to combine slightly modified versions of all three elements into an integrated view of catharsis [Kruse, 1979 p. 169].

5.1.2 Catharsis in Psychotherapy

The discussion of catharsis has been taken up early on by psychotherapists. They were of course less concerned with what exactly Aristotle meant and more with how catharsis can be useful in psychotherapy. From this point of view the purgation interpretation is certainly the most practical, since it can most easily be adapted to therapy.

A question that is of major importance to psychotherapists and that is still being debated is: How does change (in therapy) occur?

This is most important since despite the many different orientations there is one goal that all psychotherapy has in common: they want to affect some form of change in the patient. Paradoxically this is even true of those schools who believe that the goal is for the patient to totally accept who he is right now and to give up the feeling that there is anything that he needs to change. This acceptance would already constitute a major shift from where the patient was before he went into therapy.

The main controversy is whether change comes from experience or from insight/understanding/analysis (or a combination of both). Catharsis is usually, though not always, counted as a form of experience. When catharsis is facilitated in therapy the goal is to effect some change in behavior or feeling, preferably lasting beyond the immediate session.

One of the earliest mentions of catharsis in psychotherapy came in 1895 when Sigmund Freud[28] and Josef Breuer described a treatment of hysteria through catharsis [Freud & Breuer, 1895]. Freud summarized their findings as follows:

> Breuer's discoveries ... were the fundamental fact that the symptoms of hysterical patients are founded upon scenes in their past lives[29] which have made a great impression on them but have been forgotten (traumas); the therapy founded

---

[28]Jacob Bernays, who was quoted above, was the uncle of Freud's wife [Brunius, 1966 p. 65]. (Goldon [1992] claims, probably incorrectly, that Bernays was Freud's father-in-law [p. 30].)

[29]Here Freud is *not* talking about reincarnation, but rather about childhood experiences. Today however, there are therapists who extend the age regression of patients under hypnosis to before birth and conception, and sure enough many patients come up with detailed memories of past lives/incarnations.

upon this, which consisted in causing them to remember and reproduce these experiences in a state of hypnosis (catharsis); and the fragment of theory inferred from it, which was that these symptoms represented an abnormal employment of amounts of excitation which had not been disposed of (conversion). [Freud, 1966 p. 5]

In his later work however, Freud tended almost entirely towards analysis.[30]

Moreno is clearly one of the foremost and also earliest proponents of experience over analysis and he was a strong antagonist of Freud's view. "Analysis does not help; action is required" [Fox, 1987 p. 55]. According to Moreno analysis is often not necessary after a psychodrama. There are nevertheless psychoanalysts who use psychodrama and some insist that even in psychodrama change occurs because of the insight offered by a psychodramatic exploration. The American Society for Group Psychotherapy and Psychodrama, originally founded by Moreno in April 1942, has recently formed a Special Interest Group on Psychodrama and Psychoanalysis with the following statement of purpose: "This group is dedicated to exploring the integration of the various schools of psychoanalytic theory and technique with the practice of psychodrama. We will work towards the advancement of knowledge in this area via study, papers, and presentations" [Psychodrama Network News, January 1995, p. 9].

---

[30]For a discussion of Freud and Breuer's experiments with catharsis and Freud's subsequent change of direction, see especially [Scheff, 1979 p. 26-47].

It is of course often difficult to separate experience from understanding since they commonly occur together and hence many therapists suggest that healing comes from a combination of both. More and more therapists and patients do however experience that talk-therapy alone is not enough and look for alternatives. The recent successes of drama therapy (cf. chapter V.2) support the view that profound change can come from experience without analysis. In fact, students often report that deep healing occurred from studying and practicing certain schools of acting. They never consciously worked on any issues and there was no analysis; they had certain experiences on stage which then resulted in changes in their lives.

This is indeed how Moreno first got his ideas for psychodrama in his Theatre of Spontaneity in 1922 in Vienna. This episode is known as the _Case of Barbara_ and is frequently quoted by Moreno and his followers. Because of its importance as a cradle for psychodrama, I will include Moreno's description of the incidence for the reader not already familiar with Moreno's writings.

> We had a young actress, Barbara[31], who worked for the theatre and also took part in a new experiment I had started, the extemporaneous, living newspaper. She was a main attraction because of her excellence in roles of ingenues, heroic and romantic roles. It was soon evident that she was in love with a young poet and playwright who never failed to sit in the first row, applauding and watching every one of her actions. A romance developed between Barbara and George. One day their marriage was announced. Nothing changed

---

[31]The real name of the actress was Anna Höllering [Marineau, 1989 p. 70].

however, she remained our chief actress and he our chief spectator, so to speak. One day George came to me, his usually gay eyes greatly disturbed. "What happened?" I asked him. "Oh, doctor, I cannot bear it." "Bear what?" I looked at him, investigating. "That sweet, angel-like being whom you all admire, acts like a bedeviled creature when she is alone with me. She speaks the most abusive language and when I get angry at her, as I did last night, she hits me with her fists." "Wait," I said, "you come to the theatre as usual, I will try a remedy." When Barbara came back-stage that night, ready to play in one of her usual roles of pure womanhood, I stopped her. "Look, Barbara, you have done marvelously until now, but I am afraid you are getting stale. People would like to see you in roles in which you portray the nearness to the soil, the rawness of human nature, its vulgarity and stupidity, its cynical reality, people not only as they are, but worse than they are, people as they are when they are driven to extremes by unusual circumstances. Do you want to try it?" "Yes," she said enthusiastically, "I am glad you mention it. I felt for quite a while that I have to give our audience a new experience. But do you think that I can do it?" "I have confidence in you," I replied, "the news just came in that a girl in Ottakring (a slum district in Vienna), soliciting men on the street, had been attacked and killed by a stranger. He is still at large, the police is searching for him. You are the streetwalker. Here (pointing to Richard, one of our male actors) is the apache. Get the scene ready." A street was improvised on the stage, a cafe, two lights. Barbara went on. George was in his usual seat in the first row, highly excited. Richard, in the role of the apache, came out of the cafe with Barbara and followed her. They had an encounter, which rapidly developed into a heated argument. It was about money. Suddenly Barbara changed to a manner of acting totally unexpected from her. She swore like a trooper, punching at the man, kicking him in the leg repeatedly. I saw George half rising, anxiously raising his arm at me, but the apache got wild and began to chase Barbara. Suddenly he grabbed a knife, a prop, from his inside jacket pocket. He chased her in circles, closer and closer. She acted so well that she gave the impression of being really scared. The audience got up, roaring, "Stop it, stop it." But he did not stop until she was supposedly "murdered." After the scene Barbara was exuberant with joy, she embraced George and they went home in ecstasy. From then on she continued to act in such roles of the lower depth. George came to see me the following day. He instantly understood that it was therapy. She played as domestics, lonely spinsters, revengeful wives, spiteful sweethearts, barmaids and gun molls. George gave me daily reports. "Well," he told me after a few sessions, "something is happening to her. She still has her fits of temper at home but they have lost their intensity. They are shorter and in the midst of them she often smiles, and, as yesterday, she remembers similar scenes which she did on the stage and she laughs and I laugh with her because I, too, remember. It is as if we see each other in a psychological mirror. We both laugh. At times she begins to laugh before she has the fit, anticipating what will happen. She warms up to it finally, but it lacks the usual heat." It was like a catharsis coming from humor and laughter. I continued the treatment, assigning roles to her more carefully, according to her needs and his. One day George confessed the effect which these sessions had upon him as he watched them and absorbed the analysis which I gave afterwards. "Looking at her productions on the stage made me more tolerant of Barbara, less impatient." That evening I told Barbara how much progress she has made as an actress and asked her whether she would not like to act on the stage with George. They did this and the duettes on the stage which appeared as a part of our official program, resembled more and more the scenes which they daily had at home. Gradually her family and his, scenes from her childhood, their dreams and plans for the future were portrayed. After every performance some spectators would come up to me, asking why the Barbara-George scenes touched them so much more deeply than the others (audience therapy). Some months later, Barbara and George sat alone with me in the theatre. They had found themselves and each other again, or better, they had found themselves and each other for the first time. I analyzed the development of their psychodrama, session after session, and told them the story of their cure. [Moreno, 1946 p. 3-5]

This case beautifully illustrates how Moreno discovered the therapeutic, cathartic effect of theatre on actor *and* audience. It was after this episode that Moreno started to develop his psychodramatic techniques and theories.

Going back to the debate over experience versus analysis/insight, there are those on either side who stay squarely to their position no matter what the evidence. For example in the above case of change after an acting experience they simply insist that the very fact that there was therapeutic change shows that there must have been insight, even if it wasn't articulated.

Conversely Symonds, a proponent of change through catharsis (which he calls "abreaction") did a study of 68 cases of successful therapeutic change. After finding that "59 of these followed abreactions, 7 followed interpretations by the therapist, and 2 were related to change in perception which may or may not have been caused by the therapist's comment" [Symonds, 1954 p. 699], he is still not satisfied and has to bend over backwards to explain why the other 9 cases might also be based on abreaction:

I should like to propose as a hypothesis that all changes in behavior and adjustment occurring as a result of psychotherapy follow abreaction in the therapeutic situation. It is quite possible that in the 9 cases in which the changes apparently followed the therapist's interpretation or were related to changes in the clients perception, the changes actually followed an abreaction that was not noticed or recorded by the therapist, and it is possible that the abreaction might not even have been observable but might have been more in the nature of internal reaction. That is, it is hypothesized that the change took place as a result of the client's abreactive response to the therapist's interpretation or that the shift in perception was accompanied by an abreactive reaction. [Symonds, 1954 p. 699-700]

Symonds study is quoted by Scheff who makes a very strong case for change through experience/catharsis and dedicates the larger part of his book to it:

My hypotheses is that catharsis is a necessary condition for therapeutic change. [Scheff, 1979 p. 13]
Neither Freud nor any other psychotherapist provided any systematic evidence showing that catharsis was ineffective. The one study that has been done suggests the opposite, that catharsis is by far the most frequent cause of success in psychotherapy. [ibid. p. 22]

Today there are many more forms of experiential therapy, most of which were influenced by Moreno and make explicit or implicit use of catharsis (such as gestalt therapy, primal therapy, rebirthing and other forms of breath work, Reichian therapy and bioenergetics, and most recently Arnold Mindell's process work).

5.1.3 Morenian Catharsis

Next we will have a closer look at where Moreno stands on the discussion of catharsis. We have already seen that Moreno clearly favors experience over analysis. There is also no doubt that Moreno falls into the category which interprets Aristotle's use of catharsis as talking about purgation:

> ... mental catharsis (stems from the Greek, it means purging, purification). [Moreno, 1946 p. d]
> Catharsis, as a concept, was introduced by Aristotle. He used this term to express the peculiar effect of the Greek drama upon its spectators. In his *Poetics* he maintains that drama tends to purify the *spectators* by artistically exciting certain emotions which act as a kind of relief from their own selfish passions. [ibid. p. XIII]

In his bibliography Moreno refers to Butcher's translation of Aristotle [ibid. p. 425]. We have seen above that Butcher also proposes the purgation view and it is unlikely that Moreno was familiar with Else's explanation.

Moreno makes it quite clear that his own theory of catharsis goes further than Aristotle's in a number of ways:

> This concept of catharsis has undergone a revolutionary change since systematic psychodramatic work began in Vienna in 1919. This change has been exemplified by the movement away from the written (conserved) drama and toward the spontaneous (psycho) drama, with the emphasis shifted from the spectators to the actors. [Moreno, 1946 p. XIII]

Moreno's own definition of catharsis thus reads: "By a warming up process to full living out the individuals liberate and purge themselves from a mental or cultural syndrome" [Moreno, 1983 p. 125 Glossary].

Since Moreno's comments on Aristotle and catharsis are spread throughout his work, it will be useful to organize Moreno's thought in a list of the ways in which he augmented Aristotle's ideas:

5.1.3.1 Spontaneity as a source of catharsis

According to Moreno the Aristotelian catharsis is limited since it stems from a cultural conserve (cf. chapter II.1). He studied the different sources of catharsis and concluded: "I discovered the common principle producing catharsis to be: spontaneity" [Moreno, 1946 p. d]. Catharsis is most likely to occur when the subject is warmed up to a high level of spontaneity. Conversely, the more often a conserve is repeated the less catharsis can be obtained from it. Catharsis and spontaneity can in fact cause each other in both directions and Shearon, a German psychodrama director, reversed Moreno's statement: "Catharsis is the liberation of the individual's spontaneity" (quoted in [Feldhendler, 1994 p. 100]).

5.1.3.2 Catharsis focused in the Actor

Whereas Aristotle's catharsis affects the spectator, Moreno writes: "catharsis takes place: not only in the audience - secondary desired effect - and not in the dramatis personae of an imaginary production, but primarily in the spontaneous actors in the drama who produce the personae by liberating themselves from them at the same time" [Moreno, 1946 p. 29]. This liberating effect is illustrated in the *Case of Barbara* quoted above in section 5.1.2. Ultimately Moreno wanted to accomplish catharsis in both the spectator and the actor. As we have seen (cf. chapter II.3) he also hoped to overcome the actor/spectator separation.

5.1.3.3 Action Catharsis

Closely related is Moreno's point that Aristotle's catharsis in the spectator is passive. "The greater catharsis achieved through action is undeniable. The patient is able to express kinesthetically many feelings for which he has no words" [Moreno & Enneis, 1950 p. 13]. Moreno based his idea of active catharsis on the religions of the East and Far East. "These religions held that a saint, in order to become a savior, had to make an effort; he had, first, to actualize and save himself. ... In the religious situation the process of catharsis was localized in the actor, his actual life becoming the stage. This was an active catharsis" [Moreno, 1946 p. XIV]. In Aristotle's Greek theatre catharsis stems from observing what other people go through and resonating in some way. For Moreno catharsis comes from fully expressing your own emotions through your own flesh and blood - everything takes place within the subject.[32]

---

[32]In his German writings Moreno uses the fitting term *Handlungskatharsis*. "Handlungskatharsis resultiert aus den spontanen Handlungen eines oder mehrerer Mitglieder der Gruppe" [Moreno, 1959a p. 57].

5.1.3.4 Tragedy as an Extension of Life

Aristotle defined "Tragedy, then, is a process of imitating an action which has serious implications" [Else, 1967 p. 25]. Moreno responds: "Psychodrama defines the drama as an extension of life and action rather than its imitation" [Moreno, 1946 p. 15]. On Moreno's stage life is not being replayed simply as it is, but it is a safer, freer and socially acceptable place to express emotions more fully than in real life, to portray dreams and fantasies or to rewrite your life and enact the childhood you wanted to have. Moreno came to call this *Surplus Reality* (cf. chapter III.1.6).

5.1.3.5 Group Catharsis

While also using individual catharsis, especially of course in monodrama/individual therapy, Moreno emphasized how the whole group is going through catharsis together (be it in group therapy or in the theatre). This is more than just the sum of the individual catharses since it changes not only the individuals, but the group as a whole becomes more integrated and develops a feeling of belonging together, compassion for one another, trust and safety. Group catharsis can happen in at least two ways. In psychodrama the emphasis is still on the protagonist's issues, but it is very common that many other group members resonate with the drama enacted. This might bring up strong feelings in most members of the group and it is not uncommon to see an entire group in tears after a moving psychodrama.

The other possibility is to use what Moreno called *sociodrama*. Here the focus is on an issue which concerns the entire group such as social conflicts between cultures, nationalities, races, classes or (especially popular today) the sexes. Moreno described this as follows:

> The director is searching for a conflict which may stir up the group to the deepest possible catharsis, and for actors to portray this conflict. Everyone in the group goes through a similar process. Everyone warms up with varying degrees of intensity, positively or negatively towards the situation to be dramatized and towards the characters to be portrayed. The director says: There is a Negro who is lynched by a mob. Who wants to take the part of the Negro? There is a man who leads the white mob against the Negro. Who wants to be that man? Everyone may be the vehicle for the enactment of these roles. There is no ready-made dramatic conserve, not even a final plot, everything is fluid. Everyone undergoes a process of initial excitement, stirred up by physical and mental starters. [Moreno, 1946 p. 364]

5.1.3.6 Catharsis of Integration

For Moreno the goal was not to get rid of certain emotions, but rather an integration by expressing and owning different parts of oneself. The only thing to get rid of are repressions or blocks that keep us from experiencing our feelings. Moreno writes of the subject in psychodrama:

> His own self has an opportunity to find and reorganize itself, to put the elements together which may have been kept apart by insidious forces, to integrate them and to attain a sense of power and of relief, a "catharsis of integration" (in difference from a catharsis of abreaction). [Moreno, 1953 p. 85]

Fritz Perls, the founder of gestalt therapy, who was also influenced by Moreno (more on him in chapter IV.3.6), expresses the same view even more vividly:

> My second objection to the armor theory is that it reinforces the Aristotelian-Freudian defecation theory: "Emotions are a nuisance. A catharsis is required to rid the organism of these disturbers of the peace."
> Nature is not so wasteful as to create emotions as a nuisance. Without emotions we are dead, bored, uninvolved machines.
> [Perls, 1969b p. 50]

Integration of disowned parts is one of the main goals in Perls' gestalt therapy. The first to emphasize integration (especially of what he called the *shadow*) was probably Carl Gustav Jung: "We refer here to the exploration of the contents of the unconscious. This constitutes the one great purpose of the process of integration" [Jung, 1957 p. 41].

5.1.4 Boal on Catharsis and Moreno

One of the few dramatic theorists who not only comments on Aristotle, but also on Moreno, is Augusto Boal. This Brazilian playwright, politician, theatre director and theoretician is mostly known as president of his *Theatre of the Oppressed* in Rio de Janeiro and Paris and author of a book by the same title. It's first chapter is devoted to *Aristotle's Coercive System of Tragedy* [Boal, 1979 p. 1-50].

Boal's interpretation of Aristotle falls again in the purgation category since he follows Butcher's translation: "To him we owe mainly the clarification of the concept of catharsis" [Boal, 1979 p. 27]. He does however modify Butcher's view considerably:

> This reasoning is correct and we can accept it totally, except for its insistent attribution of impurities to the emotions of pity and fear. The impurity exists, no doubt, and it is in fact the object of purgation in the character's mind, or as Aristotle would say, in his very *soul*. But Aristotle does not speak of the existence of pure or impure pity, pure or impure fear. The impurity is *necessarily distinct from* the emotions which will remain once the spectacle of the tragedy is ended. That extraneous matter - the eliminated impurity - can only be an emotion or passion other than the ones that remain. Pity and fear have never been vices or weaknesses or errors and, therefore, never needed to be eliminated or purged. [Boal, 1979 p. 31]

Boal then goes on to explain that the impurity (for Aristotle) must be something directed against the laws, not in harmony with what society regards as acceptable, and he concludes:

> Let there be no doubt: Aristotle formulated a very powerful purgative system, the objective of which is to eliminate all that is not commonly accepted, including the revolution, before it takes place. His system appears in disguised form on television, in the movies, in the circus, in the theaters. [Boal, 1979 p. 47]
>
> Catharsis takes away from the character (and thus from the spectator, who is empathically manipulated by the character) his ability to act. [ibid. p. 106]

This reminds us of Moreno's distinction between Aristotle's passive catharsis and his active catharsis. Boal apparently was not familiar with Moreno's work when he wrote his first book. But he just published a new book, *The Rainbow of Desire* [1995], subtitled *The Boal Method of Theatre and Therapy* which contains a number of references to Moreno and is in fact dedicated to Moreno's wife Zerka and Grete Leutz, a psychodramatist and long-time student of Moreno, who invited Boal in 1989 to speak in Amsterdam to the International Association of Group Psychotherapists on the centenary of the birth of Moreno. This invitation made Boal decide to write his book [Boal, 1995 p. 8].

In the section on catharsis Boal suggests that while catharsis always refers to some form of purgation, purification or cleaning out of some disturbing element, there are four principal forms which differ in the nature of what is purged: medical catharsis, Morenian catharsis, Aristotelian catharsis and catharsis in the Theatre of the Oppressed.

Medical catharsis is the taking of a relevant medicine or purgative in order to get rid of some element that caused sickness. Aristotelian catharsis is explained along the lines of Boal's description in his *The Theatre of the Oppressed* to which he also refers. Again his analysis is highly critical: "This form of theatrical production - disempowering and tranquilizing - seeks, by means of catharsis, to adapt the individual to society. For those who are happy with the values of that society, obviously this form of catharsis is useful" [Boal, 1995 p. 71f].

While in his first book Boal completely rejected the concept of catharsis, he now adapts it to his own work. (The same could be said of the more general concept of "therapy".) First he emphasizes (as did Moreno) that in his theatre the spectators are not merely watching and contemplating as in the conventional theatre, but are intervening participants. Since they see *and* act, he calls them "spect-actors". In line with what Moreno calls *Surplus Reality* (cf. chapter III.1.6), Boal writes:

> The action shown on stage is a possibility, an alternative, and the intervener-spectators (active observers) are called upon to create new actions, new alternatives which are not substitutes for real action, but rehearsals, pre-actions which precede - rather than stand in for - the actual action, the action we want to transform a reality we are trying to change. [Boal, 1995 p. 72]

As in psychodrama, the stage is used to practice and explore different ways of acting in life. The goal of the Theatre of the Oppressed is not a calm equilibrium, but a dynamic disequilibrium which compels the spect-actor to liberating action, to fight his oppression within and outside of himself.

> This dynamisation ... destroys all the blocks which prohibited the realization of actions such as this. That is, it purifies the spect-actors, it produces a catharsis. The catharsis of detrimental blocks! [Boal, 1995 p. 72f]

As I have argued earlier for Moreno's view, the things to get rid of or purge are *not* the emotions and desires, but on the contrary the blocks and repressions which inhibit us from fully experiencing and expressing our emotions and desires.

All the above observations suggest that Boal's and Moreno's use of catharsis (and perhaps of therapeutic theatre in general) are very much in agreement. Boal however writes: "In the 'Morenian' catharsis, what is expelled is, in a kind of way, a poison. We can say that its goal is the happiness of the individual" [Boal, 1995 p. 71]. He refers to Moreno's well known *Case of Barbara* (cf. section 5.1.2), who he says was purified of violence and hatred in order to adapt to her social life.

All this is a rather superficial reading of Moreno.[33] For Moreno emotions are not poison to be eliminated. "Negative" emotions are not expressed to get rid of them, but it is a common experience that after the subject is able to express repressed hatred, other feelings, such as love, emerge. Moreno also never talks of happiness as the goal. For him psychological health is the ability to experience and express the full range of human emotions and to have full access to one's creativity and spontaneity.

In the German journal *Psychodrama* Thorau [1991] published a comparison of Boal and Moreno in which he shows the many parallels between the two theories. Both want to change society in similar ways, the main difference being that Moreno starts with

---

[33]In an interview in which he was asked to comment on Moreno, Boal admits: "I don't know Moreno well enough to make a big statement about it" [Taussig & Schechner, 1990 p. 26] and then continues nevertheless: "I believe that sometimes the work of Moreno may differ from mine in that I favor the dynamicization of people - making people do. I don't want people to use the theatre as a way of not doing in real life" [ibid. p. 27]. Neither does Moreno, I would like to add.

the individual and the group in which she lives, trusting that many changes on that level will eventually lead to a new society. Boal focused originally on revolutionary change of society; interestingly his new book suggests that he has now moved towards meeting Moreno's approach. Thorau even concludes that Boal's theory and practice is closer to Moreno's original ideas than most of today's psychodramatists are.[34] This actually makes a lot of sense: today psychodrama is well regulated with rules for certification, ethical conduct, safety, confidentiality, follow-up, etc. and has lost some of the theatrical excitement and spontaneity of Moreno's days.

I will end this section with a beautiful account of those good old days, which also illustrates the power of catharsis:

> My most revered session occurred during the social upheavels of the early 60's. The open sessions were advertised on the back pages of the Village Voice, the major organ of the counter-cultural hippie movement so that a part of the audience consisted of bohemian rebels eager to use the psychodrama stage to press their social agendas. At the same time the phenomenon of "mystery groups" appeared. Certain conventional suburbanites fended off the boredom of their regulated lives by joining with a group of neighbors in

---

[34]"Von solchen Vorstellungen und Forderungen, vom sozialkritischen, psychosozialen Engagement Morenos, seinem gesellschaftsverändernden Anspruch, haben sich Morenos Nachfolger inzwischen, wie die heutige Psychodramapraxis und die Entwicklung der theoretischen Diskussion zeigt, eher fortentwickelt, und Soziodrama scheint für Psychodramatiker eher als historischer Begriff bedeutsam zu sein. Augusto Boals Theater der Unterdrückten hingegen scheint in seiner Theorie und Praxis Morenos ursprünglichen Vorstellungen vom Psychodrama, vor allem des Soziodramas, näher als die heutige Praxis des Psychodramas selbst" [Thorau, 1991 p. 18].

explorations of the big city. Each month a different couple would select a surprise activity. At the last moment they would announce the time and address of the destination where the group was to assemble having absolutely no idea of what to expect. Somehow the Moreno Institute became known to a number of the more adventuresome chair couples and groups of twenty or thirty people would regularly find themselves at the Institute expecting to see a play or something of the sort. One evening a mystery group of New Jersey policemen and their wives arrived. The same night a group of outrageously dressed East Village hippies also arrived. Oil and water. The police were proud, macho, and disdainful of the hippies. The police wives were prim, proper and embarrassed. The hippies were sassy and defiant and as defensive as were the authority figures they despised. After three hours of Moreno's method two sobbing policemen were surrounded by compassionate hippies confiding personal memories of their own to the co-protagonists. The wives were as tenderly understanding toward the bohemians as they were to their husbands. As they say about our nearby Broadway neighbors, there wasn't a dry eye in the theater, but this theater was about the real lives of the audience! Who could say that this was not a worth while way for these people to have spent three hours and three dollars? [Sacks, 1994 p. 2]

5.2 Goethe

Moreno mentions Goethe mainly in his book *The Theatre of Spontaneity*. The second, enlarged edition in 1973 contains for the first time a chapter entitled *Goethe and Psychodrama* in which Moreno proclaimed "the importance of Goethe as a forerunner of both therapeusis through drama and his esthetic sense for spontaneous production" [Moreno, 1983 p.1]. This is surprising since Goethe is rarely related to therapy and spontaneity. We will show that Moreno's first claim, that Goethe was already aware of the therapeutic effects of drama, is well substantiated. But his second claim, that Goethe promoted spontaneity, is neither supported by Goethe's theoretical writings nor by his practical work as director of the Weimar Court theatre. In fact, it will become apparent that Goethe and Moreno adhered to opposite ideals of acting.

First a brief look at who Goethe was. Johann Wolfgang von Goethe (1749-1832) is probably the most important and prolific German speaking author of any time. He was already famous by the time he was 25 and is widely acknowledged as a "universal genius", excelling equally as a politician, poet, novelist, playwright, actor, theatre director and scientist. His work culminated in the well-known epic *Faust*, Part I and II, written in stages over 60 years, in which he consolidated his life and art in a poetic and philosophical exploration of man's search for absolute experience and knowledge. His fame only grew after his death and to this day he is one of the most written about figures of European history and continues to be an idol for many German speaking youth.

Moreno, on the other hand, never reached the recognition he felt he deserved. He joins in the admiration for Goethe:

> It is therefore a special honor to know that the great poet and philosopher Johann Wolfgang von Goethe thought along psychodramatic lines and that he wrote plays on the subject. There is no writer in the Anglo-saxon literature, not even Shakespeare, who has attained Goethe's rank as an overall creator in the sciences and arts. [Moreno, 1983 p. 122]

5.2.1 Therapy through Drama: Goethe's *Lila*

Moreno's main evidence for Goethe's knowledge of the therapeutic effects of dramatic enactment is his little-known "Singspiel" *Lila*. The play tells the story of the baroness Lila, who is being cured from madness. Her doctor Verazio indeed appears to be speaking of psychodrama:

> If we could cure delusions through delusions, we would have created a masterpiece. ... Let us enact for the lady the story of her delusions. ... At last delusion and reality will meet.[35]
> [Goethe, 1968 p. 191f]

---

[35]"Wenn wir Phantasie durch Phantasie kurieren könnten, so hätten wir ein Meisterstück gemacht. ... Lassen sie uns der gnädigen Frau die Geschichte ihrer Phantasien spielen. ... Zuletzt wird Phantasie und Wirklichkeit zusammentreffen."

Goethe's words here remind us of Moreno's prescription for the use of psychodrama with psychotic patients, as described for example in a chapter entitled *Psychodramatic Treatment of Psychoses* in [Fox, 1987 p. 68ff]. First the therapist enters the patient's reality and places his delusions and hallucinations in front of him through a psychodramatic enactment with the help of what Moreno calls *auxiliary egos*, psychiatric aids or other patients who play the different parts. Thus the patient sees his psychotic experiences objectified. In this fashion the patient is brought out of his internal fantasy world and starts to relate to these new "anchors" on the psychodramatic stage. As more and more of these anchors are introduced to the stage, he regains his connection to his environment.

This is exactly what happens in Goethe's *Lila*.[36] The baroness Lila turns mad after she is mistakenly notified that her husband has died. She no longer recognizes anybody, not even her husband when he returns. Questioned by Doctor Verazio[37], she proves to be living under the delusion that her husband has been imprisoned by evil spirits. She also thinks that these spirits are after her, and that it is up to her to find a way to rescue her husband. Doctor Verazio now starts to direct everybody in a "psychodrama" in which Lila's friends and family portray Lila's subjective world, complete with fairies and evil spirits. Lila goes on a long journey in which she interacts with the fairies and fights with the evil

[36]We use the final version from 1790 in [Goethe, 1968 p.181-214].
[37]Originally in 1777 played by Goethe himself [Carlson, 1978 p. 28; Diener, 1971 p. 33].

spirits. Only after she has "conquered" the demons, her husband is introduced to her. Now she recognizes him and thus regains her sense of reality.

It is remarkable to see how Goethe's *Lila* contains all the elements of Moreno's psychodrama, though the term was of course unknown in Goethe's time. Goethe himself, however, was well aware of the psychotherapeutic significance of his play as stated in a letter dated October 1, 1818: "The subject is actually a psychological cure in which one lets madness enter in order to heal madness"[38] [Goethe, 1968 p. 682]. The conclusion can only be that Goethe wrote the play in order to demonstrate psychodramatic principles. Even the name he chose for the doctor, *Verazio*, supports this: it is derived from *verax*, Latin for truthful, speaking the truth. This reminds us of Moreno's definition of psychodrama as "exploring the 'truth' by dramatic methods" [Moreno, 1946 p. a].

Historians have generally attached little importance to the play. As one critic puts it: "*Lila*, an operetta presented on the Duchess Luise's birthday, was a work of less literary significance, apparently hastily put together by Goethe for the occasion" [Carlson, 1978 p. 28]. Even more unimaginatively another writes: "The Singspiel *Lila* is a piece of occasional poetry, whose origin and deeper meaning cannot be directly deduced from the text" (Gertrud Rudloff-Hille in [Goethe, 1968 p. 679]).

---

[38]"Das Sujet ist eigentlich eine psychische Kur, wo man den Wahnsinn eintreten lässt, um den Wahnsinn zu heilen."

In *Goethe: A Psychoanalytic Study* we learn not only that "Goethe was constipated on the day when he started to write *Lila*" [Eissler, 1963 p. 246], but also that he was really a precursor to Freud:

> Far away as Verazio's therapeutic methods were from Freud's marvelous therapeutic instrument, it is valid to see in them a remote historical precursor. Thus *Lila* bears witness to Goethe's preoccupation with finding an intellectual program for removing the shadow that the unconscious throws upon the conscious mind. [Eissler, 1963 p. 237].

Moreno and Freud were of course antagonists; among other things since Moreno emphasized dramatic action over intellectual analysis. How Goethe's *Lila* can be seen as advocating Freudian analysis is beyond me.

In his own tribute to Goethe, Moreno is quick to point out that, while the play is *about* psychodrama, it is by no means itself a psychodrama. As a written play it is, rather, what Moreno calls a *cultural conserve* (cf. chapter II.1), even if it is, as Goethe proclaims, "written spontaneously"[39] (Goethe to Seidel, February 3, 1816, in [Goethe, 1968 p. 682]).

A more general analysis of portrayals of healing mental illness in Goethe's writing is provided in Georg Reuchlein's *Die Heilung des Wahnsinns bei Goethe: Orest, Lila, der Harfner und Sperata*. Besides Lila, he considers Orest in *Iphigenie* and Harfner and Sperata in *Lehrjahre*. Comparing Goethe's ideas with other

---

[39]"aus dem Stegreife geschrieben".

psychological views of his time, he concludes that the healing methods exhibited in Lila, while part of a literary tradition, are also founded on views about psychotherapy proposed and practiced by progressive therapists of the period [Reuchlein, 1983 p. 57]. He reports for instance that as early as 1758 Ernst Anton Nicolai had commented on the cure of a psychotic who believed that he carried an elephant's trunk instead of his nose. A surgeon cut in his nose and claimed he removed the trunk. Nicolai argued that this was an example of a cure effected through a trick by pretending to believe in the patient's delusion and then removing it [Reuchlein, 1983 p. 52f].

Reuchlein focuses mostly on Goethe's literary work. Despite many accounts of Goethe adopting the role of psychological healer [Diener, 1971 p. 60, 104ff], I could not find any report of Goethe's *actually* using drama to heal mental illness. However, most commentators suggested that *Lila* was first performed at the duchess Luise's birthday on January 30, 1777 in order to present to her and the duke a kind of mirror of their antagonistic relationship. Goethe as Verazius played a moral doctor who recommended that they treat each other with loving empathy [Diener, 1971 p. 29]. Moreno's psychodrama also uses this *mirror technique*: when a patient is unable to play his own drama, he instead gets to watch auxiliary egos play him.

Moreno's discussion of *Lila* reaches the following conclusion:

> And if one wants to give full credit to Goethe, one can say that,
> at least to my knowledge, no other playwright has constructed

an entire play, that is, *every scene, every word*, the *entire structure of the play*, to demonstrate drama itself as cure. [Moreno, 1983 p.123]

5.2.2 Spontaneity in Goethe's Work

While Moreno's previous point is well substantiated, it is more questionable to link Goethe to spontaneity and improvisation. Goethe is mostly known as part, if not the beginning, of the tradition of German tyrannical dictator/directors. He mainly directed scripted plays. Moreno states nevertheless:

> I was aware that Goethe was interested in impromptu theatre. In his book *Die Lehrjahre*, second book, ninth chapter, he wrote: "Spontaneity theater should be introduced into every theater. The ensemble should be trained regularly in this manner. The public would benefit if an unwritten play were produced once a month." [Moreno, 1983 p. 122]

Moreno is talking here about Goethe's novel *Wilhelm Meisters Lehrjahre*. In the chapter referred to, the protagonist and a group of friends are on a boat ride, when one of them suggests that they should improvise a scene. Everyone takes on a role and they have to pay a forfeit whenever they fall out of character. They all enjoy the game with great wit and humor. During this game, they also pick up a stranger who immediately joins in and plays the role of a country priest. It is this man who is speaking in the passage Moreno quotes:

"I find this exercise," said the stranger, "among actors, even in the company of friends and acquaintances, very useful. It is the best way to lead people out of themselves and after a detour back into themselves. It should be introduced to every company, that they have to practice sometimes in this way, and the audience would surely benefit if every few months a non-scripted piece would be performed, for which the actors of course would have to be prepared through several rehearsals."

"One should not," added Wilhelm, "think of an impromptu piece as composed on the spur of the moment, but rather as having known plot, action and division into acts and leaving the way of performing to the actor."[40] [Goethe, 1962 p. 123]

While this may be questionable, it is certainly not uncommon to attribute statements by characters in Goethe's novels to their author. But even if we grant Moreno to argue in this fashion, the above quotation, especially Wilhelm's response, conjures up images of Commedia dell'arte rather than Moreno's spontaneity theatre. We have already seen in chapter II.4 that Goethe appreciated Commedia dell'arte, but also that Moreno rejected it as a possible precursor to psychodrama.

---

[40]"Ich finde diese Übung", sagte der Unbekannte, "unter Schauspielern, ja in Gesellschaft von Freunden und Bekannten sehr nützlich. Es ist die beste Art, die Menschen aus sich heraus- und durch einen Umweg wieder in sich hineinzuführen. Es sollte bei jeder Truppe eingeführt sein, dass sie sich manchmal auf diese Weise üben müsste, und das Publikum würde gewiss dabei gewinnen, wenn alle Monate ein nicht geschriebenes Stück aufgeführt würde, worauf sich freilich die Schauspieler in mehrern Proben müssten vorbereitet haben."
"Man dürfte sich", versetzte Wilhelm, "ein extemporiertes Stück nicht als ein solches denken, das aus dem Stegreife sogleich komponiert würde, sondern als ein solches, wovon zwar Plan, Handlung und Szeneneinteilung gegeben wären, dessen Ausführung aber dem Schauspieler überlassen bliebe."

Since Goethe was not only a writer, but is also known as "the first example of the modern director as the creative artist ultimately responsible for every aspect of the production" [Carlson, 1978 p. 307], we need to ask ourselves, whether his suggested interest in impromptu theatre is reflected in his work as director of the Weimar Court theatre from 1791 to 1817. There is no record of improvised performances under Goethe, while he directed many written plays - his own as well as others'. But did he at least use improvisation in rehearsal and training of actors, as the character in his novel recommends? Carlson's account of Goethe as a director contains only one reference to improvisation: "Goethe's constant attention to rhythmic delivery eventually brought his actors to the point where, it is reported, they could even extemporize in blank verse" [Carlson, 1978 p. 304].

While this suggests that improvisation was not completely foreign to Goethe and his actors, the rest of the account seems to contradict rather than support Moreno's claim. Goethe was concerned with educating the audience and with a unified aesthetic effect. This drove him to exercise total precision and control.

> Goethe seemed to be seeking a striking and carefully composed stage picture - composed even down to the placement of the individual fingers and the angle of the head, as we see represented in paintings of Weimar productions and described in detail in Goethe's instructions to the young actor Heinrich Schmidt in 1801. [Carlson, 1978 p. 305f]

There is no talk about Goethe letting his actors explore their true emotions and expressing their creativity. On the contrary, the image we get is that of a dictator reducing the actors to robots expressing his own ideals of beauty. Goethe as a director thus epitomizes the kind of directing that Moreno rebelled against: concerned with perfecting cultural conserves and reducing the actor to a tool. Directing was practically invented by Goethe and for him the director was the main creative artist in theatre production. Moreno, on the other hand, put the creative powers back into the actor's hands and for him the director's role was merely to facilitate the spontaneity and creativity of all persons involved in the production (cf. chapter III.2.6).

Both Goethe and Moreno wanted to reform the theatre that came before them. Goethe found himself surrounded by sloppy theatre and hence started to exercise strong control as a director. Moreno in turn rebelled against the theatre, which he found too controlled, predictable and removed from the lives of the actors and the audience. Thus he started to experiment with improvisation and audience involvement.

Goethe's view is, of course, reflected in his writings on the theatre, first and foremost in his *Rules for Actors* of 1803 [Carlson, 1978 p. 309-318]. These consist of 91 mechanical rules on topics such as dialect, pronunciation, posture and movement of the body on stage, avoiding bad habits, conduct of the actor in private life, grouping and positions on stage. They address such details as how the actor should hold his hand and that he should not blow his nose on stage. Goethe apparently found these rules necessary because of the low quality of his actors.

Goethe's ideal actor is nearly the opposite of Moreno's. Whereas Goethe emphasized external qualities such as pronunciation, posture, appearance, memorization, Moreno emphasized the internal such as spontaneity, truthfulness, creativity.

While Moreno was intent on exploring the actor's experience, Goethe was mainly concerned with the effect on the spectator. About the actor he wrote: "His whole profession requires continual self-concealment, and a continual existence in a foreign mask" (Goethe to Eckermann, April 14, 1825, quoted in [Nagler, 1952 p. 427]). This is almost exactly how Moreno described the *traditional* actor (in opposition to his spontaneity actor). "The professional actor of the legitimate stage is all but spontaneous. He has to sacrifice his own self and the roles he might like to contrive, to the self and the roles which a playwright has elaborated for him" [Moreno, 1983 p. 83]. The point is, of course, that Goethe actually believed that this is how a good actor *should* be and he selected and trained his actors accordingly, "...that he might thus learn to lay aside himself and assume a foreign individuality" (Goethe to Eckermann, April 14, 1825, quoted in [Nagler, 1952 p. 428]).

Goethe's view is echoed by his long time Weimar associate Friedrich Schiller (1759 - 1805) in his essay on the use of the chorus in tragedy: "The characters of the drama need this intermission in order to collect themselves; for they are no real beings who obey the impulse of the moment, and merely represent individuals - but ideal persons and representatives of their species, who enunciate the deep things of humanity" (Friedrich Schiller, 1803, quoted in [Nagler, 1952 p. 444]).

"Real beings who obey the impulse of the moment" is exactly what Moreno would like his actors to be. Modern acting teachers often tell their students accordingly to follow their impulses. This is most notably true of Sanford Meisner from the Neighborhood Playhouse (cf. chapter I.1), who thought of acting as "living truthfully under imaginary circumstances" [Meisner & Longwell, 1987 p. 15].

Summarizing Goethe's and Moreno's views of acting, as expressed in their writings and in their work as directors, we find them in the end to be quite different and, indeed, mostly opposed to each other:

GOETHE'S ACTING	MORENO'S ACTING
for the audience	for the actor/spectator
external	internal
self-concealing	self-revealing
memorized	improvised
controlled	expressive
aesthetic goals	therapeutic goals
professional actors	non-professional actors
proscenium stage	open stage
poetic language	natural language
ensemble work	spectators join actors
classic themes	personal themes

III. MORENO ON THE NATURE AND FUNCTION OF THEATRE

We have already seen that Moreno is mostly known today as a psychiatrist (cf. introduction). It is often overlooked that his theories were originally developed to bring about "a revolution of the theatre, completely to change the theatrical events" [Moreno, 1983 p. a]. This chapter will investigate what his ideal theatre would look like.

Traditional books on the nature of theatre divide the subject into sections on stage design, playwriting, producing, directing, acting, audience, scenic design, costume design and makeup, lighting design and sound or some approximation of this.[41] The theatrical production is seen as a collaboration between different kinds of artist. If we try to apply this framework to Moreno, we find that he combines the function of playwriting, producing and directing in what he calls the new dramatist, who facilitates the spontaneity of the actors into a unified expression, effectively eliminating the playwright's role. Moreno has little to say about scenery, costumes, makeup, lights and sound, except that they all should be created extemporaneously as the production unfolds. He does talk about the actor and the audience at length, but his final goal is to overcome this very distinction in a theatre in which everyone is totally involved. That leaves the stage design the only traditional category that survives in Moreno's new approach.

---

[41]See for example part III of [Brockett, 1992].

Instead of applying the old framework, this chapter is organized into sections according to the main elements of Moreno's dramatic theory. Though everything is interrelated, we can distinguish 14 categories falling into two groups. The two main notions that Moreno advocated since his work in Vienna in the early twenties are <u>healing through dramatic enactment</u> and <u>spontaneity</u>. In Moreno's theory these two ideas are inseparable; one of the main goals of therapy is to increase spontaneity and one of the main elements facilitating therapeutic change is spontaneity. Nevertheless, it is conceivable to have one without much of the other. For example someone's therapy might consist of listening to a hypnosis tape over and over again - not much spontaneity there. Or consider a tennis player who's game displays a lot of spontaneity without much therapeutic value.

This chapter is divided according to these two notions. Roughly, the first seven sections relate to the healing power of dramatic enactment. The initial section explains what Moreno means by <u>therapeutic theatre</u>. The following sections describe how the therapeutic effect is facilitated by <u>catharsis</u>, the use of <u>personal themes from the community</u>, <u>audience involvement</u>, <u>validation of subjective experience</u>, and Moreno's stage, which is first architecturally described as the <u>open stage</u> and then metaphysically as <u>Surplus Reality</u>.

The next seven elements all support spontaneity. First, I clarify how the <u>spontaneously creative state</u> of consciousness applies to theatre. Then we will see how Moreno's theatre is always immediate. When we ask how spontaneity can be reached, we find that Moreno has developed techniques for warm-up, which are part of every production and increase the level of spontaneity in everyone involved. He also proposes the use of spontaneity training to enhance the actor's spontaneity permanently, beyond the scope of a particular production. For Moreno spontaneity and memorized lines are incompatible, hence his demand for the elimination of the playwright. His theatre is instead guided by the new dramatist who spontaneously coordinates the production. Moreno introduced the concept of encounter for the coming together of two (or more) actors experiencing each other openly and immediately.

1. Healing through Dramatic Enactment

1.1 Therapeutic Theatre

The function and purpose of theatre has been debated at least since Aristotle. An associated question is that of the criterion for criticism, how we decide what is "good" theatre. Some of the main suggestions that have been made to answer the question of the theatre's function are: imitation (Greek: mimesis), entertainment, ritual, aesthetics, education, insight, stimulation, expression, and political manipulation.

Moreno's contribution adds a new item to this list: *theatre as therapy.* He is not concerned with true representation of reality nor does he merely want to please the audience. Instead he judges theatre by its therapeutic effect. Participation in (good) theatre results in some change which is therapeutic. New is also that he is not only concerned with the effect of theatre on the audience, but especially focuses on the actor.[42]

To clarify Moreno's view it is necessary to take a closer look at what he means by "therapy". He understands therapy in the

---

[42]Moreno's description of how he discovered the therapeutic effect in his Theatre of Spontaneity in Vienna in 1922 was included in chapter II.5.1.2 (*Case of Barbara*). There he first became aware of how certain enactments affected some change in his actress and improved her daily life with her husband.

broadest sense, not just as the treatment of specific mental illnesses. Moreno wants to affect all participants in theatre in a way that is healing, he strives for a transformation of the whole being towards a higher level of vitality, authenticity, expressiveness, spontaneity, and creativity. The function of theatre is to facilitate personal growth, a sense of freedom, and the full development of human potential. As Moreno conceives it, his methods apply not only to mental patients, but to *all* human beings. "A truly therapeutic procedure cannot have less an objective than the whole of mankind" [Moreno, 1953 p. 3].

> I have always tried to show that my approach was meant as much more than a psychotherapeutic method - my ideas have emphasized that creativity and spontaneity affect the very roots of vitality and spiritual development, and thus affect our involvements in every sphere of our lives. (Moreno in [Blatner, 1988a p. vii]).

Moreno's son Jonathan describes his father's goals as follows:

> Moreno's goal in therapy was never the achievement of some fictional (and dull) normalcy, but training in still higher levels of spontaneity so that, when ready, the protagonist could discard this role for another. [Moreno, 1989 p. 6]

Since Moreno wanted to address, if not solve, the problems of modern society, his concern was foremost with so-called normal people:

> The cardinal concern of professional psychotherapy has been, up to now, the mentally disturbed group. But is not the chief concern of a sick society its *normal* group? Is not its

> normal group responsible for the general, social and moral
> decay, for the wars and revolutions which bring untold
> misery upon mankind? [Moreno, 1957 p. 25]

Moreno's broad use of the term "therapy" needs to be distinguished from its use in the traditional medical model. There it is used in much the same sense as "cure", as when we say that aspirin is a therapy or cure for headache. Cure always presupposes a specific sickness or pathology. Western medicine defines health as the absence of illness. It has little to offer to someone who seeks to be more balanced or effective. Holistic medicine understands health as some ideal state in which the human potential is fully developed. While not everyone needs a cure, almost every person can benefit from personal growth and there is hardly anyone of whom we can say that her potential is fully developed with no room for improvement.

Moreno's approach *includes* of course cure. He does prescribe specific techniques for specific disorders. "It appears that to such individuals who have reached the stage of a well organized mental disorder the enactment of the inner world within a dramatic context is indispensable" [Moreno, 1946 p. 18]. But Moreno's therapeutic approach also goes beyond cure and he more often uses the term "therapy" with a meaning like "healing" or "liberation".

One important component and often the first step in this direction is emotional release. This happens when the actor expresses emotions that he had to repress in real life. He can reexperience episodes from his life and be more expressive and true to himself than when they first happened.

According to Moreno such an experience is often sufficient to affect profound change; analysis may not be required. "The patient drives the disease out himself. The magnification of reality into a drama makes him free from reality" [Moreno, 1983 p. 83].

Moreno allows the patient to be in charge of her healing process as much as possible. He is not telling the patient what her problem is and giving her some answer, like a pill. Rather he guides and supports the patient to explore her issues and express her feelings dramatically.

Since Moreno treats the patient as a whole and gives her the responsibility for her mental health, his approach is comparable to holistic medicine. He also emphasizes the growth of the whole person and talks very little about pathologies. This is in great contrast to Freudian psychoanalysis, which stresses the pathological in human behavior, from the madman to the genius. Psychoanalysis is thus comparable to traditional medicine, trying to locate a specific dysfunction and searching for an answer which will result in a cure. This puts much of the responsibility for solving the problem in the analyst.

For something to have a therapeutic effect (in the broad sense) it is not necessary for there to be a clear therapeutic intention. In the *Case of Barbara* (cf. chapter II.5.1.2) for example, the actress thought she was doing theatre, not therapy. In this particular case it was the director who had the therapeutic intention. But there is no reason to think that acting could not have a therapeutic effect if it had been prescribed by the director for purely theatrical goals. Many actors report how their experience in theatre has changed their lives.

Whether something is therapeutic depends certainly also on the subject; the same psychodrama technique may have a therapeutic effect on some individuals, but not on others. The equivalent holds naturally for medication - aspirin does not cure everyone's headaches. One nevertheless usually calls a technique or medication therapy or a cure to the extent that it has the desired effect on many or most subjects.

The broad use of the term "therapy" is sometimes criticized, since it would imply that everything can be therapy. This is indeed true of a great number of phenomena - they can be therapeutic at the right time with the right person. For example today we have music therapy, color therapy, sandtray therapy, movement therapy and many other forms.

Theatre as therapy is today more important than ever. It could be argued that this is the only function of theatre in which film and television are *not* superior. Film has threatened to replace theatre and indeed it can show reality more accurately, is better entertainment for most people, educates more people and has a much stronger political impact. But film and especially television have very little therapeutic value; in fact, many have argued that it hinders rather than fosters personal growth.

Thus the therapeutic effect of theatre might very well be the main reason why we need to continue to practice this art. That view is becoming more and more wide spread, and as a result drama therapy (cf. chapter V.2) is slowly becoming a field of study and practice in its own right.[43]

Jerzy Grotowski in *Towards a Poor Theatre* [1968] echoes many of Moreno's points. Grotowski, the founder and director of the Polish Laboratory Theatre and the Institute for Research into Acting, is widely regarded as a leading theoretician of the theatre in this century.[44] He has argued that theatre should stop trying to compete with film by being ever more technically extravagant and impressive. Along this route, it can never win, since scene changes in film will always be faster than in the theatre, no matter how much expense and technology we use. Instead the theatre artists should focus on what is essential and unique to theatre: the actor-audience relationship.

The following quotation contains many of the elements of Grotowski's theory. It is included here mainly because he explicitly acknowledges in it the therapeutic function of theatre.

---

[43]According to one of its leaders, the field started in 1979 [Emunah, 1994 p. xix], five years after Moreno's death.

[44]In the widely used textbook *The Essential Theatre* we read: "During the 1960s, Grotowski became a major influence on theatre in Europe and America. His company performed widely, and he did workshops for various other theatres and for some of the world's best directors. His influence was further disseminated through his book *Towards a Poor Theatre* (1968)." [Brockett, 1992 p. 264f]

Peter Brook was among the directors Grotowski did workshops for. He writes: "[N]o-one else in the world, to my knowledge, no-one since Stanislavski, has investigated the nature of acting, its phenomenon, its meaning, the nature and science of its mental-physical-emotional processes as deeply and completely as Grotowski." [Grotowski, 1968 p. 13]

Theatre - through the actor's technique, his art in which the living organism strives for higher motives - provides an opportunity for what could be called integration, the discarding of masks, the revealing of the real substance: a totality of physical and mental reactions. This opportunity must be treated in a disciplined manner, with a full awareness of the responsibilities it involves. *Here we can see the theatre's therapeutic function for people in our present day civilization.* It is true that the actor accomplishes this act, but he can only do so through an encounter with the spectator - intimately, visibly, not hiding behind a cameraman, wardrobe mistress, stage designer or make-up girl - in direct confrontation with him, and somehow "instead of" him. The actor's act - discarding half measures, revealing, opening up, emerging from himself as opposed to closing up - is an invitation to the spectator. This act could be compared to an act of the most deeply rooted, genuine love between two human beings - this is just a comparison since we can only refer to this "emergence from oneself" through analogy. This act, paradoxical and borderline, we call a total act. In our opinion it epitomizes the actor's deepest calling. [Grotowski, 1968 p. 255f (my emphasis)]

1.2 Catharsis

The liberating, therapeutic effect of Moreno's theatre is to a large extent accomplished through catharsis. This concept was discussed at length in the previous chapter. Suffice it here to state again that Moreno wants to encourage catharsis in *all* participants of his theatre.

> ...catharsis takes place: not only in the audience - secondary desired effect - and not in the dramatic personae of an imaginary production, but primarily in the spontaneous actors in the drama who produce the personae by liberating themselves from them at the same time. [Moreno, 1983 p. 97]

Most other commentators who speak of catharsis in the theatre have only the spectator in mind. For example Scheff's book on *Catharsis in Healing, Ritual, and Drama* contains a chapter entitled *A Theory of Catharsis in Drama* [Scheff, 1979 p. 149-179], but has nothing to say about the effect of catharsis in drama upon the *actor* and contains only one minor reference to Moreno/psychodrama [ibid. p. 224]. Scheff analyzes only the effect on the audience, and that in great detail.

> My thesis concerns the playwright's use of audience awareness and identification with the characters to bring on catharsis: a theory of catharsis will help us to understand the structure of many, or perhaps even most, classical dramas. [Scheff, 1979 p. 150]

Scheff is however aware of the similarities between catharsis in the theatre and in therapy: "Both dramatic and psychotherapeutic theories involve the reexperiencing of past emotional crises in a context of complete security: in the safety of the theatre or the therapist's office" [Scheff, 1979 p. 23]. Moreno's psychodrama is partly about reexperiencing of past emotional crises by the protagonist and sometimes also by the audience.

Moreno stresses that his theatre strives to be personal, to touch actors and audience with themes from their lives. For Scheff it is enough for the audience to relate to the drama in a very general way. He does not require the reexperiencing of past emotions in the audience to be conscious. Thus, unlike Moreno, he does not reject the cathartic value of what Moreno would call "cultural conserves, written dramas about foreign characters," (cf. chapter II.1) such as *Romeo and Juliet*.

> To state it in a very brief and simplified form, the theory of catharsis argues that thrill-seeking is an attempt to relive, and therefore resolve, earlier painful experiences which were unfinished. When we cry over the fate of Romeo and Juliet, we are reliving our own personal experiences of overwhelming loss, but under new and less severe conditions. [Scheff, 1979 p. 13]

1.3 Community Theatre

In order to be therapeutic, theatre has to be made by and for the people. "It can be said that compared to the legitimate theatre, as the theatres of the nobility in the middle ages and the theatre of the intellectual classes in our time, the theatre for spontaneity can be considered *the theatre of the people*" [Moreno, 1983 p. 81]. This theatre is used to build a sense of community, a sense of belonging together and relating to each other. "It turns the lonely inhabitants of the house into a community" [Moreno, 1983 p. 90].

Ideally Moreno would like to bring everybody together. "Spectators of the therapeutic theatre are the entire community. All are invited and all gather before the house. The psychodrama cannot begin unless the last inhabitant of the town is present" [Moreno, 1983 p. 91]. In reality of course many psychodramas had to begin without everyone present. Moreno's goals were often idealistic, he wanted to change mankind into a *therapeutic community* where everyone is therapist and patient at the same time, helping each other to reach their full potential, facilitating the emotional growth of each member (cf. chapter V.4).

In order to reach the community, the theatre has to touch its members on a *personal* level. It has to reflect the life of the community, instead of telling the stories of kings and queens. "The theatre has to date mirrored the sufferings of foreign things, but here, in the Theatre of Spontaneity, it plays our own woe" [Moreno, 1983 p. 26].

To move the audience on a personal level, Moreno suggests that the actor, who is also a member of the community, has to play himself and not a foreign character. "In playing yourself you see yourself in your own mirror on the stage, exposed as you are to the entire audience" [Moreno, 1983 p. 27]. Thus the theatre functions as a mirror, not only for the audience, but also for the actor. The community sees itself.

Moreno demanded that the actor completely reveal himself before the audience. "In order that they may be driven out from their cages, they tear up their deepest and most secret wounds, and now they bleed externally before all the eyes of the people" [Moreno, 1946 p. 28]. This is also what Grotowski demanded of his *holy actor*. "[W]e may experience what is real and, having already given up all daily escapes and pretenses, in a state of complete defenselessness unveil, give, discover ourselves" [Grotowski, 1968 p. 257].

Nothing should be held back. "Once we had permitted the actor a full spontaneity of his own, his full private world, his personal problem, his own conflicts, his own defeats and dreams came to the fore. I recognized gradually the therapeutic value which this kind of presentation had for the actor himself and when properly manipulated, the therapeutic value it had for the audience" [Moreno, 1983 p. 102].

1.4 Audience Involvement

In order to affect the entire community the audience has to get involved. We have seen in chapter II.3 how Moreno criticized the traditional theatre for rendering the audience passive. In contrast, he wants to smash the barrier between actor and audience, inspire the spectator to become active, to participate and to become an actor himself. "From the point of view of a spontaneity theatre everyone is a player, not only the people on the stage, but also every spectator in the audience" [Moreno, 1983 p. 84]. Moreno suggests the following structure for the participation of the audience:

> The participation of the audience must be gradually freed from chaos and lawlessness and it must be made to fit esthetic rules. Leadership is assigned to a specific member of the audience, *the audience director*, parallel to the stage director on the scene. Around him, the audience director, an active group of spectators gather whereas a large majority remain in a passive role. At times, however, the whole audience is active. [Moreno, 1983 p. 23f][45]

In this model there are different degrees of involvement for different spectators and also at different times throughout a performance. This can be seen as a step in the move towards the ideal, where the distinction between spectators and actors becomes meaningless, since everyone is fully participating.

In a typical psychodrama there is a distinction between those members of the group who have been assigned specific roles and others who are watching, maybe sharing later. Nevertheless even the mostly passive audience has a function in relation to the

---

[45]This idea can already be found in [Moreno, 1924 p. 12]: "Die Wandlung der Zuschauer in Zuschauspieler, des Zuschauerraumes in ein Zuschautheater versetzt die Regie in ein neues Versuchsfeld. Die Teilnahme des Publikums muß von Willkür befreit und ästhetischen Gesetzen gefügig gemacht sein. Einem bestimmten Zuschauer wird die Führung übertragen, dem Zuschauerdirektor. Um ihn schart sich eine mittätige Gruppe, während die große Mehrheit den Hintergrund bildet."

desired therapeutic effect. They enhance the healing effect on the protagonist. By witnessing his inner world as portrayed on the stage they validate his feelings and he feels more recognized and less isolated. As actors often report, having an audience can transport one into an altered state of consciousness, with heightened awareness of inner and outer reality.

Conversely the audience benefits from seeing one of its members reveal herself. In many cases members of the audience will resonate with the action on the stage and relate it (consciously or unconsciously) to episodes from their own life.

1.5 Open Stage

To facilitate the participation of the audience Moreno had to redesign the stage.

> In an ordinary theatre the position of the spectator is arbitrary as the interest is focused upon the stage and the only thing that matters is that the spectators can see what happens there. In a psychodramatic theatre the situation is changed. Here it is important that the director, too, be able to see every spectator. This has two reasons; the polarity is double. The psychodramatic director should see every member of the audience and thus establish, if not more, at least an illusion of direct communication with them; and it is of equal therapeutic value that every spectator be able to see the

director. ... In advanced sessions moreover every member of the audience should be visible to every other member. [Moreno, 1946 p. 325]

Moreno describes his proposal for a stage for the new theatre as

one which is placed in the center instead of the periphery; one which permits movement unlimited instead of limited; one which is open to all sides instead of in front; one which has the whole community around it, instead of only a part; one which has the form of a circle instead of a square; one which moves up in vertical dimension, instead of maintaining a single level. [Moreno, 1983 p. 4]

Moreno's ideas for the open stage were inspired by the free, open spaces in the gardens in Vienna in which he moved and played with children [Moreno, 1983 p. 100].

In his most detailed description of the open stage he states:

In the center of the space is built the stage of the spontaneous actors. It is not built at the back of one end of the space, hidden like the peep-show stage, but it is built so that all its parts can be seen from all seats. It is not built in the depth and left there down on the ground, but it is erected in the vertical dimension. It is raised. Its back is not protected by backdrops, it does not look for help and defenses in the rear, it has nothing to fall back on. From the central stage steps lead up and down in an amphi-theatrical form. They lead to the special stages which are built within the auditorium itself, on every level of the amphitheatre, ready to be used by spectator-actors who may enter into dramatic action. [Moreno, 1983 p. 31]

The stage is augmented by a backdrop that can be adjusted to different dramatic scenes as they evolve in the theatre of spontaneity. "It consisted in impromptu settings, a number of wooden pieces in various sizes, colors and forms" [Moreno, 1983 p. 69]. Similarly there are materials to make impromptu drawings and impromptu costumes. Everything should be created before the eyes of the public. There is no backstage and no curtain to hide behind [Moreno, 1983 p. 99].

In 1924 with the help of the architect Rudolf Hönigsfeld, Moreno presented diagrams of a stage called *Theater ohne Zuschauer* (theatre without an audience), first in his book *Das Stegreiftheater* [Moreno, 1924 Tafel 1] and then at the *Internationale Ausstellung Neuer Theatertechnik* in Vienna (cf. Kiesler controversy, introduction.3). The diagrams display the elements in Moreno's description quoted above. They were first printed in the catalog of the *Internationale Ausstellung neuer Theatertechnik* [Kiesler, 1924 p. 67] and can now be found reprinted in many places, such as [Lesák, 1988 p. 115; Marineau, 1989 p. 83; Moreno, 1946 p. 267; Moreno, 1964a p. 21, 23; Moreno, 1983 frontispiece].

It was not until 1936 that Moreno was able to actually build a stage for his therapeutic theatre, at his sanitarium in Beacon, N.Y.[46] A photograph of this model can be found in [Moreno, 1946

---

[46]Moreno dedicated this psychodrama theatre to Mrs. Gertrude Franchot Tone who was a patient of his and sponsored the building of the stage. It was later used by her son, the actor Franchot Tone, to explore some of his marital problems with his wife, Joan Crawford [Marineau, 1989 p. 131ff].

p. 268] and a description in [ibid. p. 263]. It is less elaborate than the Vienna model and seats only 85 people, but still displays some of the main elements of his first design: a circular stage with different levels, accessible from all sides. New is a balcony, about 9 feet above the stage. This can be used to represent heaven, highest perfection, superego, etc. There is however also a more traditional looking auditorium with regular rows of fixed chairs. The stage was later copied at many other places, such as St. Elizabeths Hospital, Washington, D.C. in 1940 and New York, 1942 [Moreno, 1946 p. 264ff].

1.6 Surplus Reality

The physical design of the stage supports a metaphysical or psychological function: the actor enters a different reality, what Moreno coined "Surplus Reality", which allows the actors to "be on the stage what they are, more deeply and explicitly than they appear to be in life reality" [Moreno, 1946 p. c]. Moreno describes the metaphysics of the stage:

> Why a stage? It provides the patient with a living space which is multi-dimensional and flexible to the maximum. The living space of reality is often narrow and restraining, he may easily lose his equilibrium. On the stage he may find it again due to its methodology of freedom - freedom from unbearable

stress and freedom for experience and expression. The stage space is an extension of life beyond the reality tests of life itself. Reality and fantasy are not in conflict, but both are functions within a wider sphere - the psychodramatic world of objects, persons and events. In its logic the ghost of Hamlet's father is just as real and permitted to exist as Hamlet himself. Delusions and hallucinations are given flesh - embodiment on the stage - and an equality of status with normal sensory perceptions. The architectural design of the stage is made in accord with therapeutic requirements. Its circular forms and levels of the stage, levels of aspiration, pointing out the vertical dimension, stimulate relief from tensions and permit mobility and flexibility of action. [Moreno, 1946 p. a]

Thus Moreno's theatre does not merely imitate reality, but rather magnifies it, makes it bigger than life. "Here, acts are richer in inspiration than acts in life or in a legitimate drama" [Moreno, 1983 p. 52].

The reality of the stage can best be compared to the reality of dreams. Anything is possible: time is non-linear, time and space can be changed at any moment, animals and even furniture etc. can speak, fears as well as fantasies get acted out, dead persons can come to live, we can experience the past and the future, both as it happened or will happen and with all kinds of modifications.

The purpose of dreams can be seen as therapeutic. We dream in order to heal ourselves. Studies have shown that we can not live without dreams, we literally die. Analysis on the other hand, though beneficial, we can do without. Similarly Moreno says that it is necessary that we express our feelings and not so much that we analyze them.

Dreams are of course often the subject of psychodramas (and other theatrical events, such as plays and improvisations). Here the purpose is not to interpret the dream, but to allow the dreamer to reexperience the dream on stage and to intensify the experience. "The objective of psychodramatic techniques is to stir up the dreamer to produce the dream instead of analyzing it for him. Even if one could be sure that the analysis is objective and reliable it is preferable if analysis is turned into production by the dreamer" [Fox, 1987 p. 199]. An interpretation might emerge from this. The interpretation can only come from the subject and should not be imposed from the outside.

An example of Surplus Reality that occurs in psychodrama is the enactment of a scene from your childhood in the way in which you *wish* it had happened, for example with a loving mother. In this way, at least to a degree, we can give ourselves the childhood that we always wanted. Or we can act out a fantasy about what we want (or fear) our life to be like in five years.

The stage is a safe place to be dangerous. We can express ourselves in new ways without suffering the consequences of real life. For example, we might yell at our parents or even beat them in the form of a pillow. In this way we can have the benefit of releasing unexpressed emotions, without suffering the consequences of hurting our parents. How much we later *actually* express to them is a different question.

I want to end this section with a poetic description of Surplus Reality:

> When God created the world in six days he had stopped a day too early. He had given Man a place to live but in order to make it safe for him he also chained him to that place. On the seventh day he should have created for Man a second world, another one, free of the first world and in which he could purge himself from it, but a world which would not chain anyone because it was not real. It is here where the theatre of spontaneity continues God's creation of the world by opening for Man a new dimension of existence. [Moreno, 1983 p. 7]

1.7 Validity of Subjective Experience

Moreno's Surplus Reality contains the individual's dreams, hopes, fears, fantasies, imaginations, etc. Thus when he spoke of the "Theatre of Truth" he meant subjective, psychological truth. He always emphasized the validity of subjective experience. When a subject wants to enact a scene about her mother who did not love her, he would not question whether it was true that her mother did not love her. Rather the scene would be played as the subject experienced it subjectively. The director, actors and audience are invited to enter her private world. According to Moreno this can be the first step in healing. Often for the first time the patient feels understood and taken seriously.

Moreno wants to give "all forms of subjective existence, including the prophetic and the deviate, a place where it can fulfill and perhaps transform itself, unencumbered by the restrictions of the prevailing culture" [Moreno, 1959b p. 215]. What better place for this than the theatre, where we are free and safe to explore our highest aspirations as well as our madness (and not get arrested - though there are exceptions to this as well, cf. the section on the Living Theatre, chapter IV.3). Moreno distances himself from the psychoanalytical movement which he accuses of declaring "prophetic behavior, indeed, all deviate behavior, as suspect of pathological origins" [Moreno, 1959b p. 215]. Moreno seems to anticipate some clever psychoanalyst analyzing his own aspirations as pathological. This may very well have been done by now.

According to Moreno the psychoanalytic movement started "an era of disenchantment and fear of emotional creativity" [Moreno, 1959b p. 215]. Despite Moreno's tremendous influence, it could easily be argued that this era still continues today. But this is not a point I want to pursue here.

Moreno requires "the full involvement of the actor in the act ..., and emphasis is continually placed upon a subjectivistic frame of reference to the extreme" [Moreno, 1959b p. 215]. In therapeutic treatment Moreno carried the patient's autonomy to a maximum. "The patient becomes the chief guide in the research about him as well as in his cure" [Moreno, 1959b p. 216].

Immediate, subjective experience is validated by itself. "The experience, for instance, of two lovers or two friends does not require any validation beyond the consent and enjoyment of the participants. ... What matters is that the therapeutic experiences are valid for the participants themselves, at the time they take place" [Moreno, 1959b p. 216].

Because of these and other aspects of his philosophy Moreno is often counted as an existentialist.[47] In 1918 he edited *Daimon*, the leading existentialist and expressionist magazine of the Vienna period (cf. introduction.3 and appendix.1). Moreno himself not only agrees that he is an existentialist, but claims that he has brought the movement to its logical conclusion. "Existentialism as a movement predates psychoanalysis and has reached its high point in the psychodrama of our time" [Moreno, 1959b p. 224].

In his analysis of the historical development of the existentialist movement Moreno distinguishes "three phases, a *frustrated, heroic* and *intellectual* phase" [Moreno, 1959b p. 224]. The first period is exemplified by Kierkegaard's protest against the dishonest church of Christianity who he accused of betraying Christ, and against Hegel's philosophy which he considered as intellectualizing the spirit. It is called *frustrated* since "Kierkegaard never became in life itself the active, dynamic prophet of this fantasy, but he left for the next generation a testament to follow" [Moreno, 1959b p. 208]. Similarly Nietzsche

---

[47]"A review of the complete philosophical writings Moreno produced during these years shows that he deserves to be included among the early existentialists" [Blatner, 1988b p. 18].

never became the superman (Übermensch) that he postulated as a goal for man to attain.

Moreno places the second period from around 1900 to 1920, characterized by individuals who threw themselves into a full and genuine life in the here and now, often withdrawing from intellectual life and writing. There has been comparatively little written about this period, since "writers usually write about other writers" [Moreno, 1959b p. 211]. Moreno mentions a few names, such as Leo Tolstoy, Charles Péguy, Albert Schweitzer, Otto Weininger and especially John Kellmer, "who, in order to taste life of a different order, gave up his university career and turned from being a philosopher and writer into a simple farmhand, living with plain hardworking peasants. He broke off contact with all his earlier friends and his books, never wrote another line" [Moreno, 1959b p. 211f].

Interestingly, Moreno also includes Hitler in this category, representing the "pathological variety of existentialism" [Moreno, 1959b p. 224].

> Far more than the Nazi doctrine and racist theory, there was characteristic for Hitler a self-realization drive, a hunger to live and to fill existence with himself to the limit, with the good and the bad which was in him, regardless of all values, including all the Germanic values. He was more of an existentialist than he was a Nazi. [Moreno, 1959b p. 224]

The third period in Moreno's division is the modern intellectual existentialism of men like Jaspers, Heidegger and Sartre, all of whom Moreno rejects as intellectuals rather than doers. "Its chief concerns are the philosophical problems of existence, not existing and existence itself" [Moreno, 1959b p. 213]. They write books and avoid becoming fully involved in life. According to Moreno they have little to do with Kierkegaard's original ideas.

Moreno himself has of course written so many books that it is only natural to ask whether he himself was not an intellectual rather than a doer. He was probably both. We don't need further evidence to show that he was a prolific writer and thinker. He was even thinking and writing about the meaning of books and the written word. Some of his German writings in the early twenties expressed his distaste for books [Marschall, 1988 p. 32], and he seems to be fully aware of the inherent contradiction in publishing his thoughts. "I, the reader against my will, have to write the book against my will" [Moreno, 1923 p. 221].[48]

I know Moreno mostly through his writings, but through those I have also gained a picture of Moreno as a doer, as someone who lives his ideas in action. For example, *The First Psychodramatic Family* [1964] contains many descriptions of how he uses psychodrama techniques when there are conflicts in his daily life with his wife and son.

---

[48]The German original reads: "Ich, der Leser wider Willen, muß das Buch wider Willen schreiben," and is quoted in [Marschall, 1988 p. 34].

Role Reversal at Dinner

Mother says to Jonathan, "Eat-eat-eat!"
Jonathan is annoyed and says to himself,
"But why? - I'm not hungry."

Mother says to Jonathan, "Finish the meal,
You have so much on the plate."
Jonathan thinks, "Why should I finish
If I don't feel like it?"
Mother thinks he looks pale,
He had the flu, and lost weight.
Jonathan cries.

Mother says, "Let's reverse roles."
Jonathan in the role of mother:
"Eat, eat everything on your plate,
You can't leave the table yet
Because you are not through."
Mother as Jonathan:
"But I am full. I can't take another bite."
Jonathan as mother calmly replies:
"So don't eat!"

Jonathan becomes himself
And returns to his seat.
Mother returns to her seat deeply impressed
And says:
"Jonathan, eat only as much as you want
And when you are through you can leave the table."
Here Jonathan is not only his own therapist,
But the therapist of his mother as well.
[Moreno, 1964a p. 81f]

Moreno concludes that his own techniques and ideas have fulfilled Kierkegaard's premise: "Finally, it is amusing to think that Kierkegaard is attaining a belated rehabilitation, not by modern existentialists who have given him a gentle phenomenological burial, but via the psychodramatic stagedoor" [Moreno, 1959b p. 217].

2. Spontaneity

2.1 The Spontaneously Creative State

We have already seen in chapter I.3 that spontaneity is one of the most important concepts in Moreno's theory, and I described what spontaneity consists in. This section adds some observations on how the concept is applied to theatre.

In Moreno's ideal theatre both actor and audience enter a new state of consciousness, the spontaneously creative state. "In the theatre all men are stirred up and they move from the state of consciousness to a state of spontaneity, from the world of actual deed , actual thoughts and feelings, into a world of fantasy which includes the reality potential" [Moreno, 1983 p.31].

While the above suggests that the spontaneously creative state is a product of participating (as actor or audience) in the new theatre, Moreno also suggests the reverse, namely that good theatre results when actors enter the spontaneously creative state.

> The impromptu agent, poet, actor, musician, painter finds his point of departure not outside, but within himself, in the spontaneity "state". ... It is the state of production, the essential principle of all creative experience. If the technique

of the spontaneity state is applied to the drama, a new art of
the theatre develops. [Moreno, 1983 p. 44]

So the new theatre and the spontaneity state always go hand in
hand. Moreno declares it to be the starting point for his theatre
and compares its importance to that of lines for the conventional
theatre. He follows this with an attempt to describe the state more
internally:

> When the stage actor finds himself without a role conserve,
> the religious actor without a ritual conserve, they have to "ad
> lib", to turn to experiences which are not performed and
> readymade, but are still buried within them in an unformed
> stage. In order to mobilize and shape them, they need a
> transformer and catalyst, a kind of intelligence which
> operates here and now, *hic et nunc*, "spontaneity". [Moreno,
> 1946 p. XII]

As stated in chapter I.3, Moreno compares spontaneity to
intelligence as both describe a certain ability, and we have seen
that spontaneity can be described as the ability to improvise well.
Since Moreno's ideal theatre is mostly improvised, it follows that
its success is linked to the actual spontaneity the actors can
muster. But again there might be some actors who start off with
very little spontaneity and then develop it as a *result* of
participating in Moreno's theatre.

Moreno's demand for spontaneity does not only apply to the
actors, but to all participants in the theatre. The director (cf.
section 2.6, The New Dramatist) and also the people responsible
for lights, sound, music, etc. must be able to create on the spur of

the moment, while being very much aware of each other in order to create a unified experience. "The performance itself is the free, unpremeditated, spontaneous product of the director and his co-workers" [Moreno, 1983 p. 40].

2.2 Immediate Theatre

In Moreno's theatre there is no longer a separation between the creation and the performance of a play. "The entire work of art is formed before our eyes" [Moreno, 1983 p. 37]. Everything happens at once. "The act of creation is contemporaneous with the production; there is harmony of situation and word" [Moreno, 1983 p. 47].

The immediate theatre is full of surprises. The actors not only surprise the audience, but also themselves. This is in contrast to the traditional actor who "once he has started to play his role on the stage, does not face any surprises to which he is not carefully conditioned" [Moreno, 1983 p. 80]. Even in the conventional theatre the most interesting moments are often when something unforeseen happens, "a mistake", and we can observe how the actor handles the situation by improvising.

Moreno's new theatre always happens in the present moment: "A spontaneous performance presents things only as they are at the moment of production. It is not directed towards any past moment nor is it directed towards any future moments" [Moreno, 1983 p. 37]. All the elements of the theatre have to be created on the spur of the moment and in front of the audience and thus Moreno speaks of "impromptu settings", "impromptu drawings", "improvised costumes" [Moreno, 1983 p. 69], etc.

One of the forms Moreno developed, not only to facilitate immediacy, but also to prove it to the audience in no uncertain terms, is the *living newspaper*. Moreno directed living newspaper (Lebendige Zeitung) performances at the Vienna Stegreiftheater (1922-1925) and again at the Guild Theatre, New York City, on April 5, 1931 [Moreno, 1983 p. 38]. (See also *New York Times* article from April 6, 1931, quoted in the appendix.) He described them as follows:

> The dramatized or "living" newspaper is a presentation of the news of the day as it occurs. It is the synthesis between the spontaneity theatre and a newspaper. The intention is to make the expression on the stage spontaneous in form (impromptu) as well as in comment[49] (the news of the day). The dramatized newspaper has another asset from the point of view of an art of the moment: the absolute evidence of true spontaneity it has for the onlookers - and not simply for the actors, as in some form of the spontaneity theatre - because of the daily news character of the material projected. A good dramatized newspaper tries to produce the news as quickly as it can be

---

[49]This is probably a misprint and should read "content" as it does at a later place in the same book: "The immediacy of *form* is meant here, the spontaneity of the actor versus the acting of a rehearsed piece, and the immediacy of content - a problem which is relevant to the audience and to the actors on the stage, instead of a problem which is relevant to an individual playwright, whether past or present" [Moreno, 1983 p. 77].

gathered by the reporters; thus the production may change in content from hour to hour. [Moreno, 1983 p. 38]

For a description of the enactments following a murder case from the daily paper see [Moreno, 1983 p. 75-77].[50] The purpose of these explorations is not so much to figure out objectively what exactly happened, but rather to examine the possible motivations that led to the murder case, acknowledging the subjectivity of individual readers. "Among the many versions which had been acted out before the director, this one was chosen because it appeared to motivate a murder out of anxiety more convincingly than the newspaper report itself, and other versions constructed by the subjects" [ibid p. 75].[51]

Another more recent account is by Lewis Yablonsky who participated in a number of living newspaper events directed by Moreno. In 1961 he was chosen, for example, to play Adolf Eichmann in a number of enactments conducted by Moreno with about three hundred people at the Chicago meeting of the American Psychiatric Association. This was inspired by the newspaper reports of Eichmann's trial in Israel which had deeply affected many participants. Yablonsky reports:

> The results were electrifying during the entire three hours of the session. Many psychiatrists in the group were refugees from Germany and had lost members of their family in the

---

[50]It is not clear from the text if and when this enactment actually happened.

[51]The *Case of Barbara* is also an instance of the living newspaper Moreno conducted in the early twenties in Vienna, a description was included in chapter II.5.1.2.

death camps administered by Eichmann. Although it was only a psychodramatic living newspaper, it became immediate and emotional to everyone present. People rose up in tears and began to vilify me in the role of Eichmann with horrendous curses and denunciations.

The central impacts of the session were a profound catharsis for the group and the articulation of deeper feelings about the catastrophe that until this enactment lay festering in the participant's psyche. Many people in the group "found each other," cried together, and discussed a psychic pain that was formerly felt in loneliness and despair prior to the session. Many people embraced, and the group of several hundred developed a marvelous cohesion and empathy. [Yablonsky, 1981 p. 201]

This episode is also a good example of what Moreno called "group catharsis" (cf. chapter II.5.1.3.5). Moreno himself has also written an account of this "Psychodrama and Sociodrama of Judaism and the Eichmann Trial" [Moreno, 1964a p. 108ff], where he states: "The meaning of the psychodrama was not to duplicate the trial but to replace it by a trial of a different order in which the true and hidden experiences are brought before the conscience of the world" [Moreno, 1964a p. 109].[52]

[52]According to Moreno all this happened at a meeting of the American Academy of Psychodrama and Group Psychotherapy, an organization of his followers founded by him, and not the American Psychiatric Association, as Yablonsky claimed.
Moreno's account ends with the following "recommendations to the Israeli court as to how to carry out and conclude their trial" [Moreno, 1964a p. 109]:
"1. Adolf Eichmann shall be taken out of his cage and be given the full range of the courtroom to act out crucial episodes of his life, carefully selected and known to be true, under the direction of a skilled psychodramatist with a staff of auxiliary egos. ...
2. The first part of the psychodrama should be the process of reenactment; the second part should be the process of catharsis. For Eichmann himself, his attorney, the court, and the world witnessing, in order to make the

The living newspaper technique is still used today by some psychodramatists and is usually considered a part of sociodrama, a form similar to psychodrama, that explores social issues in a group setting without a designated protagonist; for instance [Carvalho & Otero, 1994 p. 143] and [Feldhendler, 1994 p. 103] report using it.

Moreno was not the first to experiment with performances based on the daily news. Goethe already reported its use in the Commedia dell'arte:

> The Pulcinella is usually a kind of living newspaper. Everything noteworthy that happened during the day in Neapel is reported by him in the evening. [J. W. Goethe, 1830][53]

Moreno's early and extensive work with the living newspaper is little known among theatre historians. If we look up "living

---

catharsis truly world-wide and meaningful, all mass media should be used to make a mass co-experience possible. Television, motion pictures, simultaneous psychodramatic re-trials in many parts of the world. ..." [ibid. p. 109f].
Here we see again how far-reaching Moreno's vision is and indeed he sent his recommendations to the proper authorities. Sadly, but predictably, the response by the Israeli Attorney General was negative:
"In reply to your letter of May 30 with enclosure, I wish to dissociate myself unequivocally from your suggestions. What we are conducting in Jerusalem is not a psychodrama nor a sociodrama. It is a case against an accused under due process of law and will not be turned into anything else" [ibid. p. 111].
Prof. H. F. Infield of Hebrew University, Israel responded: "...I personally am decidedly in favor. ...All I could do so far, is to discuss your paper with a group of psychiatrists... They were quite interested in the theoretical implications of your proposal, but felt that its implementation would at present be quite beyond the mental horizon of the people involved" [ibid. p. 111f].
[53]"Der Pulcinell ist in der Regel eine Art lebendige Zeitung. Alles, was den Tag über sich in Neapel Auffallendes zugetragen hat, kann man abends von ihm hören." Goethe as quoted in [Esrig, 1985 p. 163].

newspaper" in contemporary theatre dictionaries or histories, we find (if anything) the story of the performances by the Federal Theatre Project (USA) from 1935 to 1939. The spirit of these productions was however very different from Moreno's, since they consisted of written and rehearsed performances (hence were in Moreno's terminology *cultural conserves*) resembling documentary films, including film clips and photographs projected onto screens. They used text from newspapers, speeches and other documents and focused on a political topic, such as slum housing (*One Third of a Nation*, 1938) or the farm-subsidy program (*Triple-A Plowed Under*, 1936) [Brockett, 1992 p. 209f].

A history of the development of the living newspaper form does not mention Moreno and dates the invention of the title later than Moreno's early experiments in Vienna in the early twenties:

> Dramatizations of news stories were by no means original with the Federal Theatre. They had been done in political cabarets in Europe for decades and had been used by the workers' theatres in the United States, most effectively by the Workers' Laboratory Theatre in sketches like *Free Thaelmann* and *Newsboy*. The title "Living Newspaper" had been invented by the Soviet Blue Blouses, mobile theatrical troupes that had been organized in the late 1920s by journalists who aimed their work at the semi-literate peasants and workmen in the provinces. [Williams, 1974 p. 224]

Living newspaper presentations that were improvised based on the *daily* news, and thus more in line with Moreno's original idea, were later performed in Chicago by Viola Spolin (cf. chapter IV.2) in 1940[54] and by the Compass in 1955[55].

2.3 Warm-up

Since the spontaneously creative state is so important to Moreno, the question arises: How can it be obtained? Moreno answers: "..It is not created by the conscious will, which frequently acts as an inhibitory bar, but by a liberation, which is, in fact, the free uprising of spontaneity" [Moreno, 1983 p. 44].

This process of liberation Moreno called "warm-up". The term is taken from sports or dance, where it is clear that a dancer needs to go through a warm-up before performing jumps and turns. Similarly an actor cannot be expected to do a complex improvisation or enactment without a warm-up. The warm-up *gradually* leads the actor from a low level of spontaneity to a high level. The actor in psychodrama or theatre starts with a certain level of spontaneity, depending on many factors, for example if he

---

[54]"Today's news is tomorrow's play" Chicago *Sunday Times* of September 22, 1940. [Sweet, 1978 p. xix]

[55]"A week before opening, Bowen devised a format for the segment Shepherd had envisioned as the Living Newspaper, which was to be gleaned straight from the pages of the press each day. ...
At the Compass, a narrator (Bowen) and three or four actors would enter with newspapers and proceed for twenty minutes to satirize selected news items and articles by interpolating pantomimed or spoken bits." [Coleman, 1990 p. 99]

has been working in an office all day his level might be very low. He cannot be directed right away to enact an intense murder scene, in fact such a direction might shut him down. Rather he must be gradually warmed up, maybe first making some physical sculptures with his body, then adding his voice, etc. Slowly he will increase his movement and physical awareness, use his voice in different ways and carry out more and more complex improvisations. A theme will emerge or be given to him on which he will focus more and more. Before enacting a scene the different roles will be introduced and the physical space is defined according to where the scene takes place. The director with the help of the actors introduces as many details as possible, such as where windows and doors are, what the floor is like, the places of furniture and any smells or sounds.

As the actors warm up, the group as a whole also warms up to a higher level of cohesion, openness and focus. The spectators warm up to more empathy and active involvement.

This process of fostering spontaneity has to be facilitated and simply allowed to take place, rather than forced. In particular it is not of much use to command the actors: "Be spontaneous!"; this will invariably have the opposite effect and only make them more tense. "If a performance is called forth too early and abruptly, the tension in the individual will be greater than if it were called forth when ripe for presentation" [Moreno, 1983 p. 49]. The warm-up can build up to a peak and this is often the best time to begin the enactment - if one waits too long the spontaneity might decrease again. "We see here that *there is for a creative unit , one most favorable moment of actualization*" [Moreno, 1983 p. 51].

Classical psychodrama always consists of three phases: the warm-up, the enactment of a scene, and the sharing among the group members. For a description of warm-up techniques used by psychodramatists see e.g. [Blatner, 1988a p. 42-57] and [Leveton, 1992 p. 21-43]. Many of these were originally developed by Moreno, but others are drawn from sources such as Spolin's theatre games [Spolin, 1963] or dance improvisation [Blatner, 1988a p. 49].

2.4 Spontaneity Training

We have seen that Moreno's ideal actor is not the conventional, perfectionist actor who gives the exact same performance every night, cleverly worked out to the last detail, but rather the actor who is always living in the moment, always fresh and different. To this end Moreno also had to change the actor's training. "By necessity, therefore, the study and rehearsal of parts are replaced by training in spontaneity states" [Moreno, 1983 p. 74].[56]

---

[56]This idea can already be found in [Moreno, 1924 p. 69]: "Die Stegreifübung ist der Hauptgegenstand der künftigen Theaterschule."

While the warm-up is designed to increase the actor's spontaneity to get him ready for a particular performance, the spontaneity training is designed to increase his spontaneity level permanently - it will still fluctuate throughout the day, but on an overall higher level. The trained actor will warm up more and more quickly and will not lose as much of his spontaneity in between.

> For the presentation of spontaneous states and spontaneity ideas, individuals are required who have undergone a specific training. This training will produce people who have learned rapidly to embody their own inspirations and to react rapidly to those of others. [Moreno, 1983 p. 40]

Since as children we are naturally spontaneous, Moreno sees the training of spontaneity foremost as an *unlearning* of the blocks we have obtained through our upbringing.

> The actor must therefore learn to unchain himself from old clichés. By means of exercises in spontaneity he must learn how to make himself free gradually from habit formations. He must store in his body as large a number of motions possible to be called forth easily by means of an emerging idea. [Moreno, 1983 p. 66]

So what does Moreno's training look like? First here is what it is *not*: "To let children loose to do what they wish in play or work may occasionally be a valuable outlet, but it must be recognized that such procedure has no relation whatever to Spontaneity Training" [Moreno, 1946 p. 133]. In improvisation classes we can often observe that students, instructed to do whatever they want for 5 minutes, act in a rather unfocused manner and rarely come up with anything original. But if they are given a specific situation or are told they can only express themselves with the fingers of their right hand, what seems at first merely restrictive allows them quickly to come up with immediate and creative acting.

When we look for Moreno's description of his spontaneity training, we search in vain for a sophisticated and elaborate system of exercises, such as the one's developed for example by Viola Spolin [1963] or Keith Johnstone [1979]. Instead we read:

> A series of situations as they may occur in community life - in home life, domestic life, business, and so on - are constructed. Depending upon the needs of the student, the situations are either chosen by him or suggested to him by the instructor. The life situations constructed are at the beginning as simple as possible, and the student enacts a specific function in them. When these are well performed, the students are gradually placed or place themselves in more and more complex situations. No new step is undertaken until the preceding one is satisfactorily mastered. The students are told to throw themselves into the situations, to live them through, and to enact every detail needed in them as if it were in earnest. The emphasis is placed upon how true to life a certain procedure is. The detailed presentation of things and relations usually omitted in the conventional drama is often essential. No situation is repeated. [Moreno, 1946 p. 134]

In 1932-34 Moreno directed spontaneity training sessions at the New York State Training School for Girls in Hudson, New York, which were recorded in motion pictures [Marineau, 1989 p. 113; Moreno, 1994]. Moreno also described some of these sessions in his book and gave examples of the situations in which the students were placed: "Olga acts in the role of a business executive facing a group of employees. ... Norma acts in the role of the head nurse of a hospital staff in an emergency situation" [Moreno, 1946 p. 136]. Next Moreno describes how this technique can be applied to foreign language learning and training for a vocation. These are now very common applications of role-playing. For example Sternberg & Garcia report applying Moreno's spontaneity training techniques to police training in which "trainers set up 'as if' situations similar to those the trainees are likely to encounter on the job - for example, hostage situations, suicide attempts, crime investigation interviews, motor vehicle violation encounters, and family crisis situations" [Sternberg & Garcia, 1989 p. 111].

Moreno suggests the spontaneity training not only for the actors in the theatre or therapists and patients, but wants to introduce it as a general tool in education, a preparation for a fluid life. "Spontaneity Training is to be the main subject in the school of the future" [Moreno, 1946 p. 130].

2.5 Elimination of the Playwright

This is probably the most controversial point in Moreno's dramatic theory. Many other theatre theorists and practitioners have adopted elements of Moreno's theory. Spontaneity and improvisation are commonly accepted as important and valuable elements of theatre training and performance. But practically no one agrees with Moreno's call for "the elimination of the playwright and of the written play" [Moreno, 1983 p. a].

The improvised theatre without a playwright brings a totally different experience to the audience (and the actors). When we watch a production of Goethe or Shakespeare or any other playwright, we are well aware of the fact that we are watching one of many possible interpretations of a particular play. Often we have already seen or read the play and know more or less what will happen. We expect the experience to be nearly the same, whether we go to the Saturday evening performance or the Sunday matinee.

Not so in Moreno's theatre. We never know what will happen and the performance is different every night. Each show happens only once and will never be repeated - if we miss it, we cannot go some other time. There is no other performance of the same material to compare it to.

We have seen in the last chapter how radical Moreno's critique of the traditional theatre and its playwrights is. "The root of the theater disease is expressed in one phrase: rigid given lines" [Moreno, 1983 p. 108]. There are mainly two reasons[57] why Moreno would like to get rid of the written play: The first is that

---

[57]Derived from the two main notions in Moreno's theory: spontaneity and healing through dramatic enactment, cf. beginning of this chapter.

the memorization of lines kills spontaneity. The second is that the themes and plots of most plays are too far removed from the real concerns of actors and audience and thus do not serve the desired therapeutic/cathartic effect. "It is clear that the tragedy, to be truly cathartic material has to be created by the actor-patients themselves out of their own psychic stuff, and not by a playwright" [Moreno, 1946 p. 179].

Despite the many places where Moreno clearly states that spontaneity and written plays are incompatible, there is at least one occasion at which Moreno admitted such a possibility:

> Another illustration is the drama. The dialogue and the thoughts of the playwright are sacred and inviolate, but the actor trained along spontaneity lines becomes able to turn out a new play at every performance. Feeling and often gestures are here the vehicles for reinvigoration. [Fox, 1987 p. 46]

Jonathan Fox in his article on *Moreno and his Theater* suggests that Moreno may have overemphasized his contempt for the written play. He points out that Moreno mentions Shakespeare positively in a number of places and writes:

> Moreno's concept of the conserve was limited by his need to defy established cultural conditions of his era. The fact is, and Moreno sensed it if he did not state it, even a play drawn from the conserve can achieve cathartic power because the story touches us where we feel the burden of our own experience. At the same time, an improvisational piece, no matter how spontaneous, can fail to reach us precisely because it fails to reach that place where our own stories reside. [Fox, 1978 p. 115]

Of course Moreno never stated that *every* improvisation constitutes good theatre. In his theory spontaneity is a necessary but not a sufficient condition for good theatre. He valued spontaneity for its own sake, not just because it gives rise to more personal stories. So while Fox is correct to point out that even a written play can touch us on a personal level, he does not tell us how spontaneity is possible in a scripted (and repeated) performance and according to Moreno spontaneity is necessary for catharsis to occur (cf. chapter II.5.1.3.1).

Fox is right to say that spontaneity is not opposed to *plot*. In fact his own Playback Theatre company which spontaneously enacts stories told by audience members provides evidence for that. But in order to maintain that Moreno's rejection of the playwright does not follow from the rest of his theory, Fox would have to explain why spontaneity is not opposed to written, *memorized* lines.

While Fox does not answer this question, we might find an answer in Meisner's theory which was explained in chapter I.1. His acting style demands that the actor responds truthfully to the impulses of the moment, while using the playwrights given lines.

2.6 The New Dramatist

Moreno combines the functions of the playwright and the director in the new dramatist:

> The new dramatist does not write; he is the prompter of ideas. He warms up his actors to the ideas which, at the same time, are maturing within him. ... The spontaneity theatre revolutionized the function of the dramatist. He is a part of the immediate theatre. [Moreno, 1983 p. 51]

Moreno describes how the new dramatist facilitates the performance from beginning to end, all in front of the audience and on the spur of the moment. He outlines the theme or the plot, assigns the roles to the chosen actors, allows them to warm up and put on costumes and make-up, regulates and unifies their inter-action, adjusts the timing and speed as necessary, sends in a "rescue player" with new ideas when a crisis is imminent and brings the production to an appropriate ending. At a crucial point in the drama he might confer with the audience about the possible solutions a conflict might have, asking them which of the alternatives they themselves would like to see portrayed. He is always ready to step in, introducing new ideas into the play and smoothing over inconsistencies and flaws [Moreno, 1983 p. 69-72].

This spontaneous directing does not leave room to focus on details. It is unlikely that the dramatist would tell the actor how to hold his hand, etc. as Goethe did (cf. chapter II.5.2.2). Moreno's theatre is one of the least directed. He gives most of the creative power to the actor.[58]

Traditionally one of the functions of the director is to give the actor feedback on how he appears from the audience's point of view. This is also seen as a main reason for why the actor (even in a solo-performance) needs a director, unlike other artists such as painters who can clearly see their product. In Moreno's theatre the director cannot give such feedback, the whole notion of giving corrections and then doing it again doesn't apply. Furthermore the director herself is usually on stage with the actors and has the same view as the actors. This is acceptable to Moreno since it is

---

[58]This is the kind of directing that many actors would prefer. For example, Dustin Hoffman said in an interview: "The director's job is to open the actor up and for god's sake to leave him alone" [Gussow, 1968 p. 145]. Dustin expressed how frustrated he was that few directors fulfill this premise.

Interestingly Zerka Moreno [1994] reports that Dustin worked as a psychiatric attendant at Moreno's hospital in Beacon and was also a regular at Moreno's open sessions in New York (especially remembered for always coming late). He decided that it was time to leave Beacon when the patients began to beat him at Scrabble.

The fact that he worked as a psychiatric aide for some time (and lost at Scrabble) is reported in some of the biographies of Dustin Hoffman, e.g. [Freedland, 1992 p. 38], however without mentioning the name Moreno or Beacon. Freedland goes on to tell that Dustin was shocked by the misery and humiliation he witnessed, but copied some of the insane behavior he observed in an acting class.

In February 1983 the magazine *Sexual Medicine Today*, published an article entitled *Tootsie and Dr. Moreno*. Tootsie [Columbia Pictures, 1982] is one of Dustin Hoffman's major successes, in which he plays an unemployed actor who dresses up as a woman and gets hired to play a female role. The article gets off to a great start: "...*Tootsie* owes a considerable debt to Dr. J. L. Moreno, the Viennese-educated creator of psychodrama and a New York psychiatrist" [Henderson, 1983 p. 22]. The essay contains some illuminating observations on male/female relationships, but unfortunately the association made between *Tootsie* and Moreno has very little substance, mainly pointing out that both use role-playing. There is no mention of a direct connection to Dustin Hoffman or anyone else. It ends with: "When you see *Tootsie*, remember Dr. Moreno, who is now nearly 90 years old" [Henderson, 1983 p. 23] - the article appeared in 1983, nine years after Moreno died at the age of 85.

less important for him to accomplish some aesthetic look for the audience. He cares more about what kind of an experience the actors and the spectators have.

Despite Moreno's rejection of Commedia dell'arte as a forerunner of his theatre (cf. chapter II.4), there are striking similarities between his new dramatist and the *corago* of the Commedia.

> The duties of a *corago* seem to have included reading a new scenario to the assembled players, distributing parts which were less than obviously assignable, pointing out aspects of character and kinds of dialogue appropriate to particular scenes, indicating key emphasis in the plot lines, arranging the location of the action and the use of space, streets and houses, identifying exits and entrances, settling on relevant props and stage accoutrements, and suggesting possible ways of 'blocking' a scene and orchestrating stage 'business' and *lazzi*. His or her function seems to have been decidedly more than just that of an explicator and advisor. The *corago* was perhaps the closest an improvising company came to having a resident troupe dramatist, for it was the business of the *corago* to give structure and coherence to a play that was 'composed' by the players through the accumulation and intermeshing of various units of action, all of which had to be co-ordinated with dramaturgical precision and theatrical flair. [Richards & Richards, 1990 p. 191]

2.7 Encounter

Since Moreno's theatre is created by the players on the spot, it not only requires the actors to be spontaneous, they also have to be in tune with each other. They have to be able to pick up cues without much discussion or explanation.

> There are players who are connected with one another by an invisible correspondence of feelings, who have a sort of heightened sensitivity for their mutual inner processes. One gesture is sufficient and often they do not have to look at one another, they are telepathic for one another. They communicate through a new sense, as if by a "medial" understanding. The more this sense is developed the greater is the talent for spontaneity, all other conditions being equal. [Moreno, 1983 p. 68]

This sense of connection Moreno came to call telic sensitivity or *tele*. "It is the intuitive 'click' between the participants - no words need be spoken between mother and infant, or two lovers. An intimate feeling envelops them; it is an uncanny sensitivity for each other which welds individuals into unity" [Moreno, 1964b p. 470]. It is essential for the relation between therapist and patient as well as between the actors in the theatre. It makes true encounter possible. "Telic reciprocity is the common characteristic of all encounter experience" [Moreno, 1964b p. 470].

Encounter (German: *Begegnung*) is a crucial idea in Moreno's thinking, beginning with his earliest writings in 1914 and up to one of his last writings where he states: "The relationship between

I and Thou in the form of the encounter is the burning issue in our time" [Moreno, 1972 p. 212]. He discusses the concept at many places and defines it as follows:

> *Begegnung* conveys that two or more persons meet not only to face one another, but to live and experience one another - as actors, each in his own right. ... It is a meeting on the most intensive level of communication. The participants are not put there by any external authority; they are there because they want to be - representing the supreme authority of the self-chosen path. The persons are there in space; they may meet for the first time, with all their strengths and weaknesses - human actors seething with spontaneity and zest. It is not *Einfühlung*; it is *Zweifühlung* - togetherness, sharing life. It is an intuitive reversal of roles, a realization of the self through the other; it is identity, the rare, unforgotten experience of total reciprocity. The encounter is extemporaneous, unstructured, unplanned, unrehearsed - it occurs on the spur of the moment. [Moreno & Moreno, 1970 p. 8f]

Such an encounter is exactly what Moreno would like to see in the theatre, as well as in life. In it we experience the essence of what it means to be human; more so than in solitude or, at the other extreme, in the mass. Modern technology threatens to make direct, physical dialogue more and more rare and supplies ever new substitutes. "The psychotherapist is vitally concerned with the effect of a replacement of the direct human contact by robots, e.g., a bottle for the mother's breast, a book for the real encounter, a playback-from-a-tape-recorder for a therapeutic session, a worker of parts for the craftsman of an entire job" [Moreno, 1957

p. 6]. One wonders what Moreno would have to say about the increasingly popular information super-highway. Here human contact takes place in front of computer screens - hardly a suitable setting for encounter.

Yablonsky had the pleasure to experience a real-life *Begegnung* with Moreno and from his account we can see that Moreno lived his ideas in action: "The thing I remember most about Moreno at our early meetings in the fifties were his eyes. I never met anyone who looked at me so directly, honestly, and with such intensity" [Yablonsky, 1981 p. 279].

The concept "encounter" is usually attributed to Martin Buber who published his *Ich und Du* (I and Thou) in 1923. Buber was an associate of Moreno's whom he had met in a Vienna café around 1918 [Moreno, 1989 p. 70]; he was a contributing editor of *Daimon* (cf. introduction.3) for a while. Like Moreno, he drew much of his inspiration from the theatre. "Martin Buber's 'dialogism' originated in his student days at the Viennese theatre; his existential 'I and Thou,' the mutuality we have with others as a model for social interaction, was based on the interaction of two players on a stage" [Courtney, 1990 p. 5].

Moreno claimed later that he influenced Buber: "Buber, however, clearly got the idea of the encounter from me and elaborated on it in his book" [Moreno, 1989 p. 72]. While it is always difficult to prove influences, Moreno was at least chronologically the first. His earliest publication, *Einladung zu einer Begegnung* (Invitation to an Encounter) introduced the concept as early as 1914, albeit in a poetic form.

> Ein Gang zu zwei: Auge vor Auge, Mund vor Mund. Und bist du bei mir, so will ich dir die Augen aus den Hölen reisen und an Stelle der meinen setzen, und du wirst die meinen ausbrechen und an Stelle der deinen setzen, dann will ich dich mit den deinen und du wirst mich mit meinen Augen anschauen.

> A meeting of two: eye to eye, face to face.
> And when you are near I will tear your eyes out
> and place them instead of mine,
> and you will tear my eyes out
> and will place them instead of yours,
> then I will look at you with your eyes
> and you will look at me with mine.
> [Moreno, 1969 p. 12][59]
> (Translation by Moreno.)

The poem is reprinted by Paul E. Johnson in his book *Psychology of Religion* as "evidently the first literary definition of encounter, the concept which has become central in the existentialist movement" [Johnson, 1959 p. 42]. He also points out the close relation between Buber's and Moreno's thought and writes: "How much they may have influenced each other is not altogether clear, but they moved in a common stream of fertile significance, the interpersonal theory of man and God" [Johnson, 1959 p. 45].

---

[59] I could not get hold of the 1914 original. This poem seems to have been dear to Moreno and is reprinted in a number of places, e.g. [Fox, 1987 p. 4; Marineau, 1989 p. 48; Moreno, 1946 frontispiece; Moreno, 1969 p. 8, 12; Moreno & Moreno, 1970 p. 9]. It certainly contains a beautiful description of role-reversal, one of the main psychodrama techniques.

Later in 1918 Moreno published another poem with that same title *Einladung zu einer Begegnung*:

> ... Nothing stands between me and others.
> I am immediate: in the encounter.
> I am not unique: only in the encounter.
> Whether I am a god, a jester or a fool.
> I am sacred, healed, liberated in the encounter,
> Whether I meet the grass or the godhead. ...
> [Moreno, 1918 p. 206][60]

Henri Ellenberger in his history of psychotherapy *The Discovery of the Unconscious* acknowledges Moreno in the section about the year 1918:

> A young physician who actively participated in the literary life, Jakob Moreno Levy, launched a new journal, *Daimon*, whose first issue opened on a lyrical manifesto: "Invitation to an Encounter," a disguised plea for peace that later was considered as a milestone in existentialist literature. [Ellenberger, 1970 p. 828]

About 1923 he writes: "In that same year, Buber published a little book, *I and Thou*, that was to become one of the classics of existentialism" [Ellenberger, 1970 p. 843].

---

[60]".. Es gibt kein Mittel zwischen mir und andern.
Ich bin unmittelbar: in der Begegnung.
Ich bin nicht einzig: bloß in der Begegnung.
Ob ich ein Gott, ein Narr oder ein Dummer.
Ich bin geweiht, geheilt, gelöst in der Begegnung,
Ob ich das Gras oder die Gottheit treffe. ... "

We end this chapter with Moreno's own voice:

Thus I was opposed to the theatre because of my extreme affirmation of life. My concern was that life should be as dynamic, intensive, comprehensive, beautiful, and resourceful as possible. No agency, not even the theatre, should rob it of any finality of grandeur, wisdom, or love. If there is anything worthwhile in the theatre, it is that we should make life more theatrical and intensive. We should make the human encounter the supreme essence of existence, rather than an abbreviation, reduction, or diffusion of life. [Moreno, 1969 p. 26f]

IV. MORENO'S INFLUENCE ON AMERICAN THEATRE

Moreno's ideas are embodied in many aspects of modern American theatre. The emphasis on the actors internal experience originally goes back to Stanislavsky, but Moreno took it one step further by asking the actor to portray his personal issues instead of a character. He was a pioneer in the investigation of the transformative power of theatre on the actor, an idea that motivated many avant-garde companies in the sixties, such as the Living Theatre and the Open Theatre, and also inspired much writing during that period, as exemplified by Grotowski's *Towards a Poor Theatre* [1968] (cf. chapter III.1.1 and chapter V.1), which in turn influenced many American theatre artists, such as Richard Schechner and Joseph Chaikin [Chaikin, 1972 p. ix]. As indicated in chapter III.1.1 the transformative or therapeutic effect of acting can be seen as the main reason why we still need theatre today, in the age of cinema.

Moreno's inquiry into the relation between the actor as a person and the character portrayed on stage (which started with *The Godhead as Comedian* [1919], cf. appendix.1) was taken up again by Schechner's The Performance Group in *Dionysus in 69* [Schechner, 1970]. All the above mentioned avant-garde companies also experimented with audience participation.

Psychodrama's theme of a healing catharsis through re-enactment of traumatic events can be found in the works of a number of American playwrights, such as Philip Barry's *Hotel*

Universe (1930) and *Here Come the Clowns* (1938) [cf. Dietrich, 1974 p. 249-256][61], Arthur Miller's *After the Fall* (1964) [cf. Moreno, 1964a p. 113] and Peter Shaffer's *Equus* (1973). The theme was also explored in *Spellbound* (1945), directed by Alfred Hitchcock, screenplay by Ben Hecht, and starring Ingrid Bergman, Michael Chekhov and Gregory Peck [cf. Moreno, 1946 p. 19f].

It is often impossible to trace a direct line of influence, but the indirect influence of Moreno's work will become clear, especially in the section on the Living Theatre. Theatre artists became exposed to his ideas in a number of ways (and then passed on what they learned to others, etc.):

• Moreno's open sessions in New York during the forties, fifties and sixties frequently had visitors from the theatre world, such as Eric Bentley [Bentley, 1969 p. 322] (cf. introduction.2) and Dustin Hoffman (cf. footnote 58), who were regular guests at Moreno's institute [Moreno, 1994].

• Actors and directors often had a strong interest in psychology and were drawn to his books by titles such as *The Theatre of Spontaneity* and *Psychodrama Volume I-III*. Thus many theatre artists have at least heard of psychodrama as a way

---

[61]In her history of modern drama Margret Dietrich notes Moreno's influence on American (written) drama, exemplified by Barry's plays. "Nicht um dieses im europäischen Sinne Tragische in der existentiellen Ortung des Menschen geht es im amerikanischen Drama, das sich an Moreno anschloß, sondern um die soziometrische Auslotung von Menschen, die in einer Gemeinschaft leben und meist über eine Reihe von Komplexen verfügen. Psychoanalyse und Soziometrie reichen sich in ihnen die Hand. Ihr bedeutendster Vertreter in der Zwischenkriegszeit war mit dargestellten Psychodramen Philip Barry (1896-1949)." [Dietrich, 1974 p. 249]

of using theatre techniques for therapeutic purposes. Moreno's work started a whole new way of thinking about effecting positive change through guided experience, rather than intellectual analysis.

• Many actors considered themselves to be on a path of self-discovery and were naturally drawn to psychotherapy (for example Judith Malina, see Living Theatre section below). They sought out especially experiential techniques, most of which derive from Moreno's work, such as not only psychodrama, but also encounter groups and gestalt therapy. The awareness exercises used in these kinds of therapy are sometimes indistinguishable from those used in the training of actors. Therapy and acting can complement each other since they have many goals in common: self-awareness and self-knowledge, exploration and expression of different parts of oneself, overcoming blocks to full expression and spontaneity, capacity to respond with sensitivity to other people, integration of body, mind, and emotions, and ability to allow as well as to control emotions. "The qualities needed for the best acting are also those qualities required for the fullest living" [Hodgson & Richards, 1966 p. 11].

• Some theatre directors and teachers are also trained in psychodrama.[62] For example, Herb Propper, Professor of Dramatic

---

[62]In fact a large number of psychodramatists have initially worked in theatre as actors and directors and then changed professions to become therapists - sometimes out of economic necessity, since they found it to be the only way to make a living doing work at least related to theatre. Here

Arts at Emerson College, Boston, MA, is a certified psychodramatist and uses psychodrama techniques in teaching acting and in directing plays. He reports the use of psychodrama in rehearsals of Molière's *Tartuffe* [Propper, 1979].[63]

At least since the sixties Moreno's ideas can be found in the works of numerous theatre companies and in acting training programs (most of which include classes in improvisation and sometimes also in psychodrama). More research still needs to be done, especially on Moreno's connection with the Group Theatre and Viola Spolin. Since I had an opportunity to interview Judith Malina in person, most of this chapter will be devoted to the Living Theatre.

---

we are only interested in those who continued working in theatre, and thus brought their knowledge of psychodrama back to that field.

[63]Classical (protagonist-centered) psychodrama can be used in the rehearsal process in one of two ways: Either the character or the actor becomes the protagonist. When the character is the protagonist, she can enact her fantasies or dreams, or simply her view of what happened, with the help of the other actors playing the other characters. If the actor is the protagonist the group can enact scenes from his own life that evoke emotions similar to those required to play the character (this serves a similar function than the use of Stanislavsky's emotional memory technique, cf. [Gordon, 1987 p. 232; Smith, 1990 p. 38; Stanislavski, 1936 p. 163-192]).

1. Group Theatre

The Group Theatre (New York, 1931-1941) is often considered the most important American theatre company, especially recognized for bringing Stanislavsky's system to America. Like Moreno, they were known for emphasizing psychological truthfulness and immediacy. In 1930, Moreno experimented with spontaneity exercises at the Civic Repertory Theatre under Eva Le Gallienne, where he worked with actors such as John Garfield, Burgess Meredith, and Howard da Silva, who later became associated with the Group Theatre [Marineau, 1989 p. 99; Moreno, 1983 p. c].

In 1937, Moreno directed Franchot Tone and his wife Joan Crawford on the psychodrama stage at his sanitarium in Beacon, N.Y. where they explored some of their marital problems. It is there where he met Elia Kazan and Stella and Luther Adler [Moreno, 1989 p. 102; Moreno, 1995].

I hope to include a more complete assessment of Moreno's influence on the Group Theatre in the future. Meanwhile I close with a quotation from the German magazine *Theater Heute*:

> How much Moreno influenced the <Group Theatre> and the Actors Studio of Lee Strasberg has not yet been researched, at least Elia Kazan later used the psychodrama method at the <Actors Studio>. [Pörtner, 1967 p. 12]

2. Viola Spolin's Improvisations

Viola Spolin (Chicago, New York and Los Angeles, 1906-1994) has been one of the strongest forces in introducing improvisation into theatre and education. "Viola Spolin has reigned as the 'High Priestess of Improvisation' for fifty years. She is the author of the seminal, Biblical words on the matter, *Improvisation for the Theater*, and the creator of more than 200 amazing exercises called 'theater games'" [Coleman, 1990 p. 23]. Spolin's classic book was published in 1963 by Northwestern University Press and has now gone through more than a dozen printings. The text has been translated into a variety of languages and is used by theatre artists and educators worldwide. It contains detailed descriptions of more than two hundred theatre games and also some theoretical writing about the experience of creativity and spontaneity.

Spolin received her early training from Neva Boyd at her Recreational Training School in Chicago in the mid-twenties where she learned about the transformative potential of play for both children and adults [Coleman, 1990 p. 29; Spolin, 1963 p. ix; Sweet, 1978 p. xvii]. She developed many of her games while working as a drama supervisor on the Recreational Project with the WPA (Works Progress Administration), with which she became associated in 1938 [Spolin, 1963 p. ix; Sweet, 1978 p. xviii].

Her ideas and techniques spread through her workshops for players of the Compass (founded in 1955 by her son Paul Sills and others) and Second City companies in Chicago which are well documented in [Coleman, 1990] and [McCrohan, 1987], respectively. "In 1955, professional improvisational theatre, as we know it today, was born. The Compass Players nurtured their improvisational talents in workshops conducted by Paul Sills and Viola Spolin" [McCrohan, 1987 p. 25]. "Spolin's collaborations with her son and the improvising actors of the Compass, The Second City, Story Theatre, and Sills and Company are the main conduit between the professional theatre and Spolin's work" [Coleman, 1990 p. 23f]. Since then her work has shaped much of contemporary work in theatre and film. "Yet Spolin's techniques have influenced avant-garde, experimental, and political theatres, comedy writers, stand-up comedians and comedy teams, Broadway, off-Broadway, Hollywood, network television, and advertising" [Coleman, 1990 p. 24].

Spolin is generally seen as the mother of the improvisational theatre movement, but her work was at least chronologically later than Moreno's. *Yale/Theatre* magazine published in 1974 a tree-like diagram showing the history of improvisational theatre in the US with Spolin, 1938, Chicago on top, followed by the Compass and Second City [Coleman, 1990 p. 211]; no mention of Moreno.

Like Moreno[64], Spolin received her early inspiration from the inherent spontaneity in children's play activities. She used similar techniques, including warm-ups and learning through spontaneous experience, but rarely worked directly with the actor's personal issues.

Unfortunately I was not able to reach Viola Spolin before she recently passed away (*New York Times* obituary, November 23, 1994). According to Zerka Moreno she acknowledged Moreno's influence [Moreno, 1994], but further research needs to be done.

---

[64]"It was in my work with the children that my theories of spontaneity and creativity crystallized" [Moreno, 1989 p. 37].

3. Living Theatre

3.1 Short History

The Living Theatre is among the most influential and long-lasting avant-garde companies in America. It was founded in 1948 by Judith Malina (born 1926) and her husband Julian Beck (1925-1985), with Judith directing and acting and Julian designing sets and costumes.

Until 1964 the Living Theatre performed in New York in living rooms, lofts and various theatre spaces producing plays by Paul Goodman, Gertrude Stein, Bertolt Brecht, Garcia Lorca, Jean Cocteau, Strindberg, Pirandello, and most notably *The Connection* by Jack Gelber (1959), about heroin addicts awaiting a promised fix, and *The Brig* by Kenneth Brown (1963), an account of the daily brutal routine in a US Marine Corps brig. They were continually plagued by financial difficulties which culminated in IRS agents arriving to seize the theatre and dispossess the troupe. The final performance of *The Brig* took place in a padlocked theatre where the audience had to climb in through the windows.

After being closed down by the IRS, the Living Theatre went into exile touring all over Europe from 1964 to 68. The company became an experiment in communal living and collective creation using exercises and improvisations. During their stay in Europe they created *Mysteries and Smaller Pieces* (October 1964), Jean Genet's *The Maids* (February 1965), *Frankenstein* (September 1965) and Brecht's *Antigone* (February 1967). This period culminated in what is probably their best-known production *Paradise Now* (July 1968), a "spiritual and political voyage for actors and spectators" [Neff, 1970 p. 206].

The peak of the Living Theatre's popularity was the American tour of 1968-69, when it was at the forefront of the theatrical experimentation of the 1960s. Shortly thereafter in 1970 they issued the "Action Declaration" [Biner, 1972 p. 225ff] and split up into four cells, pursuing a political, environmental, cultural and spiritual orientation, respectively. However, only the one directed by the Becks endured.

The company wanted to break away from performing in established theatre buildings to a privileged audience. In 1971 the Becks led them to Brazil where they performed with and for the poor worker families, again experimenting with collective creation. Their stay ended with the arrest of the company on charges of subversion. While in prison they created and performed three plays with the other inmates [Malina, 1979 p. 2]. Back in the US in 1974 they began working with coal miners, steel mill workers, and their families in Pittsburgh [Shank, 1982 p. 28].

Partly for economic reasons the Living Theatre started again in 1975 to tour in Europe, especially Italy, at first performing only in factories, shipyards, mental hospitals, town squares, and other public places and later again in theatres for a more intellectual audience. While on tour in northern Italy, they worked with patients in 12 psychiatric hospitals. They created street theatre with them and performed it in the towns [Buchholz & Malina, 1980 p. 11]. In 1978 they collectively created *Prometheus*, a play about the ways in which humans have been bound - physically, spiritually and culturally [Shank, 1982 p. 31].

After traveling widely across the continent, in 1984 the company brought some of the productions it had developed to the Joyce Theater in New York. Julian Beck died in 1985 in New York of cancer (*New York Times* obituary, September 17, 1985). From 1989-1993 the Living Theatre found once again a permanent home on East 3rd Street and also continued performing in New York City parks and neighborhoods.

The company is very much alive today in New York under the direction of Judith Malina and Hanon Reznikov. They are currently collectively creating *Not In My Name*(1994), a protest play against the death penalty, which they are performing on the days when someone is being executed in the United States. The Living Theatre today could very well be the oldest American theatre company of any kind.[65]

---

[65]The Living Theatre is one of the most well-documented theatre companies. For a complete history of the Living Theatre up to 1970 see esp. [Biner, 1972] and also [Neff, 1970], and [Rostagno, 1970]. A cultural biography of the Living Theatre up to today has just appeared [Tytell, 1995].

3.2 Similarities with Moreno

The Living Theatre incorporated many of the ideas that Moreno advocated as early as 1924. They were concerned with smashing the barrier between performers and audience and encouraged or even provoked the spectators to participate actively. For the first time this was attempted in Paul Goodman's *Faustina* (May 1952). At the end of the play the actress who played Faustina stepped forward and chastised the audience for not jumping on stage to rescue the victim who had just been murdered. Apparently it was difficult at the time to find an actress willing to step out of the illusion and play herself.

Further examples are: *The Connection* (July 1959) in which the actor-junkies were panhandling during the intermission [Cole & Chinoy, 1970 p. 652]. In *Paradise Now* (July 1968) they went all the way in their attempt to grip the spectator and literally made love to members of the audience. In *Six Public Acts* (May 1975) they performed rituals in which the actors and the audience were mingling their blood:

> The last performer to execute the ritual addressed the public, offered the needle, and asked if anyone else wished to join them. About forty spectators approached, one by one, and performed the ritual, recalling examples of oppression by the state and smearing their blood on the flagpole. [Vicentini, 1975 p. 87]

Prometheus (1978) involved the audience from the very beginning: "When the audience enters, performers are discovered bound with ropes in theatre seats. The performance begins when spectators untie them" [Shank, 1982 p. 31]. In the second act spectators are joined in groups to play Bolsheviks, anarchists, pacifists, terrorists, prisoners, soldiers, etc. Each group rehearses with a company member before the play continues.

While audience participation was clearly one of the Living Theatre's main goals, this doesn't mean that they always succeeded. An audience member who attended performances of *Paradise Now* at The Roundhouse, London in 1969, reported that of the hundreds of spectators only few became actively involved. For most of the audience the performance was just another spectacle to go see - like the opera or ballet they've seen the night before [Sluga, 1994]. This view is also expressed in some of the more devastating reviews of their performances:

> There is precious little significance, wit, fun or substance in the Living Theatre. The actors behave like plastic computerized automatons who only come to life when they are programmed with a revolutionary slogan. Communication, the alleged goal of the troupe, is conspicuously absent. (Jeanne Miller, San Francisco Examiner, Feb. 22, 1969) [Rostagno, 1970 p. 91]

The Living Theatre was striving for authentic, truthful expression of the actor's innermost self. He is called upon to completely reveal himself and to be stripped of inhibitions, sometimes outwardly reflected by complete *nudity*. Echoing

Moreno's Surplus Reality (cf. chapter III.1.6) the actors were asked to "present your real self, as real as you can get, as close as you can get to your authentic self" (Julian Beck in [Cole & Chinoy, 1970 p. 653]). The actor was called upon to immediately follow and embody his impulses. Company member Henry Howard proclaimed: "Acting is not making believe, but living exquisitely in the moment" [Neff, 1970 p. 74].

Moreno also required the actor to be in the moment (cf. chapter III.2.2). This is even true in psychodrama when the protagonist might enact an incident from his childhood. He acts according to what feelings are brought up by enacting the scene *now*. Moreno would never waste much time trying to figure out what exactly happened in the *past*.[66] What matters is what it means *today* (the same holds for gestalt therapy, see below).

Especially in the Living Theatre's later productions, which were not based on written plays, the actors were playing themselves and not pretending to be some fictitious character. They destroyed the barrier between traditional art and real life. The performer would not indicate to be in any other time and place or to be talking to someone other than who he was indeed talking to - there were no imaginary circumstances. This is what we called *Non-Matrixed Performing* in chapter I.1 and what the Living

---

[66]This approach would circumvent the currently trendy debate about the validity of childhood memories of sexual abuse often brought up in therapy. For Moreno these memories are valid and need to be expressed and possibly enacted in some form for healing to occur. Whether they "actually" happened is irrelevant from a psychodramatic point of view. Healing needs to come from exploring the feelings and not from suing one's parents (or one's therapist for that matter).

Theatre called *Non-Fictional Acting*. The actors would wear their ordinary clothes and no costumes.

For example, in the prologue to *Paradise Now* the actors would wander among the startled audience and address spectators with phrases like: "I'm not allowed to travel without a passport. I'm not allowed to take off my clothes" [Neff, 1970 p. 207]. (Upon which the spectators would frequently take off their clothes.) They were not playing a character, but merely speaking for themselves to the people they encountered. The lines they would use were however mostly memorized and rehearsed.

This development towards non-fictional performances was intensified by the increasingly frequent arrival of police forces on the scene, as in the three-day sit-in after a performance of *The Brig* (October 1963) when "the cast refused to leave the theatre as the Internal Revenue agents arrived to seize it and dispossess the troupe" [Cole & Chinoy, 1970 p. 652]. These incidents soon became as much a regular (and planned) part of the performances as nudity and other elements and only increased their popularity.

> When the police surround the theatre they are always more dramatic than the play. Especially the French C.R.S. with their black helmets. Their theatrical presence charges the air - their shining formation, their exquisite costuming as the forces of hell, their weapons, their tensions. Their presence eclipses Paradise. I am impressed by their theatre. We have to make good a lot more interesting. [Beck & Malina, 1970 p. 660]

These performances are frequently analyzed by theorists [e.g. Kirby, 1972 p. 6f], since they stretch the boundaries of what it means to be acting. There are apparently no imaginary circumstances involved, but one may still call it acting. There is an awareness of an audience accompanied by a heightened emotional expressiveness. The performances were also rehearsed and repeated many times, of course differing depending on the audience.

The Living Theatre had a different definition of acting than the one we discussed in chapter I.1: "Acting is earnest communication of everything you are with the people who have earnestly assembled to be guided through the mysteries" [Beck & Malina, 1970 p. 658]. The distinguishing characteristic of acting for them is not the imaginary circumstances, but a heightened level of awareness in which the actor tries to exert himself to give his best truth[67].

Echoing Moreno's ideas of *tele* and *encounter* (cf. chapter III.2.7) as a meeting of two or more people not only to face each other, but to live and experience one another in intense personal communication in the here and now, the Living Theatre practiced "an increasing, an uncanny, an extraordinary sensitivity to one another. ... We sense each others' details like lovers" [Beck & Malina, 1970 p. 655] .

The goals of the Living Theatre were therapeutic (for actors *and* audience) in much the same sense as in Moreno's theatre. It is important here to point out again (as in. chapter III.1.1) that,

---

[67]Like Moreno they mean inner, psychological, subjective truth (cf. chapter III.1.7).

when Moreno speaks of therapy, he not only means psychiatric care of illness, but a transformation of the whole being towards greater aliveness, authenticity, expressiveness, spontaneity and creativity; facilitating personal growth and full development of human potential. As Moreno conceived it, his methods apply not only to mental patients, but to *all* human beings. "A truly therapeutic procedure cannot have less an objective than the whole of mankind" [Moreno, 1953 p. 3].

The Living Theatre also wanted to "change the world" [Beck & Malina, 1970 p. 654] and exhibited similar values. "When the spectator begins to feel the pain, then the actor begins to accomplish a vivid purpose: to heighten awareness. ... If we could feel the pain, we could not tolerate it and would find the means to eliminate it" [Beck & Malina, 1970 p. 654f].

When interviewed by the author, Judith Malina stated that "what we do is not therapy" [Malina, 1994]. This surprising difference seems to be mostly semantic, however, since she used the word "therapy" in its narrow sense (cure of psychological ailments) and she agreed that the Living Theatre has transformation and liberation (of individuals and of society) as its goal. There is still some difference though, since Moreno included cure of psychological ailments in his approach, even though the scope of his work is much wider.

Many commentators have also compared some of the Living Theatre's performances, esp. *Paradise Now*, to group therapy, e.g.

In parts of some performances the company functioned more as group therapists or recreation leaders than as traditional actors. All of these techniques and others served to focus on the live performer in the here and now rather than absorbing the spectator's psyche into a fictional illusion of character, time and place. In short, the audience was made to focus on the real world. [Shank, 1982 p. 35]

The trip is the experience, an exorcism of personal demons which at the same time will be therapeutically beneficial. As the psychotic experience goes beyond the rationale of common sense, so the "technique" of the Living Theatre may more rightfully belong to the realm of psychiatry than to that of theatrical preparation. [Neff, 1970 p. 74]

While video recordings of *Paradise Now* bring up images of group therapy, the use of non-verbal sounds and vocalized breathing reminds us not so much of psychodrama, but of other more recent forms of therapy, such as rebirthing, primal therapy[68] or encounter groups[69].

---

[68]Primal therapy has many similarities with psychodrama such as guiding the patients to talk *to* their parents rather than *about* them. Both encourage the expression of deep and authentic feeling. Arthur Janov, the founder of primal therapy, nevertheless displays a negative (and somewhat distorted) view of psychodrama:
"The patient may take the role of his mother, father, brother, or teacher. But of course, he is not any of those people, so he must put on an act and try to feel like someone else when often he doesn't even feel like himself yet.
Psychodrama does have some limited use, as, for example, in loosening up a group in conventional therapy, but essentially, it seems to offer one more unreal role for a person to portray when he has been acting the role of himself for many years.
... Primal patients are not acting. They *are* the little children totally out of control" [Janov, 1970 p. 229f].
Here again we encounter the use of the term "acting" as being phony, unreal (cf. chapter I.1). Moreno also often uses this meaning as when he states: "The aim of these sundry techniques is not to turn the patients into actors, but rather to stir them up to be on the stage what they *are*, more deeply and explicitly than they appear to be in life reality" [Moreno, 1946 p. c].

Paradise Now arranged the stage in a way that resembles Moreno's design of the *open stage* (cf. chapter III.1.5). The stage was usually open to all sides and the actors would wander among the audience, confronting them directly and encouraging the spectators to join in the action at various locations throughout the auditorium.

Like Moreno (cf. chapter III.1.3), the Living Theatre was using theatre to build a sense of community. "The creative as communal art surpasses the individual act because we are men, and our existence and well-being depend on one another" [Beck & Malina, 1970 p. 659]. They also shared his believe in the importance of direct experience and action over intellectual analysis, as well as his confidence in the human creative potential. "We are all supremely gifted people, every human being" (Judith Malina in [Biner, 1972 p. 221]).

Their dislike of traditional theatre is as radical as Moreno's:

> The Theatre of Fictional Character thus becomes reactionary
> by confining man to the limits of character. ... The Rational
> Theatre of intellectual discussion in which we all remain cool,

---

Janov's critique of psychodrama thus echoes Moreno's critique of traditional theater as being removed from real feeling. Clearly Moreno's goal in psychodrama is to express authentic feelings - the degree to which this is accomplished may of course vary.

[69]William Schutz, who was at the forefront of the encounter movement, writes about Moreno's influence: "The techniques developed by Moreno and his colleagues are similar to many used in encounter groups; in fact, some encounter techniques, including role reversal, doubling, and setting up dramatic situations, come directly from psychodrama. Moreno's emphasis on action and non-verbal methods makes his contribution particularly significant. The use of action within the group transports any content into the here-and-now, thereby making it appropriate material for encounter group work." [Schutz, 1973 p. 9]. See also [Back, 1972; Moreno & Moreno, 1970; Schutz, 1989].

unparticipating, cut off from real feeling and real experience, reinforces our own lifelessness, our feelinglessness, our state of cutoff. [Beck & Malina, 1970 p. 656]

3.3 Ways in which Moreno went further.

Moreno himself had the following to say about the Living Theatre:

> Modern revolutionary theatre, in Europe as well as in America, has actually developed in the direction of the spontaneity theatre but it is still not capable of bridging over the old, dogmatic barrier. "The Living Theatre" and "The Open Theatre" in America are still tied to the *drama conserve*. True, they have no playwright in the old sense, but the ensemble of players improvises step-by-step the parts of a play which they then melt together into an organized play. The aim of the ensemble is still to create a "theatre piece" which they then repeat over and over with minor variations. The old form of the theatre is therefore still there, with a few interesting deviations which they have taken over from the spontaneity theatre, the elimination of the playwright, participation of the audience, therapeutic motivations, greater freedom of the actors, the freedom of his body, up to the total freeing from costumes, complete nudity, all functions of life being performed in front of the public without any restraints. But everything that is performed is carefully "rehearsed," tried out, from the dialogue to sexual intercourse. ....

> In contrast, modern psychodrama is always new and fresh, unrepeated in every session. [Moreno, 1983 p. d,e]

Here again we see how essential for Moreno his demand for unrehearsed performances is. He was more radical than the Living Theatre in improvising every part of the performance, and he denies that the Living Theatre achieved true spontaneity, since they still used memorized lines.

The Living Theatre did however make use of improvisation and Julian Beck deemed it *divine*: "Perhaps all that writing must be left behind, the printed word, the library forgotten. Artaud. Then a theatre in which language pours from the throats of the actors: the high art of improvisation, when the actor is like a great hero, the partner of God" [Beck, 1964 p. 16].

Throughout its history the Living Theatre moved along the improvisation scale which was introduced in chapter I.2. They started off at the Cherry Lane (August 1951 - August 1952) where the performances were almost <u>completely rehearsed</u>: "At the Cherry Lane we prepared plays by making rather careful directing books. That is, we worked on the staging of the play in advance, considering the movements actors would make, the interpretation of lines" [Beck, 1964 p. 17].

Later plays would be <u>rehearsed using improvisation</u>:

> In *The Connection* Judith had arranged an atmosphere in which the actors could improvise lines and actions, in the context of the play, never straying too far. This often led to terrible choices, largely because we are not well trained in this area, but often terrific moments emerged. Best of all, an

atmosphere of freedom in the performance was established and encouraged, and this seemed to promote a truthfulness, startling in performance, which we had not so thoroughly produced before. With the readdition to the repertory of *Tonight We Improvise*, improvisation, of which chance is a major constituent, began to be identified with the work of The Living Theatre. [Beck, 1964 p. 27f]

This was however partly based on deception, as in productions like *Many Loves* (January 1959), *The Connection* (July 1959), and especially *Tonight We Improvise* (February 1955), where the actors would pretend to be rehearsing/improvising, when in fact everything was written in the script. The company soon started to feel uncomfortable with this "fraud".[70]

Chance was utilized in Jackson MacLow's *The Marrying Maiden* (June 1960) which was partly based on the *I Ching*. It was inspired by John Cage and presented under the title "The Theatre of Chance". At certain points the next action was determined by the throw of a dice or the actors would draw a card from an "action pack" and follow its direction.

Now we were really improvising, no faking at all. Things were beginning to happen on our stage which had never happened before. Each performance was different from the next, and the production was a notorious failure. We insisted on keeping the play in repertory for almost a year, usually playing it only once a week, usually to no more than ten or twenty persons. Not arrogance, but a stubborn belief that we needed

---

[70]"But we were finally disturbed ourselves by the device because it was, after all, basically dishonest, and we were publicly crying out for honesty in the theatre. The plays were not being rehearsed that night yet we were pretending they were" [Beck, 1964 p. 23].

the play, we the company, that it had something to teach us if only we could stick with it. [Beck, 1964 p. 29]

From the information we have it is difficult to determine to what degree this was a case of true improvisation. Especially towards the end of the run it is quite possible that most of the chance elements resulted in actions that have already been rehearsed - what we have called <u>rehearsed variation</u> (in chapter I.2). Interesting in the above quotation is also that the results of the Living Theatre's experiments with improvisation parallel Moreno's experience at his Theatre of Spontaneity - both were done more for the effect on the actors and didn't reach great popularity with the audience.

Moreno clearly distinguishes between spontaneity and chance. The throwing of a dice by itself does not guarantee spontaneity, even if the result is different each night. Spontaneity arises when the actors respond in a way that is novel, adequate and immediate (cf. chapter I.3).

The amount of improvisation used by the Living Theatre continued to vary from show to show. A few more examples:

• Brecht's *In the Jungle of Cities* (December 1960) started off with no improvisation. "The whole production was scientifically charted. Every moment, every sound cue, and there were more than 150 of them in Teiji Itos score, every position of every prop and bit of intricate scenery was plotted and continually placed with scrupulous precision" [Beck, 1964 p. 29]. This was later in the rehearsal process abandoned, and Judith Malina created "a remarkable rehearsal atmosphere in which the company became more and more free to bring in its own ideas" [Beck, 1964 p. 30].

- Gelber's *The Apple* (December 1961) had "nothing left to chance" [Beck, 1964 p. 31].

- Brown's *The Brig* (May 1963): "In all the improvisations, the indeterminate scenes that could result from a missing button on a costume, an accidental slip of a foot, the search for a Theatre of Chance" [Beck, 1964 p. 33]. This refers to the fact that in this production the guards had to respond to any *actual* imperfection in the prisoners outfit by punishing them. These and other strict rules were adhered to throughout the rehearsal process. For example, if the actor didn't pass the clothing inspection, he had to perform 15 minutes of extra work time. This was meant to help the actors to get into the emotional states of the prisoners they were portraying. With this device they didn't need to use imaginary circumstances - they were *actually* being punished.

- In *Frankenstein* (September 1965) the actors playing prisoners "improvise the agonies of their cruel solitary confinement" [Schevill, 1973 p. 308].

- *Antigone* (February 1967): "We learned all the lines and then got into a free space and then did whatever we wanted without any discussion. We went through it three times. We totally improvised the play." (Judith Malina in [Schechner, 1969 p. 39]). This is of course impossible according to Moreno; one cannot "improvise a play" with memorized lines.

- *Paradise Now* (August 1968): "Every night we go as far out in the improvisation as we can, we go as far toward the spectator as we know how" (Judith Malina in [Schechner, 1969 p. 24]).

"One-third of the play, according to the chart, is unnoted, and unknown. Unrehearsed" (Julian Beck in [Schechner, 1969 p. 31]).

"One-third of *Paradise Now* - the 'Action' sections - was not planned but left to the spectators and performers to develop through their own spontaneous actions" [Shank, 1982 p. 35].

- *Six Public Acts* (1975) consisted of rituals performed with various degrees of structure/improvisation. While the parts involving interaction with the audience necessarily had to contain improvisation, other sections did as well: "Throughout the march, the actors played with the sticks, kissed them, and whispered, 'I love this thing.' It apparently was a free improvisation on the worship of the stick" [Vicentini, 1975 p. 90].

- *Anarchia* (January 1994): "Reznikov wisely gives his charismatic cast plenty of room to improvise around the structured dialogue, a practice which has always been the company's forte" [Callaghan, 1994].

In his *The Life of the Theatre* [1972] Julian Beck went even further in his call for improvisation in a section entitled "Improvisation: Free Theatre". He states that real (as opposed to fake as in *Tonight We Improvise*) improvisation started with *The Brig* and continues: "It would never again be possible for us not to improvise. We would have to construct plays with forms loose enough so that we could continue to find out how to create life rather than merely repeat it" [Beck, 1972 p. 80]. Towards the end of the section he writes: "Free Theatre: ultimately free theatre is improvisation unchained" [Beck, 1972 p. 83]. The Living Theatre started performances of what they called *Free Theatre* in 1966 in Milan. Judith Malina wrote the following lines which were distributed among the spectators:

FREE THEATRE

This is Free Theatre. Free Theatre is invented by the actors as they play it. Free Theatre has never been rehearsed. We have tried Free Theatre. Sometimes it fails. Nothing is ever the same.

The Living Theatre

[Beck, 1972 p. 82].

This sounds very much in agreement with Moreno's call for spontaneity. Surprisingly, when interviewed Judith Malina denied that Free Theatre is similar to improvisation: "We didn't improvise in that... we didn't do anything. We let the audience do what they want to do that wonderful night. Free Theatre means everybody does whatever they want, and we let the audience make the decisions" [Malina, 1994]. I suspect that here too the disagreement is semantic. She seems to equate improvisation with games like playing mother and son:

> We don't really use improvisation very much, in spite of the myth. I will occasionally use improvisation in a rehearsal technique, but hardly ever; we don't do that. I don't say, "play now that you are my father, and I'm your daughter," this is for me unthinkabie. I can't imagine doing such a thing... I would never do that. This is fine for someone to do! But it's not at *all* the approach of the Living Theatre. The approach of the Living Theatre is: "I'm Judith Malina, and you are Eberhard, and I want to know your best truth and your strongest knowledge and I will give you mine." [Malina, 1994]

Moreno also wants the actor to express his truth - even if he is playing someone's father.

According to Malina the Living Theatre uses improvisation mainly when they talk with the audience (or when they get arrested). She emphasized that these encounters do not contain any fictional elements. "I'm not pretending anything. I'm not drawing anything from any other reality but the reality we're in. ... I'm trying to destroy the boundary between life and theatre" [Malina, 1994].

Moreno's work has also been seen as exploring the boundaries between life and theatre, most notably by Eric Bentley (cf. introduction.2): "I have set down this description of what I understand psychodrama to be because it offers the most vivid evidence imaginable of the intimate link between theatre and life" [Bentley, 1964 p. 187].

To summarize, we may say that both the Living Theatre and Moreno wanted to enable the actor to express his inner truth. To accomplish that same goal, they used somewhat different means.

While Moreno would allow for fictional elements (or imaginary circumstances), but not for rehearsed lines, the Living Theatre would allow rehearsed lines, but (in their later productions, esp. *Paradise Now*) not fictional elements.

They also both displayed some contempt for theatre that didn't play by their "rules" and claimed that authenticity and spontaneity is next to impossible when using rehearsed lines or fictional elements, respectively.

A minor point worth mentioning is Moreno's use of humor. He was well aware of the healing power of laughter and spoke of "a catharsis coming from humor and laughter" [Fox, 1987 p. 211]. Many of his colleagues and patients remember his sense of humor, e.g. Dr. Marvin Wellman in a letter dated October 15, 1963: "I think the greatest contribution which Dr. Moreno has made to medicine is the possibility of treatment with joy" (quoted in [Moreno, 1969 p. 258]). Moreno's wife Zerka writes:

> Thousands of the participants in sessions of the Moreno Institute will remember one of the oldest, most persistent sayings of Moreno: "I would like my tombstone to carry an epitaph which reads 'Here lies the man who brought joy and laughter into psychiatry'." He may well have his wish fulfilled. [Moreno, 1969 p. 258]

Moreno's urn with his ashes was transferred to Vienna by the Austrian Society for Literature and indeed the epitaph on his big, black, marble memorial stone reads exactly as he wanted it [Moreno, 1994].

The Living Theatre on the other hand was not exactly known for its sense of humor and was sometimes criticized for its lack and the resulting boredom: "The company, particularly vulnerable to ridicule because of its lack of humor, allowed no alien laughter ever to penetrate its relentless solemnity, self-righteousness, and self-importance" [Brustein, 1973 p. 319]. One actress reports that the company had a discussion about the meaning of laughter in 1977, while they were working on *Prometheus*. Some members wanted to see more laughter during the performance [Buchholz & Malina, 1980 p. 20].

When I interviewed Judith Malina and Hanon Reznikov and attended their lecture-demonstration on May 8, 1994 in San Francisco, they displayed a lot of humor as well as passion. Apparently the use of humor by the Living Theatre is a more recent development: "Such tongue-in-cheek humor has been a notable characteristic of recent Living Theatre productions, in contrast to the heavy-handed didacticism of their more well-known work in the 1960s" [Callaghan, 1994].

3.4 Ways in which Living Theatre went further

While Moreno went further in his demand for improvisation and spontaneity, the Living Theatre went further in its call for an anarchist and sexual revolution.

3.4.1 Anarchist Revolution

The Living Theatre had a very clear political agenda.

> So The Ultimate Theatre, which transforms cruelty, will participate in hastening the Sexual Revolution and the revolution that brings about the end of the use of money and the end of the authority of the state and the police and racism and all the antiman antifreedom things.
> That is, it will be the theatre that aids in precipitating The Beautiful Nonviolent Anarchist Revolution. [Beck & Malina, 1970 p. 662f]

In contrast Moreno very rarely made explicit political demands such as the abolishment of the police or the military.[71] In fact his trust in his techniques was so strong, that he believed that their effect would always be positive. He equally supported their use in the military, prisons, schools, hospitals and other places.

---

[71]For these reasons Moreno was apparently not very popular among Soviet communists: "The measures suggested by Moreno to 'rally' American society do not affect the main pillars of capitalism: private ownership, the rule of monopolies, and the exploitation of the working people" [Saifulin & Dixon, 1984 p. 278].

Both the Living Theatre and Moreno had a strong agenda of wanting to effect change in the individual as well as in society. And to some extent this can not be separated, since of course society is made up of individuals and individuals are bound by society. So strictly speaking one cannot be changed without the other.

Nevertheless there is a difference in the emphasis: Moreno, with his talk of therapy, stresses the individual. The Living Theatre, with its talk of revolution, stresses the change of society.

> But I think that the *cure* for our psychological ailments is very much connected with the cure for living in a socialistic world. I want to cure the social structure. I'm very happy that people are curing their own psychological ailments. And I think certainly that's very important, and I think we have to be healthy human beings in order to be able to create the world we want to live in. But I think under the current social sickness, this is very unlikely that anybody is going to cure their personal ailment without curing it through attention to what's happening in the world and to other people. [Malina, 1994]

Malina beautifully expresses the two ways of change: "I'm calling for a revolution, and I think that will help people express themselves more, and I think that if people express themselves more, it will help the revolution" [Malina, 1994].

The different emphasis on individual versus society is also reflected in their approach to theatre. The Living Theatre's focus is on the audience:

> We're very goal oriented; we're totally audience oriented. We are not doing this for our own therapy or illumination, though sometimes we get both from it. We are doing it in order to bring a vision to the spectator that will help to get people off the streets,....that will make us behave on a social level in a more humane way. [Malina, 1994]

Moreno on the other hand focuses more on the actor, especially in psychodrama, which is mainly enacted for the sake of the protagonist.

3.4.2 Sexual Revolution

For the Living Theatre the sexual revolution is an essential part of the process of liberation. The works of Wilhelm Reich were avidly read by the company [Biner, 1972 p. 196]. "Out of our sexual hangups comes much of the anger that expresses itself in violence" [Beck & Malina, 1970 p. 662].

The call for sexual freedom was brought to its logical conclusion in the "Rite of Universal Intercourse" (Rung IV of *Paradise Now*). "Here naked spectators and actors embraced indiscriminately, even copulating" [Innes, 1993 p. 187].

> *Paradise Now* was an experiment in how far we could go with the audience. How close to paradise we could get. Many of the members of the Living Theatre made love to audience members. A lot of love-making in the theatre. Real love-making. [Malina, 1994]

Moreno rarely talks about sexuality explicitly, even his autobiography contains few references. This is of course in great contrast to many other psychologists (in particular to Fritz Perls, founder of gestalt therapy, as we shall see below) and some clever psychoanalyst may very well suggest that his is a typical case of sublimation. On the other hand it is clear that sexuality is included in Moreno's call for greater freedom of expression and creativity.

3.4.3 Poetic Language

Especially in their early work the Living Theatre experimented many times with plays using poetic language: "In Brown and Gelber then is an intimation of poetry more elevated and profound, frail though it is, a blueprint on tissue paper, but nearer to truth, which poetry always is, than all the oratory everywhere, off stage and on, of our time" [Beck, 1964 p. 7].

There is no parallel in Moreno's work since he encourages the actor to use his own words as they emerge spontaneously (of course this doesn't exclude poetry either).

Later the Living Theatre went away from using poetic language and they expressed some dissatisfaction with the use of poetry: "I am quick to state that I have never attended verse theatre anywhere done to my satisfaction" [Beck, 1964 p. 11].

3.5 Direct Influence

Julian Beck is reported as having mentioned Moreno explicitly as one of the influences (among the original Stanislavsky and others) on the Living Theatre's early work in New York. This happened at a long meeting after the 4th Yale performance of *Paradise Now* at Smith College, North Hampton, Massachusetts in 1968 [Bierman, 1994].

Nevertheless Moreno's influence on the Living Theatre seems to be mostly indirect. When I interviewed Judith Malina, she stated that she never met Moreno, never went to his open sessions in New York, didn't know of his early work in theatre and knew him only as the founder of psychodrama [Malina, 1994]. Co-director Hanon Reznikov, a 25-year veteran of the company, didn't know Moreno, although he knew of psychodrama.

The only explicit mention of psychodrama in the Living Theatre's extensive writings I found is the following: "Paul uses the psychodrama, that horrid concoction of artless acting, exposure, and a patina of Stanislavsky. I hate it. I do it badly. We 'enact' pickups at bars. The whole thing offends me" [Malina, 1984 p. 269]. (Paul refers to Paul Goodman, more on him below.) Enacting pickups at bars is not what is typically known as psychodrama, although it is certainly possible that it would come up in a session where a protagonist has some related issues.

When I talked to Judith Malina she reiterated her view that she has not had much exposure to psychodrama, but as she sees it, it is for healing sick people, which is not what the Living Theatre is about. The goal of the Living Theatre is to do theatre to promote the nonviolent anarchist revolution. The focus is on social illness and the individual becomes transformed through the political work.

3.6 Moreno's Influence on Gestalt Therapy

Moreno had an indirect influence upon the Living Theatre through his influence on gestalt therapy which in turn influenced the Living Theatre. The gestalt approach was developed in the 1940s by Fritz and Laura Perls, Paul Goodman and others in New York. It became especially popular in the 1960s when Perls became a resident at the Esalen Institute in Big Sur, CA, where he conducted extensive workshops, many of which have been recorded and some of which were transcribed in [Perls, 1969a].

3.6.1 Similarities between Psychodrama and Gestalt

The similarities between psychodrama and gestalt are quite striking, both in theory and technique. They both share a strong emphasis on action rather than analysis: "We see that the dream or fantasy is a story, a drama, and we act it out again in therapy to make us more aware of what we are, of what is available" [Perls & Clements, 1968 p. 17].

Like Moreno, Perls had an early background in theatre - he studied play directing under Max Reinhardt, as reported by Perls himself [Perls, 1969b p. 43] and in his biography:

> By his late adolescence, he discovered the fabled director and teacher Max Reinhardt. "The first creative genius I ever met," Reinhardt was to make a lasting impression upon his young student through his mastery of nuance, his use of dramatic silences, and for creating moving images. ... Fritz, admiring the director's passion, his dedication and commitment to his vision, and his artistry, spent many hours a week at the *Deutsche Theater* studying and working for him. [Shepard, 1975 p. 22]

Perls also agreed with Moreno in his disdain for traditional theatre: "I never liked New York ... with its usually atrocious theater performances" [Perls, 1969b p. 185f]. Both forms of therapy were frequently compared to theatre, the following description of gestalt for example could also be applied to psychodrama:

Fritz managed to find that halfway point between psychotherapy and theatre. He had often talked about wanting to write, direct, and produce a play. ... so did Fritz create his own theatre. Fritz's brand of Gestalt Therapy could be seen as a drama where he, as director, would have the individual he worked with play all sorts of roles and parts, often building up to emotion-packed climaxes. It was, if nothing else, good theatre. And, more often than not, good therapy, too. [Shepard, 1975 p. 203f].

Moreno as well as Perls and his followers valued authenticity and spontaneity and promoted direct experience in the here and now. Both join in their disdain for the "robot". "Without emotions we are dead, bored, uninvolved machines" [Perls, 1969b p. 50].

Like most theatre people, they were passionate about the beauty of human emotions. This is in contrast to many psychotherapists who divide emotions into positive and negative ones. Even those who encourage the patient to get into and act out his "negative emotions" often recommend this in order for the patient to get rid of the "nuisance" of having these emotions.[72]

[72]For example some practitioners of *rebirthing* display such a philosophy: "There is a miracle available, and that is the total healing of all your negative conditions. There is even complete peace of mind available, and the end to all your problems. ...Rebirthing is a safe and gentle breathing process that releases accumulated negativity back to and including birth. ...Once you begin to breathe more, it is imperative that you learn to change all your negative thoughts into affirmations quickly. ... And the more I got myself rebirthed, the more money I made" [Ray, 1986 p. ix, 6, 18].

3.6.2 Differences between Psychodrama and Gestalt

Perls made the goal of the integration of personality through owning the different parts of the self (especially the "shadow") more explicit. For him awareness itself can be the cure.

A striking difference between Perls' and Moreno's writings is Perls' great emphasis on sexuality. Not only in his theoretical writings, but especially in his autobiographical work (which displayed considerable pride in his "conquests").

> "I used to enjoy screwing for hours, but now, at my age, I enjoy mostly being turned on without having to deliver the goods. I like my reputation as being both a dirty old man and a guru. Unfortunately the first is on the wane and the second ascending.
> Once we had a party in the "big house" at Esalen. A beautiful girl was lying seductively on a couch. I sat next to her and said something like this: "Beware of me, I am a dirty old man." "And I," she replied, "am a dirty young girl." We had a short and delightful affair after that. [Perls, 1969b p. 95f]

Books *about* Pearls are also full of references to his free sexuality. His biography contains many such remarks and Judith Malina apparently had a typical experience with Perls:

> "He put me down pretty badly a couple of times," remembers Judith Malina "I wasn't really afraid of him because he was a little bit on the make for me, so that I could always excuse his remarks as based on unfulfilled desire." [Shepard, 1975 p. 59]

Along the same lines Malina writes in her diaries:

Christmas Eve, 1951
Fritz Perls is an imposing German who conducts himself like a
"Great Man." He approached me, however, like a seducer.
Rumor has it that this is his custom. He admired my eyes and
hands, but called my mouth "all wrong." [Malina, 1984 p. 199]

Jack Gaines [1979] wrote a book entitled *Fritz Perls: Here and Now* which is a collection of interviews with numerous people who have known Perls. It is just *full* of references to Perls' open sexuality, especially by many of the women he pursued. They describe their encounters with great detail (and often pride), and they seem quite impressed by the experience - whether they went along with it or not. One typical example quotes Margaret Callahan:

He was caved in everywhere; he looked like a corpse. But he
had this *enormous* erection! It was not to be believed! I
thought, "This is absolutely unreal. How could this old man
possibly have an erection?" I didn't know whether to be
flattered or terrified by his interest in me.
When he walked me home that night from the baths he asked
me to share his bed. I think I'm the only woman in the world
who hasn't been in bed with Fritz Perls. [Gaines, 1979 p. 212]

In contrast, we know very little about Moreno's sex-life, though we know a lot about his marriages [see Marineau, 1989; Moreno, 1989].

Clearly the most apparent difference between psychodrama and gestalt therapy is that psychodrama is usually conducted in a group setting with active participation of many members. Gestalt is a form of individual therapy and even if it is used in a group, this usually means that the group members take turns doing individual therapy with the leader, while the other members are witnesses. In classical gestalt sessions *all* roles are played by the patient.

> Still I admit now 70-80 people. ... I do some mass experiments, but mostly restrict myself to working with a single person in front of the audience. [Perls, 1969b p. 217]

In this way gestalt therapy can be seen as a special case of psychodrama using the *empty chair* technique. In applying this technique, one literally uses one or more empty chairs instead of auxiliary egos to play parts in the protagonist's drama. He is for instance instructed to imagine his sister sitting in the empty chair and to talk to her. Later he might sit in the chair and take on the sister's role himself, perhaps talking to the chair in which he first sat (now symbolizing his self).

This is largely what happens in gestalt. "His style of working at that time utilized two empty chairs. One was the *hot seat*, which you approached and sat in when you wished to work with him. The other chair was there to help you switch roles; the person on the hot seat moved over to it whenever he or she enacted different parts" [Shepard, 1975 p. 204]. Thus in gestalt sessions the patient is always busy acting out and never gets to observe himself (as played by others) or anyone else.

The empty chair technique is put to use in adapting psychodrama to individual therapy. But even in this case there is also the possibility of the therapist taking on a role or role-reversing with the patient, both unthinkable in gestalt.

3.6.3 Moreno's Influence on Perls and Gestalt

Despite the obvious similarities between gestalt and psychodrama, just how much Perls was influenced by Moreno is still controversial. Perls definitely knew of Moreno's work and frequently visited his open sessions in the 1940s in New York where "he wrote his name five times as big as anyone else in the book" [Moreno, 1994].

3.6.3.1 Moreno's Followers on his Influence

Most of Moreno's followers think that he influenced Perls a great deal.

> Moreno had many visitors to his Institutes. Fritz Perls was one of them, and he was quite reluctant to give any credit to Moreno, even though it is evident that his own basic technique - the monodrama - bears many similarities to psychodrama. Moreno never missed an opportunity to let people know about Perls' visit to his Institute to New York in the late 1940s, and confronted the founder of the Gestalt therapy movement directly in front of an audience of more than 1,000 people during a meeting of the American Psychological Association in 1964 in San Francisco. [Marineau, 1989 p. 184]

In contrast to Marineau, Yablonsky writes: "Fritz Perls acknowledged that Gestalt therapy was in large measure derived from psychodrama" [Yablonsky, 1981 p. 137]. When I interviewed Yablonsky, he said that his statement was based on "a meeting about 20 years ago which both Moreno and Perls attended and at which Perls made a statement along those lines" [Yablonsky, 1994]. He thinks it was a meeting of the American Society of Group Psychotherapy and Psychodrama in San Francisco. This makes it quite likely that he was talking about the same meeting as Marineau above and thus the contrasting statements are even more surprising.

When I read Marineau's remark to Yablonsky, he replied: "Yes, it is also true that Perls did it reluctantly" [Yablonsky, 1994]. Yablonsky said that gestalt is encompassed within the framework of psychodrama and that psychodrama is a larger system. He agreed that every gestalt session can be looked at as a psychodrama, but not vice versa.

Adam Blatner sees Moreno's influence as follows:

> Gestalt therapy has already integrated a number of essential principals of psychodrama. Fritz Perls emigrated from South Africa around 1947 and attended a number of Moreno's sessions, integrating Moreno's role-taking techniques, especially the technique of the empty chair, with his own existential and psychodynamic ideas. Exchanges of techniques and principles continue, and the methods are quite compatible. Psychodrama, however, has a greater capacity to be used with approaches. [Blatner, 1988b p. 120]

Indeed many therapists today are trained in both systems and develop their own combination.

Moreno's son Jonathan writes:

> Though he and Fritz Perls, who had been a devotee of psychodrama sessions in New York, had open quarrels, Perls, without referring to Moreno explicitly, acknowledged his debt to "psycho-drama" in his memoirs, *In and Out of the Garbage Pail.* [Moreno, 1989 p. 9]

"Acknowledged his debt" is a slight exaggeration, the only reference to psychodrama in Perls' memoir reads:

> Suicide, self-torture, self-doubt are good examples. The cure: Do unto others what you are doing to yourself.
> "This sounds horrible."
> It is not as horrible as it sounds. Actually it is sufficient, even required, that you do those bad things to the other in fantasy and psycho-drama. [Perls, 1969b p. 205]

At least this shows that Perls was familiar with some of the uses of psychodrama and used it himself.

Grete Leutz, a long-time student and associate of Moreno's, who is now one of the leaders of the psychodrama movement in Germany, also confirms Moreno's influence:

> The special atmosphere of the Moreno-institute has also inspired men like Fritz Perls, the founder of gestalt therapy, Eric Berne, the founder of transactional analysis, and George Bach, the founder of marathon-groups. [Leutz, 1974 p. 186].

3.6.3.2 Perls' Followers on Moreno's Influence

Perhaps not surprisingly, Perls' followers are not as enthusiastic about Moreno's influence. Some, like Edward Smith in his essay *The Roots of Gestalt Therapy* go to quite some length in discussing "the several major sources which influenced Perls in the creation of his approach" [Smith, 1976 p. 1], without mentioning Moreno at all. "It appears that Perls was primarily influenced by five traditions: Psychoanalysis, Reichian Character Analysis, Existential Philosophy, Gestalt Psychology, and Eastern Religion" [Smith, 1976 p. 3]. Psychoanalysis in particular is of course quite opposite in technique and theory to both gestalt and psychodrama. Perls however was a Freudian analyst himself, before he developed his own approach.

Others like Polster include Moreno in a section on "Some Theoretical Influences on Gestalt Therapy":

> Furthermore, perhaps even more important in the framework of its impact on gestalt therapy, is the lesson implicit in psychodrama that one is more likely to make discoveries by *participating* in an experience rather than only by *talking* about it. This acknowledges the force of direct experience and moves beyond reliance on the interpretive function so central to the psychoanalytical ethos.
>
> Naturally, in the hands of the gestalt therapist, the psychodramatic production is quite different from what Moreno had in mind. Essentially, the difference is that in gestalt therapy the drama is more likely to evolve out of the individual's improvisations rather than starting from a given theme or with specified characters. Also, the gestalt dramas may often have the single individual - like Shakespeare's

players - playing many roles. Although both Perls and Moreno might disagree, we believe that this is primarily a difference in style rather than in theory. Perls believed that since each of the roles was only a projection of parts of the individual, nobody else could play these parts. Nevertheless, projection or no, there is still a world out there - and it is capable of everchanging configurations and susceptible to a variety of interpretations. Thus, if someone plays John's grandfather and John plays himself, the requirement for John to face the other guy's version of his grandfather could still be a valid confrontation wherein John can investigate whatever possibilities for action John needs to recover in his life. This does not have to rule out the powerful experiences John might also have in playing both himself *and* grandfather. [Polster, 1973 p. 315f]

The enactments are even more similar than Polster indicates. As he mentions for gestalt, so also in psychodrama the session evolves out of the protagonist's improvisations and he always demonstrates to the other actors how he wants them to play their parts. He role-reverses throughout and thus gets a chance to play all the different parts. Moreno puts a strong emphasis on putting the protagonist's view of his world on the stage and he usually gets to decide how his scenes are portrayed. Of course the problem remains whether other members are capable of capturing the protagonists view.

Will Schutz, one of the developers of encounter groups, who has also incorporated many ideas and techniques[73] from

---

[73]E.g. *doubling* as described in a case study: "People sitting around the room acted as alter egos (sitting behind Tom and saying what they thought he really felt - a psychodrama technique)." [Schutz, 1989 p. 32]

psychodrama, remembers Moreno's influence on himself, as well as on other techniques such as gestalt therapy:

> I went to psychodrama sessions and met Jacob Moreno, the creator, who constantly complained that he was not recognized for his myriad contributions to the field of group process - and he was right.
>
> ... I learned of gestalt therapy from Paul Goodman, who had just written the popular *Growing Up Absurd*. Gestalt was a real innovation, a development of psychodrama, and was to play a major role in my life when I met its creator, Fritz Perls, at Esalen a few years later. [Schutz, 1989 p. 3f]

Perls' biography acknowledges Moreno as one of his influences: "He took advantage of observing, attending, and being affected by such pioneers as Charlotte Selver (Body Awareness) and J. L. Moreno (Psychodrama)" [Shepard, 1975 p. 64].

Perls himself mentions Moreno only in passing (and not at all in his autobiographical writing): "Moreno, dealing with delinquents in a boarding-school, evolved a method of group-therapy, a situation that in principle should de-emphasize the phenomena of transference and make for a more amenable sociality" [Perls, Hefferline, & Goodman, 1951 p. 281].

3.7 Gestalt's Influence on Living Theatre

To complete the path of Moreno's indirect influence on the Living Theatre, we need to investigate the effect that the gestalt approach and its founders Fritz and Laura Perls and Paul Goodman had on the Living Theatre.

The Becks had many meetings with the Perls [Malina, 1984 p. 199, 303, 310, 317f, 357, 404, 429] and thus Shepard interviewed them when he was writing Perls' biography. The account gives a good picture of Perls' association with the Living Theatre - here are some excerpts:

> Fascinated from early adolescence by innovative theatre, Fritz spent a fair amount of time with The Living Theatre. Julian Beck recalls him hanging out at rehearsals and stagings, commenting on theatre in general and their acting in particular. And, of course, he spent time with them socially.
>
> "It became clear to us that Fritz was looking at that time and talking - with a kind of deep and moving excitement but also a great vagueness - about wanting to do some kind of directing or something with the actors. He had something in mind that was half-way between the kind of performances we were doing and therapeutic sessions."
>
> In his personal life, the same dramatic sense was evident. "He was always," added Julian, "trying to bring the meeting, the encounter, to its frontier. And the device was always honesty, frankness, and a certain shock technique. These forms of address were very important to our own work, for instance, in *Paradise Now*, where many of the scenes are concerned with bringing that kind of candor and that kind of honesty into a direct I-and-Thou relationship between the actor and the

audience. I think that Judith and I learned much about this as concept and reality through Fritz." [Shepard, 1975 p. 60f]

The main reason, however, why the Living Theatre was influenced by gestalt, is their close and long association with Paul Goodman. Paul Goodman (1911-1972) was a multi-talented anarchist philosopher, poet, playwright, gestalt therapist and longtime associate of the Living Theatre, who also introduced the Perls' to the Becks. Goodman became a patient of Laura Perls' and joined a training group directed by Fritz and Laura [Shepard, 1975 p. 61]. He also co-authored a book with Perls [Perls, et al., 1951].

Julian Beck first met Goodman in the summer of 1944 when he went to Provincetown [Schechner, 1971]. Judith Malina knew him first in a literary context, directed three of his plays, was psychoanalyzed by him, had lovers in common, and had all kinds of personal and profound relationships. She regards him as a primary teacher [Malina, 1994]. Paul Goodman was also among several prominent sponsors of the Living Theatre [Biner, 1972 p. 56].

Judith Malina very much acknowledged the influence from gestalt and especially Paul Goodman:

> I have done much theatrical work based on the gestalt theorists. Paul Goodman of course was a leading playwright of the Living Theatre, as well as a psychotherapist. I have worked very much in the gestalt theory with Fritz and Laura Perls and Paul Goodman.
> ...Although I do come from the gestalt and from Goodman, we worked together for almost twenty years. So there is a deep association with the gestalt therapy and sometimes in a gestalt

234

group we would get up and enact something out of Moreno and Fritz, Paul or Laura would say: "Let's try an exercise on Moreno." [Malina, 1994]

This concludes the line of influence:

Jacob Moreno >>>> Fritz Perls >>>> Paul Goodman

\\   /

Julian Beck & Judith Malina

V. CONCLUSION

I conclude with some implications of my research on Moreno's work in theatre. The first section shows why Moreno can indeed be called a theatre artist. As I have argued in chapter III, Moreno's main innovations in theatre are the use of dramatic enactment for therapeutic purposes and the promotion of spontaneity/improvisation. Sections two and three examine how widespread these two notions are today. The last section seeks to answer the question whether Moreno has succeeded in his mission.

1. Moreno was a Theatre Artist

At the beginning of my research I largely shared the view that Moreno was primarily a psychiatrist. It became more and more apparent, however, that Moreno was foremost and at heart a theatre person. He developed many of his ideas at his Theatre of Spontaneity and was directing his own theatre company early in his career. The directorial and theatrical sensibility stayed, moreover, with him while he worked as therapist and teacher and is captured in the following dialogue:

> STUDENT: Yes, we have often noticed that you differ from your
> students and other directors by the manner in which you

operate. You often appear to be in an ecstasy, filled with poetic moods. You move around with eccentric gestures; often you seem to try to hypnotize yourself and to hypnotize the group. You seem either under a spell or trying to get into a spell. It is as if you are trying to emphasize the importance of the moment.

MORENO: Yes, starting the session is always a great moment in my life; it is as if I'm trying to establish my own identity, to remove myself from the small tasks of daily life, and reach the level of genuine communication. To be a bearer of truth is to "become" a bearer of truth. [Moreno, 1964a p. 46][74]

In many of the pictures that depict Moreno in action, he appears to be a hypnotist, especially because of his grandiose hand gestures [Marineau, 1989 frontpage, p. 151; Moreno, 1964a p. 37, 94]. Audio tapes of lectures reveal his dramatic voice and way of speaking [Moreno, 1967].

Throughout his life Moreno was known for scandals he instigated, often staged dramatically like performances. For example, during the Kiesler controversy (Plagiatstreit) Moreno chose the most dramatic moment during the opening ceremony of the exhibition for new theatre techniques in Vienna. At the moment when Kiesler was introduced, he shouted: "I declare hereby publicly that Mr. Friedrich Kiesler is a plagiarist and a scoundrel!" (cf. introduction.3).

My claim that Moreno was a theatre artist is based, however, not only on his practical theatrical work, but also on the way he

---

[74]This dialogue is written by Moreno and thus we do not know whether it is based on an actual student or whether he made it up; either way it offers insight in his approach to directing psychodrama.

wrote. One of his early writings is translated in the appendix and is clearly theatrical, both in form and content. Even his later works, which are generally considered scientific writings in the field of psychology[75], are composed with a passion and artistic sensibility usually associated with theatre artists. This is by no means true of all psychodramatists. At the end of chapter II.5.1 I have already suggested that today the practice of psychodrama has lost much of Moreno's original theatricality and spontaneity. This is also reflected in different descriptions of psychodrama. Compare, for example, the following two definitions:

> Psychodrama can be defined, therefore, as the science which explores the "truth" by dramatic methods. [Moreno, 1946 p. a]

> Psychodrama is a professional practice based on the therapy, philosophy, and methodology developed by Jacob L. Moreno, M. D. (1889-1974), which uses action methods of enactment, sociometry, group dynamics, role theory, and social systems analysis to facilitate constructive change in individuals and groups through the development of new perceptions or reorganization of old cognitive patterns and concomitant changes in behavior. [Buchanan, 1984 p. 783]

The first evokes immediate excitement about psychodrama, both as a subject for philosophical investigation as well as something to experience. The second definition, while probably accurate, makes it sound rather boring. Like much writing today in psychology it sounds scientific and displays little passion, despite the fact that Buchanan is probably very enthusiastic about

---

[75]Libraries and bookstores classify Moreno's works under psychology.

promoting psychodrama - he is a long-time trainer and practitioner and is the Director of Psychodrama Services at Saint Elizabeths Hospital, Washington, D.C.

In contrast to Freud and most other psychotherapists, Moreno did not write much about pathology, but rather about the human potential for creative expression. Like most theatre artists he saw beauty in the full range of human emotions, including so-called pathological or negative ones. For example, his case study of a patient who believed that he is Adolf Hitler reads at times like the description of a great actor whom he admires [Moreno, 1959b p. 191-203].

Moreno's writing resembles not so much that of psychologists, but rather that found in theatre, as for example in Jerzy Grotowski's book *Towards a Poor Theatre*.[76] We have seen in chapter III.1.1 that Grotowski is a leading theoretician of the theatre in this century and writes about the therapeutic function of theatre. A full comparison of Grotowski and Moreno would be a project by itself.[77] But it is worth pointing out that both employ much the same terminology, in so far as they speak of catharsis, encounter, exposing, integration, liberation, masks, opening up, revealing, roles, spontaneity, therapeutic function, truth, etc.

Here are a few quotations to illustrate the similarities:

---

[76]This does not imply that their work as directors is also similar. For example, in contrast to Moreno, most of Grotowski's productions are based on written plays, use well-trained actors, and are highly directed.
[77]It would especially point out how both emphasize the transformative effect that theatre has on the *actor* (and secondarily on the audience).

> In playing yourself you see yourself in your own mirror on the stage, exposed as you are to the entire audience. [Moreno, 1983 p. 27]
>
> In order that they [the players] may be driven out from their cages, they tear up their deepest and most secret wounds, and now they bleed externally before all the eyes of the people. [Moreno, 1946 p. 28]

Grotowski also demands of his *holy actor* to look inward while completely revealing himself to the audience.

> The actor who undertakes an act of self-penetration, who reveals himself and sacrifices the innermost part of himself - the most painful, that which is not intended for the eyes of the world - must be able to manifest the least impulse. [Grotowski, 1968 p. 35]
>
> Here everything is concentrated on the "ripening" of the actor which is expressed by a tension towards the extreme, by a complete stripping down, by the laying bare of one's own intimity - all this without the least trace of egotism or self-enjoyment. The actor makes a total gift of himself. [Grotowski, 1968 p. 16]

Moreno likewise wants the actor to fully expose himself. Nothing should be held back.

> Once we had permitted the actor a full spontaneity of his own, his full private world, his personal problem, his own conflicts, his own defeats and dreams came to the fore. I recognized gradually the therapeutic value which this kind of presentation had for the actor himself and when properly manipulated, the therapeutic value it had for the audience. [Moreno, 1983 p. 102]

Since as children we are naturally spontaneous, Moreno sees the training of spontaneity foremost as an *unlearning* of the blocks that result from our upbringing.

> The actor must therefore learn to unchain himself from old clichés. By means of exercises in spontaneity he must learn how to make himself free gradually from habit formations. He must store in his body as large a number of motions possible to be called forth easily by means of an emerging idea. [Moreno, 1983 p. 66]

Similarly Grotowski's training technique is not an accumulation of skills, but rather an elimination of blocks and conditioning that inhibit free expression of pure impulse.

> The education of an actor in our theatre is not a matter of teaching him something; we attempt to eliminate his organism's resistance to this psychic process. The result is freedom from the time-lapse between inner impulse and outer reaction in such a way that the impulse is already an outer reaction. Impulse and action are concurrent: the body vanishes, burns, and the spectator sees only a series of visible impulses.
>
> Ours then is a *via negativa* - not a collection of skills but an eradication of blocks. [Grotowski, 1968 p. 16f]

Note how Moreno's and Grotowski's ideas are similar not only in content, but also in the style in which they are expressed. They both use a visceral language, rich in physical descriptions and metaphors.

2. Therapeutic Theatre Today

The widespread use of theatre techniques for therapeutic purposes today is best exemplified by <u>drama therapy</u> which has recently become a field of study, research, and practice in its own right (alongside other modalities such as art, music and dance therapy). It became legitimized in America after the founding of the National Association for Drama Therapy in 1979 [Emunah, 1994 p. xx; Landy, 1986 p. v]. In its pamphlet, the association defines drama therapy as "the intentional use of drama/theatre processes to achieve the therapeutic goals of symptom relief, emotional and physical integration, and personal growth."

This is clearly in line with Moreno's philosophy and psychodrama is considered part of drama therapy. But the field also uses other methods, from theatre games to performing full productions involving mental patients as actors, designers, etc. Unlike classical psychodrama, the enactments do not have to be centered around a specific patient's issue. At times they might not have any obvious connection to real-life problems at all. Like the actor in theatre, clients in drama therapy can be inspired to play roles which are different from themselves, to become another person (real or fictional). This allows us to experience and express all the different parts of ourselves, including shadow aspects, and to expand our limited view of who we are and what we can be. It takes advantage of the fact that we are often more open and spontaneous when we are *not* told to work on our psychological issues, but rather to have fun and try out different ways of being.[78]

Drama therapy, like psychodrama, is now used in a variety of settings, such as schools, prisons, businesses, and mental institutions. Today there are two American universities that grant degrees in drama therapy, the California Institute of Integral Studies in San Francisco and New York University. They are directed by Renée Emunah and Robert Landy, respectively, who also authored the two standard textbooks used for teaching drama therapists. Both acknowledge how the field is indebted to the pioneering work of Moreno.

Landy in his book *Drama Therapy: Concepts and Practices* states:

> In fact, drama therapy would be difficult to conceptualize outside the context of Moreno's pioneering work. [Landy, 1986 p. 29]
>
> [Psychodrama] provides both a theoretical source for drama therapy and a series of techniques widely used by drama therapists. [Landy, 1986 p. 31]
>
> As sources of drama therapy, psychodrama and sociodrama are very rich. Moreno's work is the first significant Western

[78]The benefits of drama therapy can of course also be experienced by students in acting classes. A conscious therapeutic intention is not necessary, neither for the teacher nor the student. In this way it is possible to reach people who would refuse to attend anything that uses the term "therapy".

Conversely, drama therapy is able to reach people who would not attend anything which is called "play", without some promised therapeutic benefit.

Having experienced both, I no longer care about semantics, but about enjoying myself and growing from the experience.

attempt to view dramatic action as a formalized method of psychotherapy. [Landy, 1986 p. 72].

Landy also includes a chapter on "Psychodramatic Techniques" [Landy, 1986 p. 121-134], which he considers an essential part of the drama therapists repertoire.

Renée Emunah recently published *Acting for Real: Drama Therapy Process, Technique, and Performance.* She offers the following definition: "Drama therapy is the intentional and systematic use of drama/theatre processes to achieve psychological growth and change. The tools are derived from theatre, the goals are rooted in psychotherapy" [Emunah, 1994 p. 3].

Emunah refers to Moreno and psychodrama throughout her book and acknowledges how her field is indebted to his work:

> Aside from *theatre*, the most obvious and influential conceptual source is drama therapy's immediate predecessor, *psychodrama.* [Emunah, 1994 p. 3]
>
> The most widely known utilization of theatre for curative purposes since early civilization was psychodrama. The founder of psychodrama, Jacob L. Moreno, M.D. (1889-1974), was a brilliant, prolific, and visionary man. [Emunah, 1994 p. 17]
>
> That psychodrama has been a fundamental part of the work of most drama therapists goes without saying. Psychodrama is central in my own work, particularly at certain stages in the process. [Emunah, 1994 p. 19]
>
> At the core of psychodrama, sociodrama, and drama therapy, lie role play and role reversal. These essential processes, for which we are indebted to Moreno, are about putting ourselves in the shoes of others, increasing our understanding and

empathy, and not only *seeing* but *experiencing* the world from a perspective outside of our own. [Emunah, 1994 p. 20]

Emunah also supports the point made in section 1 of this chapter: "With his interest in group dynamics, theatricality (e.g., staging, stage lighting), and spontaneity, one might consider Moreno to be more of a drama therapist than psychodramatist!" [Emunah, 1994 p. 19]. This implies that drama therapy recaptures some of the theatricality displayed in Moreno's early work.

3. Improvisation Today

While Moreno's pioneering work with therapeutic theatre is acknowledged by many people working in the field today, he is rarely seen as a father of the improvisation movement. He was surely not the first person to experiment with improvisation, but he was probably it's strongest advocate when he started working in theatre in the early twenties. Before that time it was mostly used in forms similar to Commedia dell'arte (cf. chapter II.4) or to cover up mistakes in regular theatre.

Today improvised theatre performances are commonplace in most cities with an active theatre scene. Courses in improvisation are part of every actors training program (university or conservatory).

But learning and growing through spontaneous improvisation has also entered many aspects of life outside of theatre, from elementary and secondary education through training of managers, police officers, and other professionals. This point is clearly expressed in the following quotation from Richard Courtney who is also aware of Moreno's early work.

> The theatre is hardly a frill. At first sight, however, not everyone realizes how significant it is. Perhaps the best-kept secret of the twentieth century has been the slow infiltration of spontaneous drama into the schools of the Western world. Before World War I isolated pioneers realized its potential, but it was not until the 1950s and 60s that real inroads were made

into educational systems in Britain, the Commonwealth, and the United States. By the 1970s it had spread to Europe and, by the 1980s, to Africa and Asia. The growth of educational drama and spontaneous improvisation has been phenomenal, whether as a method of learning ("drama across the curriculum") or as a subject in its own right. In Ontario, for example, few students were using spontaneous drama in schools in the 1960s, but by 1988 there were about 50 thousand in grades 8 to 12 alone. How did this change come about? Quite simply, it *worked*: Good teachers discovered that learners responded quickly and in depth through free dramatization.

Nor was the expansion limited to education. In the early twentieth century, spontaneous drama was used in therapy only by Jacob Moreno's "psychodrama." Later, this method was used with many other dramatic styles in "drama therapy" - a major mode of creative arts treatment for those with mental and physical dysfunctions.

Today, all kinds of improvisations and simulations are used in training programs for business, marketing, social work, jobs, and retraining, for nurses and medical practitioners, and for those engaged in space programs. Recent research has shown that in our post-industrial society many generic skills (those required for work and leisure that can be taught in schools) derive from the ability to read others and see things from their point of view - a specifically dramatic skill. Activities making use of drama are increasing at such an exponential rate that, perhaps, they may be a commonplace in the twenty-first century. [Courtney, 1990 p. 3f]

To illustrate just how much improvisation has entered mainstream society, here are a few quotations from *Sensual Fantasy for Lovers*, a video made to help couples enhance the passion and excitement in their sexual relationship.

Experiment with sexual scenarios that involve improvising and role-playing. All it takes is a little imagination, a little creativity, a little pretending...

Assuming specific identities allows you to give play to hidden aspects of your own personality...

Let the spontaneity of the moment carry you away to a world where anything is possible...

You may find yourself suddenly wonderfully released from the constraints of daily life, free to reveal more of yourself to your partner. Seize the moment with its potential for the unexpected, to venture into new areas of sensual gratification. Role-playing allows you to explore a different world where you create the rules. As you take on a new identity, you'll find it easier to cast aside inhibitions, enjoying the freedom to explore exciting new forms of sexual expression. Pretending provides a wonderful opportunity to infuse mystery into your love-making and renew your love affair with each other...

It has been suggested that only by putting on masks can we reveal our true selves. Loosing yourself in a role allows you to surrender to your own spontaneous passions. [*Sensual Fantasy for Lovers*, Playboy Entertainment Group, 1993]

When watching this video, a viewer familiar with Moreno would indeed be reminded of his ideas. While it is impossible to trace a precise line of influence from Moreno to the makers of the Playboy video, one can nevertheless say that the ideas that go back to Moreno were spread along two routes: through the human potential movement and through the advocates of improvisation in theatre and education. One of the major catalysts of the human potential movement was the Esalen Institute in Big Sur, California, where encounter groups, gestalt therapy and other self-awareness techniques were practiced and disseminated. We have seen in chapter IV.3.6.3 that Moreno influenced two of the founding fathers of Esalen, Fritz Perls and Will Schutz.

The other line of influence proceeds, as I have outlined in chapter IV.2, from Moreno through Viola Spolin who influenced generations of actors and educators with her landmark book *Improvisation for the Theater* [1963] and through her work with the actors of the legendary Compass and The Second City companies in Chicago, who have subsequently inspired much of contemporary professional comic and improvisational acting in theatre and film.

4. Did Moreno Succeed?

Despite Moreno's profound influence, we read in one of his last publications:

> But I have failed so utterly in turning the moment in the world's needs. The hope is gone from the faces of men. Our youth is bewildered. Many children are stopped from being born because of the worthlessness of birth and life. It is in the last calamities that my failure comes through. I must admit humbly that my megalomania is shattered. Nothing is left but the crown and the throne. The body is dead. [Moreno, 1972 p. 214]

This proclamation of failure can be understood only if we fully appreciate the extent and idealism of his vision. For his goal was nothing less than a global therapeutic community living within a therapeutic world order.

> All the above listed concepts and ideas have a serious purpose, leading up to the philosophy of a world system, to the ethical prospect of a "therapeutic world order," a unity of mankind, as foreshadowed in 1934 in the opening sentence of *Who Shall Survive?*: "A truly therapeutic procedure can not have less an objective than the whole of mankind." A therapeutic world order is mandatory, it is the next cosmic imperative if our world is to survive. [Moreno & Moreno, 1970 p. 6]

Moreno described his vision in a number of places:

> The therapeutic community settles disputes between individuals and groups under the rule of *therapy* instead of

the rule of *law*, it attacks the problem of community government through the use of one man as a therapeutic agent of the other, of one group as the therapeutic agent of the other... In the spontaneous-creative universe of therapeutic communities, the spontaneity of one individual stimulates the spontaneity of the other, and the quantitative result is the opposite of what we have at present, a robot-dominated world order in which spontaneity is an arbitrary and incidental element. [Moreno, 1957 p. 22f]

Each person has equal status and is working towards the well-being and growth of every other person, being therapist and patient at the same time. Everyone is not only free, but is actively supported to develop their full potential. "In such a society life itself will be therapeutic" [Moreno, 1957 p. 25]. Moreno thus wanted his techniques to enter all facets of life: "Imagine, if you can, the next summit meeting in which every participant would have to reverse roles with every other participant before final decisions were made!" [Moreno, 1964a p. 136].

Through "mass psychotherapy" he hoped to reach "universal peace" [Moreno, 1969 p. 7]. To this end he wanted to employ modern technology and mass media.[79]

> I foresee that in the not too distant future theatres for therapeutic television and motion pictures will be just as common place as newsreel theatres are today. Each will have a

---

[79]This suggests that when Moreno condemns the "robot" he sees the problem not so much with technology itself, but with how we use it. "The robot in its various forms - the work tool, the weapon, the cultural conserve, the zoomaton, the atomic bomb, and the calculating machine - is at the core of the process of alienation, of man from nature, from himself and from society" [Moreno, 1957 p. 4].

psychiatric consultant. They will provide the most effective vehicle for mass psychotherapy ever devised....

It is advisable to organize dramatized, living newspapers to be broadcast from television stations throughout the world. This is more than the usual photographic reel of events but an instrument by means of which the living creative genius on this planet can communicate directly and instantly with their fellowmen. [Moreno, 1946 p. 420][80]

---

[80]A chapter in *Psychodrama: First Volume* contains a fairly detailed description of Moreno's ideas for producing therapeutic motion pictures [Moreno, 1946 p. 385-420]. While he contends that "action catharsis can never be replaced by spectator catharsis" [Moreno, 1946 p. 396], he describes the possibility of a limited therapeutic effect on a large television audience: "The citizen in his home should feel that he is taking part in the session physically, he should feel that his own representative, an audio ego, is acting in his behalf on the screen, on the stage as in the audience. It produces not only the illusion of most intimate personal participation in the psychodramatic session , but a form of audience catharsis similar to the audience's experience in flesh and blood sessions" [Moreno, 1946 p. 420]. The first step in this new direction is simply the recording and televising of regular psychodrama sessions. This can later be more adapted to the medium of film, using either patients or auxiliary-egos with psychiatric training as actors.

Since we know that Moreno was always aspiring to live his theories in action, we wonder whether he actually experimented with therapeutic motion pictures. Indeed it turns out that Moreno was a pioneer in this field as well, and a number of his undertakings are reported in [Moreno, 1969 p. 252-254]. The first time he recorded psychodrama sessions was in 1933 in Hudson, N.Y., while he was Director of Research at the New York State Training School for Girls. Films for public television were produced by Moreno and his associates in Paris in 1955 and 1964, in Washington, D.C. in 1953, for CBS in 1959, for NBC in 1965, and in Los Angeles in 1966. At the Camarillo State Hospital in 1964 Moreno was televised weekly on closed circuit TV while conducting psychodrama sessions. The entire patient population was watching from their screens.

Given such grandiose visions it is clear that we are nowhere near their fulfillment and thus Moreno (and we) have failed in that respect. It might even be suggested that today we are moving further away from a humanistic society. Meanwhile, it is still possible to pursue Moreno's vision, in the hope that we will at least grow from the experience.

APPENDIX

1. Translation of Moreno's first theatrical publication.

Moreno's first publication which clearly had theatre as its subject appeared on April 1919 in German under the title "Die Gottheit als Komödiant". It contained many of the ideas which he later developed further, its main point being his call for the actor in the theatre to play himself and not a playwright's creation. There was also a description of the cathartic effect of playing scenes from one's life. He didn't use the word catharsis, but we can clearly recognize the nucleus of psychodrama. This important document, which establishes Moreno as a dramatic theorist early on, is here translated for the first time in its entirety - Moreno himself (loosely) translated only a few pages from it, which are published in *Psychodrama: First Volume* [Moreno, 1946 p. 21-24] and also in *The Theatre of Spontaneity* [Moreno, 1983 p. 24-26].

The piece is written as a play or dialogue where an actor comes on the stage to play Zarathustra, but is interrupted by a spectator who doubts his identity. Now a lengthy discussion about the nature of acting ensues between the director, the actor, the playwright and some spectators. It is not clear if and when the plot was actually performed or whether Moreno actually interrupted a theatre performance on Zarathustra.[81] Moreno himself describes the incident in his autobiography as if it had actually happened:[82]

> Back in 1911, we entered a theater in Vienna one evening just as a play was beginning. We made our way to the first row and sat down. The rest of the audience was already into the hypnotic spell of the play, *Also Sprach Zarathustra*. It was our notion to awaken the actors and the spectators from their "histrionic sleep." We accused the actor who played Zarathustra of misrepresenting himself. We wanted to draw attention to the conflict between Zarathustra, the spectator, and Zarathustra, the actor. My companion posed as the real Zarathustra, sitting in the audience, aghast at the violence done to his character by the actor and the playwright. The

[81]Moreno writes: "This plot was presented on the stage of the theatre for spontaneity. Produced: Kinderbuehne (Children's Theatre), 1911" [Moreno, 1983 p. 24]. There seems to be no clear record of such a performance and other researchers write: "At times there have been speculations whether Moreno indeed interrupted a theatre performance on Zarathustra in Vienna. I am assuming that Moreno invented his story" [Marschall, 1988 p. 38].
In Marineau's biography of Moreno we read: "One day he entered a theatre with a friend: the play being presented was *Thus Spake Zarathustra*, based on Nietzsche's book of that name. Moreno and his friend stopped the actor who was about to play Zarathustra and objected that nobody but Zarathustra himself could play the role. The director of the play and the author rapidly came to the defense of the actor. Finally Moreno announced that they were witnessing the end of traditional theatre and that the time is ripe for the birth of the only real theatre in which every actor would play himself, not a role. The police were called in, Moreno and his friend went before a judge, and they had to promise not to interfere again in other people's plays . This is one version of the story; another version, saying that this incident that happens at a play put on by Moreno himself for the children in the Augarten, is less dramatic, but the basic scenario remains the same" [Marineau, 1989 p.46].
[82]This is by no means a guarantee of historical fact, as Moreno frequently employed what he called *psychodramatic truth*: "The stories told in this book strive to be psychodramatically and poetically accurate, as they exist in the minds of the people involved and told by them. They do not strive for historic accuracy. ... A psychodramatic biography differs in this sense from a historically analytical biography" [Moreno, 1964a p. 7]. For more on Moreno's use of psychodramatic truth see [Marineau, 1989 p. 8-11].

"real" Zarathustra ordered the actor to play himself, not Zarathustra. After my friend confronted the actor and the playwright, I went up on the stage and presented my radical philosophy. I called for the tearing down of the institution of the theater in order to create a new theater which would not just "mirror the sufferings of foreign things ... but play our own woe." I wanted to create a theater of genius, of total imagination, the theater of spontaneity, in line with the work I was doing with the children in the parks of Vienna.

A scandalous situation! The actors were upset; the audience angry. Fiction had given way to reality. We were evicted from the theater by police and taken to jail, where we spent the night. The following morning we went before a magistrate. Luckily we were dismissed after we submitted to a scolding and after we promised to refrain from [doing] anything like that again. We were a tough-looking pair, and public outcry was serious. Our actions were seen as a serious threat to the peace. It could have been much worse for us than spending the night in jail.... [Moreno, 1989 p. 72f]

Whether historical fact or not, it is clearly no accident that the title of the play was taken from Friedrich Nietzsche's *Also sprach Zarathustra*. Moreno's text shows Nietzsche's influence, both in the way it is written (as a dialogue, with fools as characters, using poetic, esoterical language, symbolic images, biblical references), as well as in the topics it deals with (self-realization, subjective truth, birth of a new theatre, relation between God and man, art and beauty, life as comedy). Nietzsche was very popular at the time of Moreno's writing. "Among the philosophers in whom I was particularly engrossed were Spinoza, Descartes, Leibnitz, Kant,

Fichte, Hegel, Marx, Schopenhauer, and Nietzsche" [Moreno, 1989 p. 29].

Despite some similarities, Moreno was critical of Nietzsche for not living his convictions in action. "Nietzsche failed. He gave birth to the conceptual scheme of the superman without any fruitful effects" [Moreno, 1964a p. 42].

> They [Kierkegaard and Nietzsche] cherished highly the heroic attitude, but they never entered into the act. They moved towards it, circled around it, reflected upon every possible version of heroic acting out, including the dilemmas, prospects, and explanations as to what might happen in the course of the act, anticipating dreads and producing them. But the more they became involved in the heroic attitude towards life, the farther the real act moved away from them. It literally slipped through their fingers. [Moreno, 1964a p. 43]

All this suggests another interpretation of Moreno's text: The actor playing Zarathustra is Nietzsche himself wanting to be the heroic superman (*Übermensch*). Moreno points out how impossible his undertaking is and calls upon him to instead be himself, to "step into life itself" [Moreno, 1953 p. 9], to act spontaneously in the here and now.

According to Moreno his piece was first published in pamphlet form on October 1911 [Moreno, 1946 p. 24]. The following is translated from *Der Neue Daimon*, a continuation of *Daimon*, an expressionist literary journal edited by Moreno [Moreno, 1919b p. 48-63] (cf. introduction.3). The translation follows the German text as close as possible to give the reader the experience of reading the original. Like much of Moreno's early writing, the language is often poetic, esoteric, and, according to one's taste, exquisite or obscure. *Emphases* are those of the original document; only the footnotes are mine.

J A K O B   M O R E N O   L E V Y

THE GODHEAD AS COMEDIAN

Characters:

The Director.
The Actor, portraying Zarathustra.
The Playwright.
The Spectator Johann.
I.
The Left Fool.
The Right Fool.
The Oldest Spectator.
The Youngest Spectator.
All Spectators.

Place:

The Theatre.

ALL SPECTATORS:

(rise from their seats)

The divine comedy is dead. Where is the divine comedian?

THE LEFT FOOL:

(crawls through the curtain and cowers)

What is supposed to happen? Is God also among the comedians?

THE RIGHT FOOL:

(leaping)

Everything bad has happened to me: I will become a prophet.

THE DIRECTOR:

(hastily)

Audience!

I am sorry, the play will not be performed. The apocalypse is coming to us. Zarathustra has just forgotten his role. And the Father in heaven has just taken away my playwright's imagination.

(The spectators are increasingly amazed.)

But I don't lose control and think immediately about my business. To get rid of the crowd, I turn them quickly into the audience. Here is the theatre.

(Exits.)

THE OLDEST SPECTATOR:

The playwright is gone. The theatre is over.

THE YOUNGEST SPECTATOR:

The Great Man rises. I am the macrocosm. God's house will be built out of my male phallus. The new earth, the new heaven, the new paradise.

ALL SPECTATORS:

(rise from their seats, imploring)

God! We do not want to give birth to any more mediators.

If you do not step down to us by yourself, we will instead climb up to you.

(The curtain rises.)

(The Actor carries Zarathustra's mask.)

(Johann steps on the stage.)

JOHANN:

(startled)

These eyes are not the eyes of Zarathustra!

(Steps closer.)

The conflict is written on your face: the hair uncut and the beard cut. Your skin is smooth: where are the wrinkles and the seventy years of Zarathustra? Your back is straight: where is the hump and pain of Zarathustra?

(Throws himself on the floor.)

Help, help, Sir! I am a fool in search of Zarathustra.

(The Actor is embarrassed.)

JOHANN:

(takes a piece of paper from his pocket)

Here on the program is written: Tonight's performance will be "The Deeds of Zarathustra." His life will be performed? *That* only Zarathustra can do.

(Jumps up.)

Sir, tell us your mission, your name!

ACTOR:

Zarathustra.

(Johann is highly amazed.)

ACTOR:

I am him and I am not: a life in two hours.

JOHANN:

Two hours are not his hundred thousand!

ACTOR:

The time often slows down. For me a thousand years are like a day.

JOHANN:

If you were born in the first second of the two hours and died in the last: it would be thinkable.

Only a short while ago you were far away from this house. Who were you on the street, say? When did you become Zarathustra? When the curtain rose? When will you die? When the curtain closes?

ACTOR:

I can change roles. Caesar, Napoleon, Mahomet appear through me at some time - and today Zarathustra. The playwright picks the fruit, but I consume it. Nothing is too high for my lowness: One day the voice of God himself will sound out of my mouth through this room, as it did before through Bileam's donkey. I can do anything.

JOHANN:

(dismayed)

To think of God as descending with his heaven to the world, as human, is insane; how much more so, to think of him as a comedian on the fool's stage?

ACTOR:

Nevertheless. Here is his altar. I am the lamb. I hate myself and I act only to escape myself. I become God's comedian daily in order to be God, in the madness of life in heaven.

JOHANN:

The playwright picks the fruit and you consume it; but who is the fruit itself?

ACTOR:

The fruit itself? It is ... nobody.

JOHANN:

Nobody?

Oh! perhaps the role came suddenly over you and now you have to perform it, like the sleep-walker quickly climbing down the balcony?

Ah! no, I understand. Zarathustra was first: *your own theory*. He came to you once as the divine flower of your longing and rests in your soul; he turned more and more into your secret giant, a chorus of many voices that captured your entire inner world: Zarathustra's face, his walk and voice, his birth and death. Until one evening Sir Zarathustra himself was riding on your former body, so that today, here, in front of all these children, mothers, fathers, he could reveal his life for two hours.

ACTOR:

Zarathustra did not come to me from my longing, but from outside. I did not memorize him inside, but outside.

JOHANN:

Did you ever meet him?

Perhaps Zarathustra was alive at some time and now he watches from his grave the resurrection of his great flesh in your low and strange skin. The dead cannot defend themselves and disclaim. I celebrate the perfect, unique, dead body when it is dead; because the most painful ailment for the dead is not heii, but to be dragged through the world without becoming real. Man, let the living be alive and the dead be dead!

I am their representative. Zarathustra is here in the wrong place: it is my duty to reestablish his peace.

World-killer! Double! The dead onto you!

ACTOR:

Before you curse my work in front of the peopie, consider this: to be a real double, I would have to be at the *same time as Zarathustra*.

JOHANN:

Suppose your Zarathustra is not dead, but is alive somewhere.
Right at this moment! Or more precisely: he moves around and
teaches in the market-places of this city, well-known to everyone.
Or the most terrible for you: he is sitting in the audience. Now!
There! He watches evening after evening the farce of his life
falling out of the box of this hell: O help, stop! He walks through
this side entrance to the stage.

(Johann throws himself to the floor)

He kneels and winds himself around your knees and ...

ACTOR:

Pleads humbly for a peaceful life?

JOHANN:

The reciprocal, unavoidable conflict has broken out: between
Zarathustra the spectator and Zarathustra the actor. The
playwright destroys the encounter and with it the world, but the
actor also destroys the most radical appearance, not the
encounter, but *himself in the encounter*, his closest
next to him.

What does Zarathustra-God have to do, when he now meets the
Egyptian, you, his Zarathustra-actor face to face? The fastest
solution: *Zarathustra becomes a murderer*. The
craziest: *Zarathustra drives the mirror-being to
suicide*. The Messianic resolution: *through his look*

and his words Zarathustra brings the actor to reason.

ACTOR:

It is only remarkable how Zarathustra always wants to destroy me, but not himself!

JOHANN:

Suicide would only appear to help Zarathustra, since death makes the disease you caused him even more incurable and would leave you totally alone with the conflict, which then could only be saved by the nightmares of self-reflection, evoked by the vision of the dead man.

ACTOR:

Why do you get involved in my dispute with Zarathustra? Why does he need an advocate? If my acting on his behalf annoys him, why not also your arguing on his behalf?

JOHANN:

But, unfortunate one, aren't you afraid that I might be Zarathustra? I, who's mask you still wear? Don't you realize your defeat, proven from every possible point of view? The first possibility might be: Zarathustra, understood as your own theory, which might one day bring you down.

ACTOR:

The longing.

JOHANN:

The second possibility might be: Zarathustra is really dead and his legend brings you down. By presenting him you deny your own hidden being and become at the same time creator of the most complete hell for the dead. To be a pure double you would only have to be at the same time as Zarathustra.

ACTOR:

Oh! you slowly make me - myself - crazy!

JOHANN:

The third possibility might be: Zarathustra is alive and is trying to destroy his false actor. Since the longing for perfection motivates the comedian to play Zarathustra as identical as possible, he becomes, in the moment of highest attainment, the pure mirror-image of the master, congruent to him like one triangle to the same one, completely reciprocal, identical inside and outside. *Zarathustra's conflict is the descended protest of God-Father against the son representing him.*

ACTOR:

Could there be a more terrifying state then the encounter between equals?

JOHANN:

The perfect double is the return of the most identical. Zarathustra-actor and Zarathustra-himself are in this ideal case no longer *t w o* different (even if in every other respect identical) bodies and souls, but have suddenly become *o n e* body and *o n e* soul, completely matching each other, at the same time and space, one unity in which no sharpest eye could discover a break suggesting the former twins. Hence they are identical like a triangle is congruent with itself, like the viewer retracts his image in the mirror - exactly at the time the mirror is taken away (destroyed). *The I and the double tear each other apart in their own identical flesh.*

ACTOR:

But how could ever a human being become conscious of this most peculiar visitor, with whom he has the same eyes, ears, thoughts and pains *at the same time and together?*

JOHANN:

Usually never; and strictly speaking only in one very rare instance. For this radical unity we have to construct the *t w o things in themselves*, which have only *o n e and the s a m e* world of appearance. If the one thing in itself happens to be the Godhead itself, which has attempted to unite itself with the other one, the human being, starting at birth, then this transformation of the creator into the creature, this complete fusion, this self-destruction of the double by the double, becomes metaphorical action.

ACTOR:

I understand the terrible pains my sins have caused Zarathustra, but still I haven't unraveled the precarious situation that I have gotten myself into through my acting.

JOHANN:

After having examined the conflict from Zarathustra's point of view, we will look at it from the viewpoint of your secretly lived life. The sum of your spiritual misfortune results exactly at the point when you have reached the highest level and bliss as comedian. In that moment you can clearly be seen as *the double on both sides*. This is because from your being an actor - as your only center during your existence in the theatre - emanate two rays, one towards the *outside*, to your double in *space*, the independently existing Zarathustra, the other one towards the *inside*, to your essence in your soul, to yourself, as the usually completely existing I, which came out of itself in the theatre.

ACTOR:

How can I free myself and the audience from this spell?

JOHANN:

By determining whether Zarathustra, who according to your statement could not be your own theory and equally certain has never lived in three dimensions, might not be the *theory*, the dream-creation of someone else whom we all know!

ACTOR:

Oh! I sense the ending of my tragedy. Where is my murderer?

(The playwright hurries in from the right.)

PLAYWRIGHT:

You're acting badly today, o Zarathustra! What are you complaining about?

ACTOR:

I am searching for my murderer. Just now my doctor has diagnosed a serious illness of my mind. The only encounter which might help me is this: with God. Send him here!

PLAYWRIGHT:

If God came among the actors, he would easily turn into a comedian, but an actor would hardly turn into more than a muddle-head.

ACTOR:

Who are you then?

PLAYWRIGHT:

I am the author of this play.

ACTOR:

Finally you are here, limping angel! Quickly heal a victim of your art! You probably know Zarathustra?
Oh! this mask may no longer torture him!

(He tears down the mask from his face.)

PLAYWRIGHT:

Very well! I have created him.

ACTOR:

Then all heroes of the novel and the stage shall return to your black father-heart! Why do you allow your madness to dance in someone else's, mine limbs? Why are you not your own hero, your own playwright and your own actor at the same time?

PLAYWRIGHT:

Everyone has his own function. Mine is to write, you the actor has to act, the architect has to built magnificent stages. The one is gifted with great, nonverbal sensitivity, the other with the corresponding poetry. Only together they create great harmony. Everyone shall fulfill his function; if he fails to do this, God will leave him.

ACTOR:

I can not find within me nor without me a sign telling me exactly what I am suited for, what my talent is. I have always especially wanted to have a function for which I have no talent at all.

PLAYWRIGHT:

The most perfect guide is: the longing.

ACTOR:

Oh, but your longing seems to me shallow. Who ordered you to its master? Why is your body and your soul not as pure as your poetry? Why do you allow your magic children to become independent before they have transformed you? How can you write about heroes before you become one yourself? What gave you the right to let me, a truly low scoundrel, play Zarathustra today?

PLAYWRIGHT:

Only the dream and its word is perfect; therefore I reject the material symbol. Any material symbol. God does not come to the world from the outside, as appearance. I know him only as my longing, therefore I may not accept the world and me - my social, physical and psychological condition.

ACTOR:

The point is not whether the dream or the realization is perfect, rather I am accusing you of being perfect neither in dreaming nor in realizing, of lacking any kind of perfection. While you kept your longing in silence, you could not come into conflict with any conscience other than your own; but as soon as you broadcast your desires to the world, I have the right to implore you to take your dream completely serious and to let it affect at first yourself. *You are against the material symbol only insofar as it has consequences for yourself.*

PLAYWRIGHT:

Realizing is humbling, it makes the longing sober. Speech replaces being. I hate the arrogance of the self-improving. The internal is my domain, in it the poetry, the thought and the music, in it the apocalyptic glow of the permanent expectation, in it my self-crucifixion and the dialectical emperor of our Messianic hope.

*   *   *

(When after these words one of the actors shouted my name, I rose from my seat in the audience and walked right up onto the stage. After I arrived there, I stood still, did not move and did not want to answer any questions. As I looked up again after a while, everyone was astonished and asked me, why I did not say anything for so long. Then I answered:)

I:

Out of joy. Be happy with me! Out of joy over the fact that the children, for the first time since the theatre was given to the people as a gift from heaven, are performing *p e r f e c t* theatre.

PLAYWRIGHT:

On the contrary. You allow unpleasant truth to overshadow the beauty.

I:

All you children and mothers and fathers and actors and playwrights of this joyful house: nourish yourself completely through me with my unleavened bread and follow me on my last exodus out of Egypt, because I will explain to you completely why this night is special over all other nights.

The theatre has so far mirrored *the sufferings of foreign things*, but tonight it will present *your own woe*; it has sinned until now, overcome by false gods, but tonight it will perform *itself as a play*; until now the playwright has betrayed the actor, the actor has betrayed the spectator, but tonight they all have become one people; only in this fantastic night I provoke the highest form of laughter through rebellion, example, magic, and our own God becomes the comedian.

PLAYWRIGHT:

But the Divine must first enter the audience, to sit with us, laugh with us, and to listen with us!

I:

This conversation has become nothing but the self-talk, the *self-reflection*, the self-revealing of the theatre, forced upon its components (spectator-actor-playwright) through the presence of God as spectator, developed especially since God had not been satisfied only to listen.

PLAYWRIGHT:

What chaos is he creating! The function of the spectator is to receive a gift and not to become an actor.

I:

Nothing happens faster than the transformation of the loving into the law-making God. At first of course *the Godhead as spectator* fulfills itself through complete devotion and always following the advice to turn the theatre assigned to him into the happiest throne of his paradise. But a small disturbance is enough: the discovery of the most inconspicuous incident, of a gap, a split in his inner and outer world, transforms him into the most furious rage against himself or the others. The growing suspicion for example, that Zarathustra is not playing himself, but is precisely a comedian, transforms his gentleness into madness, rage, frenzy. The zealous God-Father descends to his son to free him from his sin, to completely heal the gaping crack in the creation. The peaceful spectator turns into a warrior, who steps onto the stage and interrupts boldly the black art of the magician, who has to pause in order to unravel the common conflict with God.

PLAYWRIGHT:

But this is also the end of the theatre.

I:

Yes, and therefore emphatically no. *Before the establishment of the essential theatre, all its previous elements have to be completely destroyed, one piece at a time, down to its original foundation.* Damned be all the machinery. Restoration of chaos. If at the end of the conversation all actors, playwrights and spectators are destroyed, then out of the original state rises anew the *birth of the theatre* and the development of the perfect appearance.

PLAYWRIGHT:

Why does God destroy what he perceives, the actor whom he dislikes; rather than the perceiving - his eye, which is allowed to see the depraved?

I:

To destroy the eye might cure the eye, but not God, who values it as much or as little as the things it perceives in space. God is forced into the dilemma between himself - his eye in the spectator - and its subject in space - the double actor-Zarathustra - and he has to affirm both sides of the conflict at the same time. He has no time to choose, but must act immediately *equally favoring both,* and the comedian, who is no longer in touch with himself, has to be corrected, retained ...

PLAYWRIGHT:

So your God is making laws, reforming and improving the world.

I:

Yes, and therefore emphatically no. At first he grows in silence for an eternity; and you can not find out what he is there, neither through talk nor through action. But a need in his environment pushes him to become closest to us, maybe even because of our infinite distance, and as a law-maker to resurrect our deepest inner secret.

PLAYWRIGHT:

I suspect that he infinitely overestimates the material symbol; our own physiology and the other material containers, even space itself, are mere magic tools, metaphors for the high level of our consciousness. I could actually imagine that the most enlightened saint experiences the conflict inside, and resolves it, without ever having to do anything in the outside.

I:

The saint could do this and I can very well imagine that he could not do *more*. Even God would grant him that all conflicts, insofar as they are directed inwards and fall completely and purely in the sphere of one's own soul, have to recognize as their only place of resolution the silence; but he would have to be equally explicit about his disagreement in those cases in which the conflicts are *related to space* and originate from an immediate, concrete relation to a Thou. For God neither can nor wants to let go of *himself*, he neither can nor wants to deviate from the *enigma*.

PLAYWRIGHT:

What does that mean: enigma?

I:

Nothing concrete, if it had a tangible meaning, it wouldn't be called enigma.

The thinker, the wise, Makanthropos, the saint, the savior: they all have a meaning, are able to do something, move forward; God alone can not do anything, solve anything. The *thinker* is able, enchanted with the frame of his experience and his concepts and systems, to eliminate the cosmos together with his own human being, but God is not powerful enough to deny the smallest dust-particle in the air, which connects him with this thinker. The *wise*, obsessed slave of his thirst for knowledge, sacrifices his redemption to the disease of knowledge, but God wouldn't have become wiser through all the wisdom of the world and of his heart. *Makanthropos*, the spiritual emperor of the cosmos, who sees the crowd below him hustle and bustle, crushes them still. He looks with contempt down upon the universe and identifies it as *a reduced human being*, the Mikanthropos. *But God is the macrocosm himself*, he can neither look up nor down, he has neither heaven nor hell. After reaching self-realization, the *saint* is consumed by the meaning of forever repeating his fulfilled existence, hence his absolute coldness on the outside. God, however, is equally concerned with the fulfillment of all parts of the cosmos and is forced to become the good Samaritan of all the lost souls he encounters. The *savior's* purpose is to redeem, and as long as there is a sinner who is waiting for his help, he will be born. God on the other hand is the perfect being, appearing as the complete existence, and *against* the purpose to redeem. Only the suffering of the world as he opens his eyes, the conflict in the encounter, the interruption of the enigma excite him: he becomes the *redeemer of the world*, even though he is not.

PLAYWRIGHT:

I understand. The others are egocentric.

I:

The high being is *theocentric*.

PLAYWRIGHT:

Now I also understand why he must emphasize the material signs and the space, as well as the spirit, and condemn their elimination: because of the *completeness*.

I:

The enigma must be full, complete.

PLAYWRIGHT:

He says *yes* to everything, therefore he has to interfere whenever something goes wrong.

I:

This is a false doctrine. It is impossible for him to say yes, only the saint, the savior, the son can do that, but the only necessary and exclusive God is God the Father. The "yes" is already a way of looking, a hymn. God the Father doesn't interrupt the continuum of creation through observations, not even a little "yes" escapes him. He is the originator of all the things which are his identical organs. He is the invisible mother, who is suddenly *t h e r e* , when her children are crying.

PLAYWRIGHT:

How can one encounter the macrocosm?

I:

In order to encounter the macrocosm, it has to appear itself.

PLAYWRIGHT:

How can "everything" appear?

I:

The universe can only be touched. The conflict makes the macrocosm appear. You can encounter the enigma neither with reason nor with allegory, but only with the body. *God's moving through space is his moving through himself. His universe is created at every moment as the clear surrounding and the mystic space covered by his glance and the encounter.*

PLAYWRIGHT:

Is God not the one guilty for any sacrilege?

I:

He shouldn't pretend to be omniscient and he doesn't accept any sin. God knows about things exactly as much as he experiences in the encounter with them. *Their fall into sin during the encounter is the cause of him becoming a helper.*

PLAYWRIGHT:

I am thinking: God has the experiences of all beings and all things, identical and at the same time with them - in himself?

I:

This would make God the monstrous double of all things: their highest Satan. The severest punishments in hell: they could be controlled through silence.

God has the Father-consciousness, but he is not allowed to have knowledge of any other I, other than his own; he learns of the things through them.

Think about it! How do you learn from them?

PLAYWRIGHT:

Oh! I am a scoundrel with seven seals: before the Highest One. But a play can not be made other than through writing. Or do you know of another way? Being is being, existence is being here and writing will always remain a mean act! Or is there such a thing as perfect writing, a perfect play, a perfect actor?

I:

All previous theatre is merely a preview and a commentary to the perfect drama, who's hero is the identical human being.

PLAYWRIGHT:

But still there has to be a playwright writing it?

I:

The playwrights are spent. *The Godhead as playwright* saves the art and may one day stop the march through the world in order to reflect upon the taken path. *Not in the beginning, at the end is the word.*

PLAYWRIGHT:

A play is a play, whether it takes place in heaven or on earth. Or does God's drama have any special virtues?

I:

The play is a form of poetry, which in turn is a special case of the various expressive arts. *The system* is founded upon the lie; it wants to suck up everything. Even what has never been carried out: past and future, the saint, the winner and Don Juan. *The essay* is founded upon cowardice: it talks around the thing and never bites. The key to *science* is collecting and observing: it is predominant in a world in which God has no place. *Poetry* is created by imagination, an offspring of longing: the worship of the word replaces God until he arrives. System, essay, science, poetry are all products of nature, subject to causality and they turn out to be the *accidental* result of practiced and unpracticed circumstances. *The first preparation for a theurgical doctrine of speech is the elimination of all unpracticed states of consciousness.*

The report as such is the representation of a practice. The states of consciousness which have actually been reached, I call: states of experience or realizations. The connections in space which have actually erupted I call: states of encounter.

PLAYWRIGHT:

I am surprised to hear that you describe the report, even for the Godhead, as the ideal way for the word. I am thinking that especially God creates out of nothing.

I:

God creates out of nothing, but precisely his *mirror image*.

The story about the elders says that in the big assembly in heaven, there is an angel on every step of the stairway which leads up all the way to the highest sphere. If one asks him, he sings high in accordance with the level of his step. If he sings too high, he dies instantly, and in the following eon he has to reincarnate as a famous playwright.

Each state of experience corresponds to a specific word, each state of encounter to a specific dialogue. The autosopher or reporter does not describe the appearances of his I and of the world, but rather the *self-creations within consciousness and within space.*

PLAYWRIGHT:

God's revelation to mankind is therefore: the report of his realizations.

I:

Yes and no; for God, who is identical in the enigma, must hide especially his most precious treasures. To have and fulfill the experience is enough; there is no need to talk about it.[83] The report of states of experience *as an end in itself* is not allowed in the encounter. *All sin comes from choosing the wrong place.*

The content of the encounter is the conflict; it breaks out, the moment God comes in contact with a lower sphere. *God's authorized revelations are reports of conflicts in space.*

PLAYWRIGHT:

God can be a playwright if he creates the comedy as a report in the form of a dialogue about his former three-dimensional existence. Will it give preference to certain conflicts?

---

[83]Cf. chapter III.1.7 "Validity of Subjective Experience".

I:

Only the theatrical report on *perfect* actions is allowed. The ideal play is created by God as a portrayal of his own destiny, his history dramatized by himself, the tragedy of his subject, *the replay of his life in an artistic mode*. Art is not my metaphysics, but I myself become the *meta* of my art. The first truly historic drama is at the same time the birth of the myth.

ACTOR:

The perfect drama is created by God. Where are the comedians? *How is the Godhead as actor possible?*

I:

The old jokers are spent! But God and the characters in his play appear themselves on the stage as the comedians playing their long since solved conflicts. They shine as the perfect radiance of their former identical being, as the unsolved enigma of the macrocosm, as the transmission of their time and their space, into the breads of the Easter celebration.

ACTOR:

The self-realization of the theatre!

I:

That is: the resurrection of God in himself, the great Passion of the lamb, the triumph of the identical art in the realm of the illusion.

ACTOR:

I destroy and transfigure my former seriousness, myself, through the radiance.

I:

By *performing* my past tragedy again, I am having a comic, liberating, relieving effect upon myself, the original hero. Inside I burst out laughing, while at the same time I am playing myself as I was, in earnest, naked, in front of all the people; for *I see my world of past suffering dissolved in this different reality*.[84] Life is suddenly no longer painful, but amusing. My former pains, rages, desires, joys, jubilations, victories, triumphs have become pain*less*, lust*less*, joy*less*, victory*less*, triumph*less*, *meaning-less*. Dear fellow spectator, was it ever me who speaks and acts from inside myself? Or do the Gods believe thus? Oh! the laughter, the laughter, the endless laughter has overcome God and the audience giggles with him.

ACTOR:

What was the origin of the endless laughter?

I:

The laughter originated when *God saw himself*. It happened during the Sabbath of Creation that God *looked*

---

[84]Though Moreno doesn't use the word, we can clearly recognize here his idea of *catharsis*, cf. chapter II.5.1.

back on the six working days and suddenly had to laugh about himself.

ACTOR:

When God lets loose, his eyes quiver with joy and below his feet suddenly a stage opens up.

PLAYWRIGHT:

Oh! three times laughing this endless laughter! The comedian laughs about himself, the spectator laughs about the actor and the playwright has turned into a spectator.

I:

In this night we found out that the theatre is *dead*. In this night we found out, that the new theatre will be rebuilt *around God himself*. Let us move in that direction! Follow me!

(All leave the theatre full of exuberant cheerfulness.)

(The curtain falls.)

(Children's Theatre 1911)

2. Moreno in the *New York Times*.

This collection offers an informative picture of how Moreno was known during his New York period.

- <u>Feb. 3, 1929</u>: "IMPROMPTU PLAN USED IN EDUCATION - Children in New Brooklyn School Are Taught to Exercise Their Spontaneity Rather Than to Depend on Standardized Habits."

This first article on Moreno reports that he has opened an impromptu school at Plymouth Institute in Brooklyn. It is based on an interview in which Moreno explained some of his theories on using spontaneous expression to break down the inhibitions of standardized education. He said that children up to the age of five are endowed with the gift of spontaneous expression, before they turn into imitative automatons. He held that "improvisation has a fundamental importance for mental and emotional growth" and saw "three important phases in the impromptu movement: its relation to the drama, to education and to clinics." The article also mentions the dramatized newspaper as "a favorite and ever-varying subject for impromptu players."

Moreno himself is referred to as "Dr. J.L. Moreno, author of the impromptu method", "a graduate of the University of Vienna", "who was managing director of the impromptu theatre in Vienna." Notice especially that Moreno is not yet referred to as a psychiatrist.

- <u>April 6, 1931</u>: "THE PLAY - Impromptu Players Appear."

This is the only *New York Times* article which writes about Moreno as a theatre person and one of the few accounts of his theatrical work in New York. The reviewed performance uses the *living newspaper* technique which was explained in chapter III.2.2. Since all of the article deals with theatre, it is quoted in its entirety:

> From their atelier in Carnegie Hall, where rumors have been rife for weeks of seismic alterations impending in the American drama, Dr. J. L. Moreno and his Impromptu players came last night to the Guild Theatre for their first performance in public. The occasion was manifestly serious. Dr. Moreno, who has delved into these impulsive theatricals in several foreign capitals, presented the idea in a somewhat impassioned introductory speech as "not only a theatrical venture but the protest of man as a biological being against the robots." His players intently awaited the spark of their new and combustible art. The Theatre Guild stage, which will try anything once, was set for improvisations in April.
>
> Such as it was, the zealous idea of impromptu acting cropped out first in two renditions by a five-piece orchestra which had admittedly rehearsed a bit but disdained the reading of music in actual performance. Starting from scratch, they stayed there for two numbers until Dr. Moreno reappeared with his troupe of strictly spontaneous actors. The first endeavor was to be a newspaper drama, and the master explained the situation and assigned the parts swiftly - "The Act of Transference," this was called. The curtain was lowered, and the American stage awaited its newest development.
>
> The first play, like the ones that followed, turned out to be a dab of dialogue uneasily rendered by its hapless players.

Although the impromptu scheme called upon them to burn with fires of creation, they appeared lucky to remember a few of the phrases of melodramatic cant, and when the dialogue was not witless or absurd it was patently looking for the nearest "out" or curtain-line.

Two or three somewhat involved stories followed, interspersed with a black-face monologue and announcements by a robotlike gentleman speaking the headlines of a newspaper. But it became more and more evident that heavy boredom, rather than "forms, moods and visions," were the product of the actors. Demanding wit above all else, the Moreno players lacked that essential as fully as the premeditation upon which they frown so heartily. The legitimate theatre, it can be reported this morning, is just about where it was early last evening. [*New York Times*, April 6, 1931]

Apparently Moreno's productions were not successful with the audience and critics. This is one of the reasons why Moreno soon afterwards turned away from working in theatre and concentrated more and more on his work in psychiatry. Moreno himself describes this development:

The theatre of "one hundred percent spontaneity" met with the greatest resistance from the public and the press. They were used to depend on "cultural conserves" of the drama and not to trust spontaneous creativity. Therefore, when the spontaneity theatre offered good theatre, honest, artistically workable spontaneity, the entire undertaking appeared suspicious to them. The spontaneity play seemed to them to be thoroughly rehearsed and prepared, in other words, a hoax. When, however, a play was bad and lifeless, they drew the hasty conclusion that real spontaneity is not possible. We lost the interest of the public and it became difficult to maintain the financial stability of the theatre.

...Later I discovered a happier solution in the "therapeutic theatre." One hundred percent spontaneity was more easily achieved in a therapeutic theatre. It was difficult to forgive esthetic and psychological imperfections in a normal actor. But it was easier to tolerate imperfections and irregularities of an abnormal person, a patient. Imperfections were, so to speak, to be expected and often quite welcome. [Moreno, 1983 p. a-b]

- <u>June 6, 1931</u>: "DR. BRILL DESCRIBES LINCOLN AS 'MANIC' - DR. MORENO IS SKEPTICAL!"

This article describes Dr. A.A. Brill's paper read at the American Psychiatric Association's convention in which he described Abraham Lincoln as a "schizoid manic personality" and then presents Moreno's critique: "An American by adoption, Dr. J. L. Moreno, New York psychiatrist, formerly of Vienna, took issue with Dr. Brill, saying that Psychoanalysis has not developed to the point where it could make a satisfactory analysis of Lincoln." Note this is the first time, at least in the *New York Times*, that Moreno is referred to as a psychiatrist. From this time onwards Moreno focused more and more on his work in psychiatry.

Moreno defended Lincoln further by declaring him a genius beyond the reach of psychoanalysis: "Dr. Moreno said Dr. Brill's conclusions were based on the statements of friends and contemporaries, who had 'all kinds of motives to relate all kinds of stories about Lincoln.' ... A genius of his sort was capable of playing roles and saying many things which could be explained in a multitude of ways besides the analysis of Dr. Brill."

Moreno himself devoted eight pages to this incident in his *Who Shall Survive?*. From this section it becomes apparent that he is particularly proud of this controversy, e.g. when he says of his critique of psychoanalysis: "I was dangerous, not as much because I knew its limitations but particularly because I had developed methods which the future will, as I claimed, prove to be superior" [Moreno 1953, p. xlix]. He almost seems to compare himself to Lincoln: "As I spoke, I felt as though, in a way, Lincoln spoke through me" [ibid p. l].

According to Moreno the incident made headlines on the same day in the *New York Times, Washington Post, Chicago Daily Tribune, Los Angeles Times, Toronto Evening Telegram, Canadian Star, London Times* and *Le Matin* [ibid p. xliii] and even became a newsreel: "And so as many people may remember, in the course of the summer of 1931 moving picture audiences could see and hear Brill getting up and trying to prove that Abraham Lincoln was a schizoid-manic personality and I standing up after him and disproving it" [ibid p. l].

- April 3, 1933: "EMOTIONS MAPPED BY NEW GEOGRAPHY - Dr. J. L. Moreno Calculates There Are 10 to 15 Million Isolated Individuals In Nation."

This article introduces Moreno's *sociometry*, though it uses a different name: "A new science, named psychological geography, which aims to chart the emotional currents, cross-currents and under-currents of human relationships in a community, was introduced here yesterday at the scientific exhibit of the Medical Society of the State of New York, which opens its 127th annual meeting here today at the Waldorf-Astoria."

We easily recognize the basic idea of sociometry when we read: "The maps represent studies of the forces of attraction and repulsion of individuals within a group toward one another and toward the group, as well as the attitude of the group as a whole toward its individual members, and of one group toward another group."

Here Moreno is referred to as "Dr. Jacob L. Moreno of New York, consulting psychiatrist of the National Committee of Prisons and Prison Labor and director of research, New York State Training School for Girls, Hudson, N.Y."

Moreno's studies of these girls and of other populations are reported and the article ends with the ambitious statement: "Dr. Moreno added that plans have been completed to chart a map of the psychological geography of New York City."

Moreno himself declared that the event had great significance:

> The closest approximation to an official start of the sociometric movement occurred on April 3-5, 1933, when the Medical Society of the State of New York exhibited a few dozen sociometric charts during its convention at the Waldorf Astoria Hotel. ... In the days to follow all the large newspapers, led by the New York Times, carried headlines, stories, editorials, pictures of sociograms and sociometric cartoons, throughout the United States. I later discovered to my amusement, that the culprit had to do some explaining to the Executive Committee as to why so many other worthy medical

contributions were pushed out of the limelight. [Moreno 1953, p. xiii]

- <u>May 14, 1935</u>: "DIET RICH IN MEAT HELD HEADACHE AID"

Under this headline several studies are summarized that were presented at the convention of the American Psychiatric Association, only two of which interest us here. "Use of a hatred of Adolf Hitler to rebuild a child's character was reported by Dr. John Levy of New York City. ... Dr. Levy said the case illustrated how the psychiatrist may put to use the natural tendency of children to express their emotional conflicts in make-believe ways."

I am almost certain that the name John Levy refers to Moreno. Up to the end of his university years, Moreno always signed his name "Jacob Levy" which was his given name. Later he added Moreno, his father's first name, and Levy became his middle name [Marineau 1989, p. 65].

The article however treats Levy and Moreno as two different people and, following the above quotation, continues:

> A new method of character and personality building by play-acting was described by Dr. Jacob L. Moreno and Helen Jennings of the New York Training School for Girls at Hudson. Dr. Moreno said that it will work well for all walks of life, including one of the most difficult, the training for executive duties.
> The girls enact spontaneous plays - that is, two or more of them join in imagining a situation either dramatic or workaday, but always like real life. This scene they try to enact, throwing their emotions into it strongly. They do not rehearse it. [*New York Times*, May 14, 1935]

- <u>March 2, 1936</u>: "STATE SCHOOL ADOPTS NEW SOCIAL TRAINING - Sociometry, Developing Spontaneity Among Girls, Aims to Reach Hidden Human Force."

This article is based on the first issue of Moreno's journal *The Sociometric Review* and tells more about his experiments at the New York State Training School for Girls: "They are called spontaneity training and sociometry, a technique developed by Dr. J. L. Moreno, in collaboration with Helen Jennings."

Helen Jennings was a longtime student and then associate of Moreno's. She wrote in his *Impromptu* journal[85] and later became editor of the journal *Sociometry* [Moreno 1953, p. lxxxv]. Moreno remembers meeting her:

> Helen H. Jennings was a young graduate student at Columbia University in those days. Always interested in new ideas, she became my enthusiastic student. Sociometry, group therapy, and psychodrama were all of interest to her. Her work, over the years, went a long way towards forwarding the spread of my ideas throughout the world. Helen was brilliant and ambitious. I gave her my state job as Director of Social Research, that is, she did the work and received the salary while I retained the title. I always thought the world of Helen. She is one of the most talented social scientists I ever met. ... Helen introduced me to her mentor at Columbia University, Dr. Gardner Murphy. [Moreno 1989, p. 97f]

---

[85]*Impromptu* vol. I no. 1, Jan. 1931, p. 26, "Experiments in Impromptu Analysis" and vol. I no. 2, April 1931, p. 12 "Psychoanalysis and Dr. Moreno".

The article then describes how the ideas of sociometry were applied at the Hudson school:

> The force is released by "spontaneity," by which the girls are given the chance to choose people and work they would like, and to get it as far as the likes and rights of the other girls will permit.
>
> Dr. Moreno says that at first this training seems to be something too trivial to be effective. As an example he cites the meeting of girls at the dining tables at Hudson.
>
> There are three ways of seating possible, he says. ... Third, is the new sociometric method, which does not even seem new. The girls write down their choices of table companions - first, second and third choices. These choices are charted, sociometrically, which is a system of bringing out the hidden likes and dislikes, the popular personalities and the isolated ones.
>
> Then the girls are seated by these charts, each one placed as nearly as possible to her own choice. The result, Dr. Moreno reports, is highly satisfactory. [*New York Times*, March 2, 1936]

• Nov. 9, 1936: "DEDICATE THEATRE TO CURE PHOBIAS - Doctors, Educators and Social Workers See Beginning of Experiment at Beacon. - ACTING IS SPONTANEOUS - Audience is to Participate in What is Described as Kindergarten for Adults."

The occasion for this article is the opening of Moreno's institute at Beacon, N.Y.:

> A therapeutic theatre, the first in the United States, where the players will act spontaneously to try to rid themselves of mental worries or serious phobias, was dedicated here today.

> The theatre is new in both form and purpose. It is a medical experiment. The associate director is Mrs. Gertrude Franchot Tone, mother of Franchot Tone, movie actor. Its head is Dr. J. L. Moreno, psychiatrist and originator of the "spontaneity" technique which the theatre will use.
> The dedication was attended by a party of physicians, educators, social work officials and psychologists. [*New York Times*, Nov. 9, 1936]

Surprisingly his institute is here referred to as a theatre. Later it will mostly be referred to as a sanitarium [e.g. *New York Times*, June 30, 1938; May 16, 1974; Marineau, 1989 p. 131]. Despite the name there were no theatre persons mentioned as attending the party. Moreno is as usual referred to as a psychiatrist.

Franchot Tone was one of the actors from the Group Theatre (cf. chapter IV.1) that Moreno worked with. His mother Gertrude became a patient of Moreno and lived at Beacon for a few years, where she recovered from her alcoholism. She was the main financial sponsor of the psychodrama theatre at Beacon [Moreno, 1989 p. 100-103].

The article then describes an example for the use of psychodrama:

> As an example of the medical purpose, Dr. Moreno cited a man unhappy, upset, unable to succeed because he could not get along with his boss.
> In the theatre this man would take part in spontaneous play-acting, unprepared in advance except as those studying his troubles would choose a topic applicable to his unsolved problem. The audience would participate in his acting. It

would be a sort of kindergarten for adults. [*New York Times*, Nov. 9, 1936]

Here one recognizes Moreno as a forerunner of play therapy and the now trendy *inner child* workshops. "It was not confined to mental cases nor to social misfits. Adults, he said, seemed, like children, to find answers to their problems in spontaneous plays."

• June 30, 1938: "PLEAD FOR COURAGE IN USING CHEMISTRY - Population Control and revised Concept of Influence of Environment Are Urged."

This is a summary of some presentations given at a meeting of the American Association for the Advancement of Science in Ottawa. The section on Moreno states:

> Dr. Jacob Moreno of the Beacon Hill Sanitarium, New York, told the association that merely shutting off immigration would not prevent race friction nor preserve the old human stock of a country from saturation. Without scientific population control within a country, he asserted, even the most rigid immigration restrictions may fail.
> Dr. Moreno, an adviser on resettlement projects in the United States, stated that, when lawmakers began to fear immigration and reduced gradually its volume and quality, internal migrations of Negroes from the Southern to the Northern States began and also an increased migration of Mexicans.
> [*New York Times*, June 30, 1938]

Seeing Moreno called "an advisor on resettlement projects in the United States", one is astounded at how many titles Moreno holds. The article ends with Moreno's recommendation to use sociometry to solve the problem: "The American community has so many cleavages on its various racial fronts that emotional tactics cannot operate indefinitely. Sociometric tests would gradually develop a basis for a rational race control."

- <u>May 25, 1941</u>: "Science In The News - Psychology and Hess"

  As might be expected, the psychologists and psychiatrists have given their opinion of Hess's dramatic flight from Germany to Scotland. To us the most convincing of these analyses is that of the distinguished Dr. J. L. Moreno, whose business in life it is to dispose of inner conflicts and take out of life worries and obsessions of which even their possessors are not aware. [*New York Times*, May 25, 1941]

Again we are amazed at the great variety of topics on which Moreno speaks. His analysis concludes as follows:

The flight may well be something that Hitler himself had in mind at one time simply because Hess is an extension, an auxiliary ego of Hitler. The head of Nazism is suddenly planted by proxy in the heart of the enemy's country. We have, then, a symbolic, single-handed invasion, the fulfillment of a threat long contemplated and publicly announced. Whatever the interpretation may be there is no doubt that Hess's act stunned and confused. [*New York Times*, May 25, 1941]

- Feb. 16, 1947: "SCIENCE IN REVIEW - The 'Catharsis' of the Drama Successfully Used in the Treatment of Mental Cases"

This is a review of the first edition of *Psychodrama* published by Moreno's own publishing company Beacon House [Moreno 1946].

> Psychiatrists call all this "mental catharsis" and do their best to bring it about. Dr. J. L. Moreno makes practical use of "mental catharsis" in what he calls "psychodrama." To achieve his purpose he needs a small theatre. ... He describes his techniques and results in the first volume of his new book, "Psychodrama" (Beacon House, Beacon, N. Y.). [*New York Times*, Feb. 16, 1947]

Next there is a detailed description of a psychodrama working out a marriage problem and then the conclusion:

> The formula is simple: Induce the patient to express himself, but always spontaneously, by letting him enact the incidents that harass him. But the technique of induction is difficult. The director is a producer, therapist and an analyst. [*New York Times*, Feb. 16, 1947]

The article also attests to the wide use of Moreno's technique by 1947:

> Psychodrama is now an accepted mode of treating mental cases in Beacon, N. Y., St. Elizabeth's, numerous Veterans Administration hospitals, university medical schools and Federal and social agencies. The technique has proved of value in rehabilitating veterans, selecting and training officers, treating personality disorders, straightening out marital tangles, and transforming unhappy families into happy ones. [*New York Times*, Feb. 16, 1947]

The review concludes:

> Even if Dr. Moreno's "Psychodrama" is a textbook it deserves the attention of a wide audience. If writers of fiction want good material for their problem romances and sound suggestions for character drawing, Dr. Moreno is the man to help them out with his striking case records and their planned interpretation. [*New York Times*, Feb. 16, 1947]

• <u>May 16, 1974</u>: "JACOB L. MORENO, PSYCHIATRIST, 82 - Pioneer of the Psychodrama Technique is Dead"

This obituary again calls Moreno a psychiatrist and considers the development of psychodrama his major achievement. It starts with a section on his beginnings in Vienna:

> It was in Vienna shortly after World War I that Dr. Jacob Levy Moreno embarked upon an experiment that was to prove itself a major advance in psychiatry. There he organized something called the Theatre of Spontaneity, which employed actors and actresses to participate in a new form of entertainment that grew out of improvisations based on cues from the audience. [*New York Times*, May 16, 1974]

Note that even his early work in Vienna, which was clearly theatrical, is called a major advance in *psychiatry* and not in theatre.

Next we learn of the wide spread of psychodrama in hospitals throughout the world. Moreno considered the scope of psychodrama to be the whole community of mankind. "For Dr. Moreno psychodrama offered not so much a 'cure' to mental problems as a device for self-discovery that would help lead to a person's well-being."

Only one root of Moreno's philosophy is mentioned: "He maintained that psychodrama was not so much an invention of his as a resurrection of the ancient technique of acting out, which goes back at least to Aristotle's conception of Greek tragedy as 'catharsis'."

Next we find a short biography that is useful to quote in it's entirety, since it gives a concise picture of the highlights of Moreno's life in the eye of the public.

> Dr. Moreno was born in Bucharest, May 20, 1892. He studied at the University of Vienna, receiving a medical degree in 1917. In Vienna, he had a private practice and served as a hospital superintendent, but became interested in the way children, especially, loved to act out stories and myths.
>
> In 1921, he founded Das Stegreiftheater, his Spontaneity Theatre, and proceeded to experiment with psychodrama, discovering that the roles he selected for his actors and actresses helped them deal better with their personal problems.
>
> Dr. Moreno moved to the United States in 1925 and settled first in New York. He found that acceptance of his theories was slow, particularly because some colleagues deplored his showmanship.
>
> He began his work with children at Plymouth Institute in Brooklyn and introduced some experiments at Mount Sinai Hospital here. In 1929, he founded an Impromptu Theatre at Carnegie Hall and later did work at the Guild Theatre.
>
> Dr. Moreno also made studies of sociometry at Sing Sing Prison in 1931 and set up conferences on the subject. In 1936, he founded the Beacon Hill Sanitarium in Beacon, where he also

set up his Therapeutic Theatre the same year. The sanitarium was later named after him. He served as an advisor to many other institutions and received many professional awards.
Among his books were "Sociometry, Experimental Method and the Science of Society," published in 1951; "Who Shall Survive?" revised in 1953, and several volumes he edited on psychodrama. [*New York Times*, May 16, 1974]

Even though some of his work in theatre is at least mentioned, Moreno is presented mainly as a psychiatrist. We are somewhat surprised to find that the last date mentioned for Moreno's activities is 1936, but as suggested above, his innovative period was from 1916 to 1936. In the almost forty years afterwards he concentrated on spreading his ideas through organizing professional associations, journals, conferences, trainings, demonstrations and publications (of which many were revisions of earlier writings).

CHRONOLOGY: MORENO AS A THEATRE ARTIST

1889   Birth of Jacob Levy Moreno in Bucharest, Romania, also birth of Martin Heidegger, Ludwig Wittgenstein, Adolf Hitler.

1894   Plays God and his angels with children of the neighborhood. Tries to fly, falls, and breaks his arm.

1908-11   Conducts creative drama with children in parks in Vienna.

1909   Enters University of Vienna, first as a student of philosophy, then of medicine.

1912   Organizes self-help groups with prostitutes in Vienna.

1913-17   Private tutor for Elisabeth Bergner. Ignites her interest in theatre and directs her and other children in plays.

1914   Publishes *Einladung zu einer Begegnung* (Invitation to an Encounter), which he later claimed has influenced Martin Buber's *Ich und Du* (I and Thou) [1923].

1917   Receives M.D. degree, February 5.

1918-20   Publishes *Daimon*, later *Der Neue Daimon* und *Die Gefährten*, an expressionist, existentialist literary journal with articles by Moreno, Max Brod, Franz Werfel, Paul Kornfeid, Martin Buber, Georg Kaiser, Oskar Kokoschka, Paul Claudel, Iwan Goll and many others.

1921   First public performance at Komödienhaus in Vienna on April 1. Ridiculed by audience and critics.

1922-24	Directs Stegreiftheater (Theatre of Spontaneity), Maysedergasse in Vienna, where he discovers the healing power of dramatic enactment. Among his actors are Peter Lorre, Anna Höllering and occasionally Elisabeth Bergner.

1924   Publishes *Das Stegreiftheater* (The Theatre of Spontaneity).

Presents design for *Theater ohne Zuschauer* (theatre without an audience, later called open stage) at *Internationale Ausstellung neuer Theatertechnik* in Vienna. Controversy with Friedrich Kiesler over plagiarism.

1925   Emigrates to the United States.

1929-31   Directs Impromptu Theatre, Carnegie Hall, New York.

1930   Experiments with spontaneity exercises at New York Civic Repertory Theatre under Eva Le Gallienne, where he works with actors such as John Garfield, Burgess Meredith, and Howard da Silva, who later become associated with the Group Theatre.

1931   Performs Living Newspaper at Guild Theatre on Broadway (a space also used by the Group Theatre).

Publishes *Impromptu,* a journal devoted to the use of improvisation in theatre and education, with articles by Moreno, A. B. W. Smith, J.J. Robbins, Theodore Appia, Helen Jennings, Hans Kafka, Robert Müller and others.

1932-34   Directs spontaneity training sessions at the New York State Training School for Girls, Hudson, N.Y., which are recorded in motion pictures.

1935   Creates *Therapeutic Motion Pictures* company to distribute films he made at Hudson and later at Beacon.

1936   Starts Beacon Hill Sanitarium, Beacon, NY with attached psychodrama theatre sponsored by Gertrude Franchot Tone.

1937   Directs Franchot Tone and his wife Joan Crawford exploring marital problems on the psychodrama stage in Beacon; meets Elia Kazan and Stella and Luther Adler.

1941   Inaugurates psychodrama theatre at St. Elizabeths Hospital, Washington, DC.

Incorporates Beacon Publishing House.

1942   Opens New York Theatre of Psychodrama at 101 Park Avenue, renamed Moreno Institute in 1952. Moreno's open sessions continue on weekend nights until the early 1970s and are frequently attended by theatre people (e.g. Eric Bentley, Dustin Hoffman).

1946   Publishes *Psychodrama, Volume I.*

1947   Translates and revises *The Theatre of Spontaneity.*

1949   Dedicates Theatre of Psychodrama, Harvard.

Conducts psychodrama at Mansfield Theatre (Broadway), New York City.

Marries Celine Zerka Toeman, who becomes his partner in life and work; she is still active today teaching and writing about psychodrama.

1951-66	Adjunct professor of sociology, Graduate School of Arts and Sciences, New York University.
1959	Publishes *Psychodrama, Volume 2* (in collaboration with Zerka T. Moreno).
1964	At the Camarillo State Hospital Moreno is televised weekly on closed circuit TV while conducting psychodrama sessions. The entire patient population is watching from their screens.
1969	Publishes *Psychodrama, Volume 3* (in collaboration with Zerka T. Moreno). Awarded Golden Doctorate, Vienna University.
1974	Dies at home, Beacon, New York, May 14.

(Since 1932 Moreno focused more and more on his work in psychodrama, sociometry, and group psychotherapy, publishing numerous books and articles, founding and editing journals, creating institutes and societies, presenting lectures and demonstrations worldwide.)

BIBLIOGRAPHY

Artaud, Antonin (1958). *The Theater and its Double* (Mary Caroline Richards, Trans.). New York: Grove Press.

Back, Kurt W. (1972). *Beyond Words: The Story of Sensitivity Training and the Encounter Movement.* New York: Russell Sage Foundation.

Banham, Martin (Ed.) (1992). *The Cambridge Guide to Theatre* (Revised Paperback Edition). Cambridge University Press.

Beck, Julian (1964). Storming the Barricades. In Kenneth H. Brown (Ed.) *The Brig* (pp. 3-35). New York: Hill and Wang.

Beck, Julian (1972). *The Life of the Theatre* (Second Limelight Edition, January, 1991). San Francisco: City Lights.

Beck, Julian (1992). *Theandric: Julian Beck's Last Notebooks* (Edited by Erica Bilder and Judith Malina). Philadelphia: Harwood Academic Publishers.

Beck, Julian, & Malina, Judith (1970). Messages. In Toby Cole & Helen Krich Chinoy (Eds.), *Actors on Acting* (pp. 654-663). New York: Crown Publishers.

Bentley, Eric (1964). *The Life of the Drama*. New York: Atheneum.

Bentley, Eric (1967). Das Drama des Lebens. *Theater Heute, 8*(9), 14-16.

Bentley, Eric (1969). Theatre and Therapy. In Eric Bentley (Ed.) *Thinking about the Playwright* (pp. 321-338). Evanston, IL: Northwestern University Press.

Bergner, Elisabeth (1978). *Bewundert Viel und Viel Gescholten.* München: Bertelsmann Verlag.

Bierman, Jim (1994). Interviewed by the Author at UC Santa Cruz, CA (May 19, 1994).

Biner, Pierre (1972). *The Living Theatre.* New York: Horizon Press.

Blatner, Adam (1988a). *Acting-in: Practical Applications of Psychodramatic Methods* (Second Edition). New York: Springer Publishing.

Blatner, Adam (1988b). *Foundations of Psychodrama: History, Theory, and Practice* (Third Edition, with Allee Blatner). New York: Springer Publishing.

Blatner, Adam, & Blatner, Allee (1988). *The Art of Play.* New York: Human Sciences Press.

Boal, Augusto (1979). *Theater of the Oppressed* (Charles A. & Maria-Odilia Leal McBride, Trans.). New York: Urizen Books.

Boal, Augusto (1995). *The Rainbow of Desire: The Boal Method of Theatre and Therapy* (Adrian Jackson, Trans.). London and New York: Routledge.

Brauneck, Manfred (1982). *Theater im 20. Jahrhundert.* Reinbek bei Hamburg: Rowohlt.

Brecht, Bertolt (1964). *Brecht on Theatre: The Development of an Aesthetic* (John Willett, Trans.). New York: Hill and Wang.

Brockett, Oscar G. (1992). *The Essential Theatre* (Fifth Edition). Harcourt Brace Jovanovich College Publishers.

Brook, Peter (1968). *The Empty Space.* New York: Atheneum.

Brunius, Teddy (1966). *Inspiration and Katharsis: The Interpretation of Aristotle's The Poetics VI, 1449 b 26.* Uppsala: Almquist & Wiksells.

Brustein, Robert (1973). The Third Theatre Revisited. In James Schevill (Ed.) *Break Out!* (pp. 314-321). Chicago: Swallow Press.

Buber, Martin (1923). *Ich und Du.* Leipzig: Insel Verlag.

Buchanan, Dale Richard (1984). Psychodrama. In Toksoz B. Karasu (Ed.) *The Psychosocial Therapies: Part II of The Psychiatric Therapies* (pp. 783-799). Washington, D.C.: The American Psychiatric Association.

Buchholz, Imke, & Malina, Judith (1980). *Living Theater Heisst Leben: Von einer die auszog, das Leben zu lernen.* Linden: Volksverlag.

Buer, Ferdinand (Ed.) (1991). *Morenos therapeutische Philosophie* (2. durchgesehene Auflage). Opladen: Leske+Budrich.

Burkart, Veronika (1972). *Befreiung durch Aktionen: Die Analyse der gemeinsamen Elemente in Psychodrama und Theater.* Wien, Köln, Graz: Hermann Böhlaus.

Butcher, Samuel H. (1951). *Aristotle's Theory of Poetry and Fine Art* (Fourth Edition). New York: Dover Publications.

Callaghan, David (1994). Anarchia. By Hanon Reznikov. The Living Theatre, Theatre for a New City, New York City. 2 January 1994. *theatre journal, 46*(4), 550-551.

Carlson, Marvin (1978). *Goethe and the Weimar Theatre.* Ithaca and London: Cornell University Press.

Carvalho, Esly Regina, & Otero, Heve E. (1994). Sociodrama as a Social Diagnostic Tool: Our Experience in Paraguay. *Journal of Group Psychotherapy, Psychodrama & Sociometry, 46*(4), 143 - 149.

Chaikin, Joseph (1972). *The Presence of the Actor.* New York: Atheneum.

Chekhov, Michael (1991). *On the Technique of Acting.* New York: Harper Perennial.

Chinoy, Helen Krich (1976). Reunion: A Self-Portrait of the Group Theatre. *Educational Theatre Journal, 28*(4), 445-552.

Clark, Barrett H. (1965). *European Theories of the Drama* (Newly Revised Edition). New York: Crown.

Clurman, Harold (1983). *The Fervent Years: The Group Theatre and the Thirties.* New York: Da Capo.

Cole, Toby, & Chinoy, Helen Krich (Eds.). (1970). *Actors on Acting.* New York: Crown.

Coleman, Janet (1990). *The Compass: The Improvisational Theatre That Revolutionized American Comedy.* Chicago: The University of Chicago Press.

Courtney, Richard (1974). *Play, Drama & Thought: The Intellectual Background to Drama in Education* (Third, Revised and Enlarged Edition). New York: Drama Book Specialists/Publishers.

Courtney, Richard (1990). *Drama and Intelligence: A Cognitive Theory.* Montreal & Kingston: McGill-Queen's University Press.

Cox, Murray (Ed.) (1992). *Shakespeare Comes to Broadmoor, 'The Actors are Come Hither': The Performance of Tragedy in a Secure Psychiatric Hospital.* London and Philadelphia: Jessica Kingsley Publishers.

Dethlefsen, Thorwald (1990). *Oedipus der Rätsellöser: Der Mensch zwischen Schuld und Erlösung.* München: Bertelsmann.

Diener, Gottfried (1971). *Goethes >Lila<.* Frankfurt: Athenaeum Verlag.

Dietrich, Margret (1974). *Das Moderne Drama: Strömungen, Gestalten, Motive* (Dritte, überarbeitete und erweiterte Auflage). Stuttgart: Alfred Kröner Verlag.

Dukore, Bernard F. (1974). *Dramatic Theory and Criticism: Greeks to Grotowski.* New York: Holt, Rinehart and Winston.

Eissler, Kurt Robert (1963). *Goethe: A Psychoanalytic Study.* Detroit: Wayne State University Press.

Ellenberger, Henri F. (1970). *The Discovery of the Unconscious: The History and Evolution of Dynamic Psychiatry.* New York: Basic Books.

Else, Gerald F. (1957). *Aristotle's Poetics: The Argument.* Cambridge, Massachusetts: Harvard University Press.

Else, Gerald F. (1967). *Aristotle Poetics.* Ann Arbor Paperbacks: The University of Michigan Press.

Emunah, Renée (1994). *Acting for Real: Drama Therapy Process, Technique, and Performance.* New York: Brunner/Mazel.

Esrig, David (1985). *Commedia Dell'Arte: Eine Bildgeschichte der Kunst des Spektakels.* Noerdlingen: Greno Verlagsgesellschaft.

Ettin, Mark (1992). *Foundations and Applications of Group Psychotherapy: A Sphere of Influence*. Boston: Allyn and Bacon.

Fanchette, Jean (1971). *Psychodrame et Théatre Moderne* (Préface de J. L. Moreno). Paris: Éditions Buchet/Chastel.

Feldhendler, Daniel (1992). *Psychodrama und Theater der Unterdrückten* (2. erweiterte Auflage). Frankfurt am Main: Wilfried Nold.

Feldhendler, Daniel (1994). Augusto Boal and Jacob L. Moreno: Theatre and Therapy. In Mady Schutzman & Jan Cohen-Cruz (Eds.), *Playing Boal: Theatre, Therapy, Activism* (pp. p. 87-109). London and New York: Routledge.

Feldman, Lee Gallup (1974). A Brief History of Improvisational Theatre in the United States. *Yale/Theatre*, *5*(2) (Spring 1974), 128-151.

Fink, Siobhan O. (1990). Approaches to Emotion in Psychotherapy and Theatre: Implications for Drama Therapy. *The Arts in Psychotherapy*, *17*, pp. 5-18.

Fox, Jonathan (1978). Moreno and his Theater. *Journal for Group Psychotherapy, Psychodrama and Sociometry*, *31*, 109-116.

Fox, Jonathan (1986). *Acts of Service: Spontaneity, Commitment, Tradition in the Nonscripted Theatre* (Published in 1994). New Paltz, NY: Tusitala Publishing.

Fox, Jonathan (Ed.) (1987). *The Essential Moreno*. New York: Springer.

Freedland, Michael (1992). *Dustin Hoffman*. München: Knaur.

Frenzel, Ivo (1966). *Nietzsche*. Reinbek bei Hamburg: Rowohlt.

Freud, Sigmund (1966). *On the History of the Psycho-Analytic Movement* (Joan Riviere, Trans.). New York and London: W. W. Norton & Company.

Freud, Sigmund, & Breuer, Joseph (1895). *Studies on Hysteria* (1966). New York: Avon Books.

Fuhrmann, Manfred (1982). *Aristoteles Poetik (Griechisch/Deutsch)*. Stuttgart: Philipp Reclam Jun.

Gaines, Jack (1979). *Fritz Perls: Here and Now*. Millbrae, California: Celestial Arts.

Gallienne, Eva Le (1934). *At 33*. New York: Longmans, Green and Co.

Gallienne, Eva Le (1953). *With a Quiet Heart*. New York: The Viking Press.

Gassner, John (1965). Catharsis and the Modern Theater. In Barrett H. Clark (Ed.) *European Theories of the Drama* (pp. 514-518). New York: Crown Publishers.

Goethe, Johann Wolfgang von (1962). *Wilheim Meisters Lehrjahre, Berliner Ausgabe 10*. Berlin: Aufbau-Verlag.

Goethe, Johann Wolfgang von (1968). *Poetische Werke, Gedichte und Singspiele, Berliner Ausgabe IV*. Berlin: Aufbau-Verlag.

Golden, Leon (1992). *Aristotle on Tragic and Comic Mimesis*. Atlanta, Georgia: Scholars Press.

Gordon, Mel (1987). *The Stanislavsky Technique: Russia*. New York: Applause Theatre Book Publishers.

Greenberg, Ira A. (Ed.) (1974). *Psychodrama: Theory and Therapy*. New York: Behavioral Publications.

Grotowski, Jerzy (1968). *Towards a Poor Theatre*. New York: Simon & Schuster.

Gussow, Mel (1968, September). Dustin Hoffman: an Interview. *McCall's,* p. 143-146.

Hagen, Uta (1973). *Respect for Acting.* New York: Macmillan.

Held, R. L. (1982). *Endless Innovations: Frederick Kiesler's Theory and Scenic Design.* Ann Arbor, Michigan: UMI Research Press.

Henderson, Harry (1983, February). Tootsie and Dr. Moreno. *Sexual Medicine Today,* p. 22-23.

Herrigel, Eugen (1951). *Zen in der Kunst des Bogenschiessens.* Bern, München, Wien: Otto Wilhelm Barth Verlag.

Hinck, Walter (1984). Man of the Theatre. In Elizabeth M. Wilkinson (Ed.) *Goethe Revisited: A Collection of Essays* (pp. 153-169). New York: Riverrun Press.

Hodgson, John, & Richards, Ernest (1966). *Improvisation.* New York: Grove Press.

Hutton, James (1982). *Aristotle's Poetics.* New York: W.W. Norton & Company.

Innes, Christopher (1993). *Avant Garde Theatre 1892-1992.* London and New York: Routledge.

Janov, Arthur (1970). *The Primal Scream.* New York: Dell Publishing.

Johnson, Paul E. (1959). *Psychology of Religion* (Revised and Enlarged Edition). New York - Nashville: Abingdon Press.

Johnstone, Keith (1979). *Impro: Improvisation and the Theatre.* New York: Routledge.

Jung, Carl Gustav (1957). *Bewusstes und Unbewusstes: Beiträge zur Psychologie.* Frankfurt am Main: Fischer Taschenbuch Verlag.

Kiesler, Friedrich (Ed.) (1924). *Internationale Ausstellung neuer Theatertechnik: Katalog. Programm. Almanach.* (Nachdruck durch den Verlag Löcker & Wögenstein, Wien 1975). Wien: Würthle & Sohn.

Kirby, Michael (1972). On Acting and Not-Acting. *The Drama Review, T-53: 16*(1), 3-15.

Kruse, Noreen W. (1979). The Process of Aristotelian Catharsis: A Reidentification. *Theatre Journal, 31*(2), 162-171.

Kumiega, Jennifer (1985). *The Theatre of Grotowski.* London and New York: Methuen.

Lain Entralgo, Pedro (1970). *The Therapy of the Word in Classical Antiquity.* New Haven and London: Yale University Press.

Landy, Robert J. (1986). *Drama Therapy: Concepts and Practices.* Springfield, Illinois: Charles C Thomas.

Landy, Robert J. (1993). *Persona and Performance: The Meaning of Role in Drama, Therapy, and Everyday Life.* New York, London: The Guilford Press.

Lazarowicz, Klaus, & Balme, Christopher (Eds.). (1991). *Texte zur Theorie des Theaters.* Stuttgart: Philipp Reclam jun.

Lesák, Barbara (1988). *Die Kulisse explodiert: Friedrich Kieslers Theaterexperimente und Architekturprojekte 1923-1925.* Wien: Löcker Verlag.

Leutz, Grete (1974). *Psychodrama Theorie und Praxis: Das klassische Psychodrama nach J. L. Moreno* (1. korrigierter Nachdruck 1986). Berlin Heidelberg New York: Springer-Verlag.

Leveton, Eva (1992). *A Clinician's Guide to Psychodrama* (Second Edition). New York: Springer.

Malina, Judith (1972). *The Enormous Despair*. New York: Random House.

Malina, Judith (1979). *The Diaries: Brazil 1970 Bologna 1977*. Devon, England: Dept. of Theatre, Dartington College of Art.

Malina, Judith (1984). *The Diaries of Judith Malina 1947-1957*. New York: Grove Press.

Malina, Judith (1994). Interviewed by the Author in San Francisco (May 10, 1994).

Marineau, René F. (1989). *Jacob Levy Moreno 1889-1974*. London and New York: Tavistock/Routledge.

Marschall, Brigitte (1988). *"Ich bin der Mythe": Von der Stegreifbühne zum Psychodrama Jakob Levy Morenos*. Wien: Böhlau Verlag.

May, Rollo (1983). *The Discovery of Being: Writings in Existential Psychology*. New York: W. W. Norton.

McCrohan, Donna (1987). *The Second City: A Backstage History of Comedy's Hottest Troupe*. New York: The Putnam Publishing Group.

McGill, Kathleen (1990). Improvisatory Competence and the Cueing of Performance: The Case of the Commedia dell'Arte. *Text and Performance Quaterly*(10), 111-122.

Meisner, Sanford, & Longwell, Dennis (1987). *Sanford Meisner on Acting*. New York: Vintage Books.

Merleau-Ponty, Maurice (1988). *Merleau-Ponty a la Sorbonne: resume de cours, 1949-1952*. Grenoble: Cynara.

Moreno, Jacob (1914). *Einladung zu einer Begegnung*. Wien: Anzengruber Verlag.

Moreno, Jacob Levy (Ed.) (1918). *Daimon.* (Kraus Reprint, Nedeln/Liechtenstein, 1969). Wien: Brüder Suschitzky Verlag.

Moreno, Jacob Levy (Ed.) (1919a). *Der Neue Daimon* (Kraus Reprint, Nedeln/Liechtenstein, 1969). Wien, Prag, Leipzig: Genossenschaftsverlag.

Moreno, Jacob Levy (1919b). Die Gottheit als Komödiant. *Der Neue Daimon, April 1919*(4), 48-63.

Moreno, Jacob Levy (Ed.) (1920/21). *Die Gefährten* (Kraus Reprint, Nedeln/Liechtenstein, 1969). Wien, Leipzig: Genossenschaftsverlag.

Moreno, Jacob Levy (1923). *Der Königsroman.* Potsdam: Kiepenheuer Verlag.

Moreno, Jacob Levy (1924). *Das Stegreiftheater.* Potsdam: Verlag des Vaters, Gustav Kiepenheuer Verlag.

Moreno, Jacob Levy (Ed.) (1931). *Impromptu.* New York.

Moreno, Jacob Levy (1946). *Psychodrama: First Volume* (Seventh Edition 1985). Ambler, PA.: Beacon House.

Moreno, Jacob Levy (1953). *Who Shall Survive?* Beacon, N.Y.: Beacon House Inc.

Moreno, Jacob Levy (1957). Global Psychotherapy and Prospects of a Therapeutic World Order. In Jules H. Masserman & Jacob L. Moreno (Eds.), *Progress in Psychotherapy: Volume II. Anxiety and Therapy* (pp. 1-31). New York: Grune & Stratton.

Moreno, Jacob Levy (1959a). *Gruppenpsychotherapie und Psychodrama* (3. unveränderte Auflage). Stuttgart: Georg Thieme Verlag.

Moreno, Jacob Levy (1959b). *Psychodrama: Second Volume, Foundations of Psychotherapy* (In Collaboration With Zerka T. Moreno). Beacon, N.Y.: Beacon House.

Moreno, Jacob Levy (1964a). *The First Psychodramatic Family* (with Zerka and Jonathan Moreno). Beacon, N.Y.: Beacon House.

Moreno, Jacob L. (1964b). The Philosophy of the Third Psychiatric Revolution. In Maurice Friedman (Ed.) *The Worlds of Existentialism* (pp. 468-471). New York: Random House.

Moreno, Jacob L. (Ed.) (1966). *The International Handbook of Group Psychotherapy.* New York: Philosophical Library.

Moreno, Jacob Levy (1967). *Psychodrama and Psychometrics.* Cassette Soundrecording 47 min., Los Angeles: Pacifica Foundation.

Moreno, Jacob Levy (1969). *Psychodrama: Third Volume, Action Therapy & Principles of Practice* (In Collaboration With Zerka T. Moreno). Beacon, N.Y.: Beacon House.

Moreno, Jacob Levy (1971a). Influence of the Theater of Spontaneity upon the Modern Drama. *Handbook of International Sociometry, VI,* 84-90.

Moreno, Jacob Levy (1972). The Religion of God-Father. In Paul E. Johnson (Ed.) *Healer of the Mind* (pp. 197-215). Nashville and New York: Abingdon Press.

Moreno, Jacob Levy (1983). *The Theatre of Spontaneity* (Third Edition). Ambler, PA: Beacon House.

Moreno, Jacob Levy (1989). The Autobiography of J. L. Moreno, MD. *Journal of Group Psychotherapy, Psychodrama and Sociometry, 42*(1,2).

Moreno, Jacob Levy (1995). *Auszüge aus der Autobiographie*. Köln: inScenario Verlag.

Moreno, Jacob Levy, & Enneis, James M. (1950). *Hypnodrama and Psychodrama*. Beacon, New York: Beacon House.

Moreno, Jacob Levy, & Moreno, Zerka T. (1970). *Origins of Encounter and Encounter Groups*. Beacon, N.Y.: Beacon House.

Moreno, Zerka (1994). Phone Interview by the Author (June 4, 1994).

Moreno, Zerka T. (1971b). Beyond Aristotle, Breuer and Freud: Moreno's Contribution to the Concept of Catharsis. *Group Psychotherapy and Psychodrama, XXIV*(1-2), 34-43.

Nagler, A.M. (1952). *A Source Book in Theatrical History*. New York: Dover Publications.

Neff, Renfreu (1970). *The Living Theatre: USA*. Indianapolis and New York: The Bobbs-Merrill Company.

Nietzsche, Friedrich (1976). *Also sprach Zarathustra*. Insel Verlag.

Nietzsche, Friedrich (1990). *Die Geburt der Tragödie aus dem Geiste der Musik* (Leipzig 1895). München: Goldmann.

Ogden, Dunbar H. (1987). *Performance Dynamics and the Amsterdam Werkteater*. Berkeley / Los Angeles / London: University of California Press.

Perls, Fritz (1969a). *Gestalt Therapy Verbatim*. Lafayette, CA: Real People Press.

Perls, Fritz (1969b). *In and Out the Garbage Pail*. Lafayette, CA: Real People Press.

Perls, Fritz, & Clements, Cooper (1968). Acting Out vs. Acting Through. In John O. Stevens (Ed.) *gestalt is* (pp. 17-37). Moab, Utah: Real People Press.

Perls, Fritz, Hefferline, Ralph, & Goodman, Paul (1951). *Gestalt Therapy, Excitement and Growth in the Human Personality.* New York: The Julian Press.

Perls, Fritz S. (1969c). *Ego, Hunger and Aggression: The Beginning of Gestalt Therapy.* New York: Vintage Books.

Polster, Erving and Miriam (1973). *Gestalt Therapy Integrated, Contours of Theory and Practice.* New York: Brunner/Mazel.

Pörtner, Paul (1967). Psychodrama: Theater der Spontaneität. *Theater Heute,* 8(9), 10-14.

Pörtner, Paul (1972). *Spontanes Theater.* Köln: Kiepenheuer & Witsch.

Propper, Herb (1979). *Psychodrama in Rehearsals of Molière's Tartuffe* (unpublished paper).

Ray, Sondra (1986). *Celebration of Breath (Rebirthing, Book II)* (Revised Edition). Berkeley, California: Celestial Arts.

Reuchlein, Georg (1983). *Die Heilung des Wahnsinns bei Goethe: Orest, Lila, der Harfner und Sperata.* Frankfurt: Verlag Peter Lang.

Richards, Kenneth, & Richards, Laura (1990). *The Commedia dell'arte: A Documentary History.* Oxford, Cambridge: Basil Blackwell.

Rorty, Amelie Oksenberg (Ed.) (1992). *Essays on Aristotle's Poetics.* Princeton University Press.

Rostagno, Aldo (1970). *We, The Living Theatre*. New York: Ballantine Books.

Sacks, James M. (1994). Those Were The Days... *Psychodrama Network News, January 1994*, 2.

Saifulin, Murad, & Dixon, Richard (Eds.). (1984). *Dictionary of Philosophy* (Translation of Fourth Russian Edition produced by the Political Literature Publishers, Moscow in 1980). New York: International Publishers.

Sarlós, Robert Károly (1982). *Jig Cook and the Provincetown Players*. The University of Massachusetts Press.

Schattner, Gertrud, & Courtney, Richard (Eds.). (1981). *Drama in Therapy, Volume II: Adults*. New York: Drama Book Specialists.

Schechner, Richard (1969). Containment is the Enemy. *The Drama Review, T-43: 13*(3), 24-44.

Schechner, Richard (Ed.) (1970). *Dionysus in 69: The Performance Group*. New York: Farrar, Straus and Giroux.

Schechner, Richard (1971). The Living Theatre. In Gabriele Mazzotta (Ed.) *The Living Book of the Living Theatre* (pp. 1-3). Greenwich, Connecticut: New York Graphic Society Ltd.

Scheff, Thomas (1979). *Catharsis in Healing, Ritual, and Drama*. Berkeley: University of California Press.

Schevill, James (1973). *Break Out!* Chicago: Swallow Press.

Schmitt, Natalie Crohn (1990). *Actors and Onlookers: Theater and Twentieth-Century Scientific Views of Nature*. Evanston, Illinois: Northwestern University Press.

Schutz, William C. (1973). *Elements of Encounter: A Bodymind Approach*. Big Sur, California: Joy Press.

Schutz, Will C. (1989). *Joy: 20 Years Later* (Revised Edition of: Joy, Expanding Human Awareness, 1967). Berkeley, California: Ten Speed Press.

Schutzman, Mady, & Cohen-Cruz, Jan (Eds.). (1994). *Playing Boal: Theatre, Therapy, Activism*. London and New York: Routledge.

Shank, Theodore (1982). *American Alternative Theater*. New York: Grove Press.

Shepard, Martin (1975). *Fritz*. Sagaponack, NY: Second Chance Press.

Sievers, Wieder David (1955). *Freud on Broadway: a History of Psychoanalysis and the American Drama*. New York: Hermitage House.

Silverberg, Larry (1994). *The Sanford Meisner Approach: An Actors Workbook*. Lyme, NH: Smith and Kraus.

Sluga, Hans (1994). Interviewed by the Author (November 10, 1994).

Smith, Edward W.L. (Ed.) (1976). *The Growing Edge of Gestalt Therapy*. New York: Brunner/Mazel.

Smith, Wendy (1990). *Real Life Drama: The Group Theatre and America, 1931-1940*. New York: Alfred A. Knopf.

Spolin, Viola (1963). *Improvisation for the Theater*. Evanston, Illinois: Northwestern University Press.

Spolin, Viola (1985). *Theater Games for Rehearsal*. Evanston, Illinois: Northwestern University Press.

Stanislavski, Constantin (1936). *An Actor Prepares* (Elizabeth Reynolds Hapgood, Trans.). New York: Routledge.

Sternberg, Patricia, & Garcia, Antonina (1989). *Sociodrama, Who's in your Shoes?* New York: Praeger.

Stevens, John O. (Ed.) (1975). *gestalt is.* Moab, Utah: Real People Press.

Stevens, S.S. (1946). On the Theory of Scales of Measurement. *Science, 103*(2684).

Sucher, C. Bernd (Ed.) (1995).   *Theaterlexikon: Autoren, Regisseure, Schauspieler, Dramaturgen, Bühnenbildner, Kritiker.* München: Deutscher Taschenbuch Verlag.

Sweet, Jeffrey (1978). *Something Wonderful Right Away: An Oral History of The Second City & The Compass Players.* New York: Limelight Editions.

Symonds, Percival (1954). A Comprehensive Theory of Psychotherapy. *American Journal of Orthopsychiatry*(24), 697-712.

Tairoff, Alexander (1924). *Das entfesselte Theater.* Berlin: Gustav Kiepenheuer.

Taussig, Michael, & Schechner, Richard (1990). Boal in Brazil, France, the USA: An Interview with Augusto Boal. In Mady Schutzman & Jan Cohen-Cruz (Eds.), *Playing Boal: Theatre, Therapy, Activism* (pp. 17-32). London and New York: Routledge.

Thorau, Henry (1991). "Durch Millionen von Mikrorevolutionen die Makrorevolutionen der Zukunft vorbereiten": Augusto Boals Teatro do Oprimido (Theater der Unterdrückten) und Jacob Levy Morenos Psychodrama. *PSYCHODRAMA Zeitschrift für Theorie und Praxis von Psychodrama, Soziometrie und Rollenspiel, 4*(1), 5-19.

Tytell, John (1995). *The Living Theatre: Art, Exile, and Outrage.* New York: Grove Press.

Vicentini, Claudio (1975). The Living Theatre's "Six Public Acts". *The Drama Review, T-67: 19*(3), 80-93.

Waldman, Max (1971). *Waldman on Theater.* Garden City, New York: Doubleday & Company, Inc.

Watts, Alan (1975). *Tao: The Watercourse Way.* New York: Pantheon Books.

Werfel, Franz (1929). *Barbara oder Die Frömmigkeit.* Frankfurt am Main: Fischer Taschenbuch Verlag GmbH.

White, Edmund (1993). *Genet: A Biography.* New York: Alfred A. Knopf.

Williams, Jay (1974). *Stage Left: An Engrossing Account of the Radical Theatre Movement in America.* New York: Charles Scribner's Sons.

Wolberg, Lewis R., Aronson, Marvin L., & Wolberg, Arlene R. (Eds.). (1976). *Group Therapy 1976.* New York: Stratton Intercontinental Medical Book Corp.

Yablonsky, Lewis (1972). *Robopaths: People as Machines.* New York: Bobbs-Merrill.

Yablonsky, Lewis (1981). *Psychodrama: Resolving Emotional Problems Through Role-Playing.* New York: Gardner Press.

325

Yablonsky, Lewis (1994). Phone Conversation with the Author (May 2, 1994).

Youngkin, Stephen D., Bigwood, James, & Cabana, Raymond G. (1982). *The Films of Peter Lorre*. Secaucus, New Jersey: The Citadel Press.

Zaporah, Ruth (1995). *Action Theater: The Improvisation of Presence*. Berkeley, California: North Atlantic Books.

54268156R00201

Made in the USA
Lexington, KY
09 August 2016